On NARRATIVE

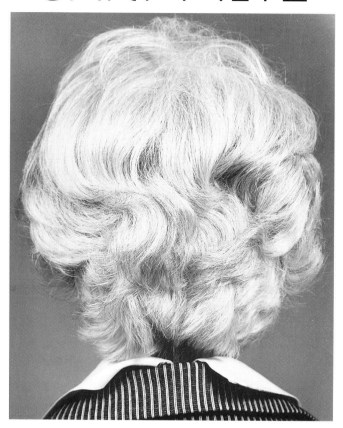

On NARRATIVE

Edited by W. J. T. Mitchell

The University of Chicago Press
Chicago and London

The articles in this volume originally appeared in *Critical Inquiry* Volume 7, number 1 (Autumn 1980) and Volume 7, number 4 (Summer 1981).

The University of Chicago Press, Chicago 60637
The University of Chicago Press, Ltd., London

Library of Congress Cataloging in Publication Data
Main entry under title:

On narrative.

"The articles in this volume originally appeared
in Critical inquiry, volume 7, number 1 (Autumn
1980) and volume 7, number 4 (Summer 1981)."
   Includes bibliographical references and index.
   CONTENTS: White, H. The value of narrativity
in the representation of reality.—Schafer, R.
Narration in the psychoanalytic dialogue.—
Derrida, J. The law of genre.—[etc.]
   1. Discourse analysis, Narrative—Addresses,
essays, lectures. 2. Narration (Rhetoric)—
Addresses, essays, lectures. I Mitchell, W. J.
Thomas, 1942–   II. Critical inquiry.
P302.06   808.3′0141   80-53137

Contents

Foreword

The following collection of essays is an expanded version of a special issue of *Critical Inquiry* (vol. 7, no. 1 [Autumn 1980]) that grew out of the symposium "Narrative: The Illusion of Sequence" held at the University of Chicago on 26–28 October 1979. Enlarged now with critical responses by Louis O. Mink and Marilyn Robinson Waldman and rejoinders by Hayden White, Nelson Goodman, and Seymour Chatman, this collection provides an interdisciplinary compendium of some of the most important recent thinking on the topic of narrative. Reflecting the debates and collaboration of literary critics, philosophers, anthropologists, psychologists, theologians, art historians, and novelists, the collection is intended to carry thinking about the problem of narrative well beyond the province of the "aesthetic"—that is, poetic, dramatic, or fictional narrative—and to explore the role of narrative in social and psychological formations, particularly in structures of value and cognition.

The rather special character of this symposium may be traced to the social design given the event by its organizers and managers, Joan Cowen and Joyce Feucht-Haviar. Unlike many such gatherings, the symposium was not fragmented into concurrent or competing sessions; no enclaves of specialization were allowed to form, and all the speakers, panelists, and guests remained throughout the weekend to discuss the issues, both in the formal sessions and late into the dark and stormy nights of Chicago's autumn. Several distinguished participants, including Paul de Man, Robert Scholes, Richard Shiff, Barbara Herrnstein Smith, and David Tracy, did not read papers but made important contributions to the discussions, which are reflected in the revisions the authors made in their papers after the symposium and in the critical responses that enliven the concluding section of this volume.

The inevitable temptation in introducing this topic is, of course, to try to tell the story of the symposium. But which story would be the right one to tell? Would it be the "plot" of the organizers of the symposium to bring together a distinguished group of speakers from a variety of disciplines to discuss narrative under the rubric of "The Illusion of Sequence"? This was the first plan to go awry, as one speaker after another quarreled with the assumption that sequence either is illusory or is definitive of narrativity. Would the right story be on the order of intellectual history, explaining how it is that in this age and place one could gather together a group of philosophers, literary critics, psychologists, art historians, anthropologists, novelists, and (rarest of breeds) narratologists to discuss the ways we tell, understand, and use stories? Or would the right story be a journalistic version, "getting the story straight" with who, when, where, what, how? Or a piece of literary journalism such as the account in *The Chicago Literary Review* which presents the symposium as a ritual drama in three acts, featuring the major speakers (I leave it to you to guess their identities) in such roles as Knave, Scapegoat, Hermeneutic Harlequin, Oracle/Sophist/Priest, Secret Sharer, Saint, Alienist, Skeptic, Professor, Critic, and Chorus?

If conflict, and not mere sequence, connexity, or a central subject, is one of the essentials of narrative, then the symposium on narrative was a storied event indeed. One thing that should make the present issue of *Critical Inquiry* of value to students of narrative in all disciplines is that it dramatizes (and, we hope, clarifies) the most fundamental debates about the value and nature of narrative as a means by which human beings represent and structure the world. It is a commonplace of modern relativism, of course, that there are multiple versions of events and the stories about them and that there is something suspect about claims to having the "true" or "authorized" or "basic" version in one's possession. The real problem, however, is not the telling of true stories from false (this seems to be a practical rather than a theoretical problem) but the very value of narrativity as a mode of making sense of reality (whether the factual reality of actual events, or the moral, symbolic reality of fictions). Hayden White came closest to taking an explicitly "anti-narrativist" stance in his symposium lecture, suggesting that narrativity *as such* tends to support orthodox and politically conservative social conditions and that the revolt against narrativity in modern historiography and literature is a revolt against the authority of the social system.

It is now possible, as Robert Scholes observes, to say of narrative what Marx said of religion, that it is an "opiate" which mystifies our understanding by providing a false sense of coherence, an "illusion of sequence." Many of the essays which follow seem, in retrospect, to be designed to answer this charge. A remedy for our addiction to the orderly consolations of narrative sequence is offered by Frank Kermode, who suggests that narratives also conceal "secrets" which may be uncovered by "overreaders . . . members of a special academic class that has the time to pry into secrets." Kermode's reassuring discovery of a scandalous, incoherent, chaotic dimension to narrativity is a theme which recurs in several of these essays: in Victor Turner's claim that narrative, like ritual, is not simply in opposition to the forces of disorder and chaos but is a way of bringing on disintegration and indeterminacy in the interests of unpredictable transformations in a culture or individual; in Paul Ricoeur's sense of narrative as an "open" interpretive structure or "model for the redescription of the world"; and in Jacques Derrida's contention that the "law of genre" (including the genre of narrative) "is threatened intimately and in advance by a counter-law that constitutes this very law" so that "the law is mad, is madness; . . . madness cannot be conceived before its relation to law."

The speaker with the most intimate professional acquaintance with the encounter between madness and the law of narrative was, of course, the eminent psychoanalyst Roy Schafer, whose interest is in redescribing psychoanalysis as an interpretive discipline (as opposed to a positive science), based on typical or normative narratives of individual development, and in helping people come to understand and redescribe their own life stories in ways that allow for change and beneficial action in the world. Whether Schafer's use of narrative reconciles the law of narrative with madness or imposes a benign but false resolution on its revolutionary energies is a story that is best completed by the reader of these essays.

The debate over the value of narrative, either as a mode of imposing order on reality or as a way of unleashing a healthy disorder, is accompanied by an argument about the nature of narrative, which focuses on three questions addressed most generally by Nelson Goodman: (1) What are the minimum conditions for narrativity? (2) How much distortion can a narrative endure before it becomes something else? and (3) What is the relationship between different versions of a story? These questions sometimes converge in the notion that there must be a basic story, an "Ur-narrative" with certain minimal features underlying all the different versions of a tale, that allows us to identify these versions as versions of something. This assumption, articulated here by Seymour Chatman in the linguistic terminology of "deep structure," has served as a basic point of departure for the discipline of narratology and is subjected to a vigorous critique by Barbara Herrnstein Smith, who contends that this binary notion of narrative "betrays a lingering strain of naive Platonism . . . which is both logically dubious and methodologically distracting." A related binary notion of narrative which comes into question in these pages is the assumption that stories refer to a chronological continuum which is neutral or unproblematic. Paul Ricoeur opposes this view with a multidimensional and existential picture of time that stresses "the reciprocity between narrativity and temporality." We have not only different versions of stories but different versions of time which are shaped by the stories we live by.

Conflict over the nature and value of narrative was, of course, not the only or most interesting story of the symposium on narrative. Probably the most important sense of the event as lived was the aura of intellectual excitement and discovery, the common feeling that the study of narrative, like the study of other significant human creations, has taken a quantum leap in the modern era. The study of narrative is no longer the province of literary specialists or folklorists borrowing their terms from psychology and linguistics but has now become a positive source of insight for all the branches of human and natural science. The idea of narrative seems, as several of the contributors to these pages note, to be repossessing its archaic sense as *gnārus* and *gnosis,* a mode of knowledge emerging from action, a knowledge which is embedded not just in the stories we tell our children or to while away our leisure but in the orders by which we live our lives. The magic of this mode of knowledge was conjured up for the symposium's closing session by Ursula K. Le Guin's witty and generically indescribable talk, "It Was a Dark and Stormy Night; or, Why Are We Huddling about the Campfire?" Whether we call it prose or poetry, narrative or meta-narrative, parody or panegyric on storytelling, if the story of the narrative symposium is to be found anywhere, it is in the secret sequences of Le Guin's jocular and haunting tale.

The symposium on narrative was sponsored by the University of Chicago Extension, C. Ranlet Lincoln, Dean (who also served as moderator). It was organized and managed by Joan Cowan, Assistant Dean of the Extension, and Joyce Feucht-Haviar, Assistant to the Dean. The symposium was funded by the Extension and by the Midwest Faculty Seminar with the support of the Andrew W. Mellon Foundation. Speakers, panelists, and special guests were Seymour Chatman, Paul de Man, Jacques Derrida, Howard Gardner, Merton Gill, Nelson Goodman, Paul Hernadi, Frank Kermode, Ursula K. Le Guin, Françoise Meltzer, W. J. T. Mitchell, Barbara Myerhoff, Paul Ricoeur, Roy Schafer, Robert Scholes, Richard Shiff, Barbara Herrnstein Smith, Richard Stern, David Tracy, Victor Turner, Tamás Ungvári, and Hayden White.

W. J. T. Mitchell

The Value of Narrativity in the Representation of Reality

Hayden White

To raise the question of the nature of narrative is to invite reflection on the very nature of culture and, possibly, even on the nature of humanity itself. So natural is the impulse to narrate, so inevitable is the form of narrative for any report of the way things really happened, that narrativity could appear problematical only in a culture in which it was absent—absent or, as in some domains of contemporary Western intellectual and artistic culture, programmatically refused. As a panglobal fact of culture, narrative and narration are less problems than simply data. As the late (and already profoundly missed) Roland Barthes remarked, narrative "is simply there like life itself . . . international, transhistorical, transcultural."[1] Far from being a problem, then, narrative might well be considered a solution to a problem of general human concern, namely, the problem of how to translate *knowing* into *telling*,[2] the problem of fashioning human experience into a form assimilable to structures of meaning that are generally human rather than culture-specific. We may not be able fully to comprehend specific thought patterns of another culture, but we have relatively less difficulty *understanding* a story coming from another culture, however exotic that

1. Roland Barthes, "Introduction to the Structural Analysis of Narratives," *Image, Music, Text,* trans. Stephen Heath (New York, 1977), p. 79.
2. The words "narrative," "narration," "to narrate," and so on derive via the Latin *gnārus* ("knowing," "acquainted with," "expert," "skilful," and so forth) and *narrō* ("relate," "tell") from the Sanskrit root *gnâ* ("know"). The same root yields γνώριμος ("knowable," "known"): see Emile Boisacq, *Dictionnaire étymologique de la langue grecque* (Heidelberg, 1950), under the entry for this word. My thanks to Ted Morris of Cornell, one of our great etymologists.

1

culture may appear to us. As Barthes says, "narrative . . . is *translatable without fundamental damage*" in a way that a lyric poem or a philosophical discourse is not.

This suggests that far from being one code among many that a culture may utilize for endowing experience with meaning, narrative is a metacode, a human universal on the basis of which transcultural messages about the nature of a shared reality can be transmitted. Arising, as Barthes says, between our experience of the world and our efforts to describe that experience in language, narrative "ceaselessly substitutes meaning for the straightforward copy of the events recounted." And it would follow, on this view, that the absence of narrative capacity or a refusal of narrative indicates an absence or refusal of meaning itself.

But what *kind* of meaning is absent or refused? The fortunes of narrative in the history of historical writing give us some insight into this question. Historians do not *have* to report their truths about the real world in narrative form; they may choose other, non-narrative, even anti-narrative, modes of representation, such as the meditation, the anatomy, or the epitome. Tocqueville, Burckhardt, Huizinga, and Braudel,[3] to mention only the most notable masters of modern historiography, refused narrative in certain of their historiographical works, presumably on the assumption that the meaning of the events with which they wished to deal did not lend itself to representation in the narrative mode. They refused to tell a story about the past, or, rather, they did not tell a story with well-marked beginning, middle, and end phases; they did not impose upon the processes that interested them the *form* that we normally associate with storytelling. While they certainly *narrated* their accounts of the reality that they perceived, or thought they perceived, to exist within or behind the evidence they had examined, they did not *narrativize* that reality, did not impose upon it the form of a story. And their example permits us to distinguish between a historical discourse that narrates, on the one side, and a discourse that

3. See Alexis de Tocqueville, *Democracy in America*, trans. Henry Reeve (London, 1838); Jakob Christoph Burckhardt, *The Civilization of the Renaissance in Italy*, trans. S. G. C. Middlemore (London, 1878); Johan Huizinga, *The Waning of the Middle Ages: A Study of the Forms of Life, Thought, and Art in France and the Netherlands in the Dawn of the Renaissance*, trans. F. Hopman (London, 1924); and Fernand Braudel, *The Mediterranean and the Mediterranean World in the Age of Philip II*, trans. Siân Reynolds (New York, 1972). See also my *Metahistory: The Historical Imagination in Nineteenth Century Europe* (Baltimore, 1973) and Hans Kellner, "Disorderly Conduct: Braudel's Mediterranean Satire," *History and Theory* 18, no. 2 (May 1979): 197–222.

Hayden White, professor in the program in the history of consciousness at the University of California, Santa Cruz, is the author of *The Tropics of Discourse: Essays in Cultural Criticism, The Greco-Roman Tradition,* and *Metahistory: The Historical Imagination in Nineteenth Century Europe.*

narrativizes, on the other; between a discourse that openly adopts a perspective that looks out on the world and reports it and a discourse that feigns to make the world speak itself and speak itself *as a story.*

The idea that narrative should be considered less as a *form* of representation than as a *manner of speaking* about events, whether real or imaginary, has been recently elaborated within a discussion of the relationship between "discourse" and "narrative" that has arisen in the wake of structuralism and is associated with the work of Jakobson, Benveniste, Genette, Todorov, and Barthes. Here narrative is regarded as a manner of speaking characterized, as Genette expresses it, "by a certain number of exclusions and restrictive conditions" that the more "open" form of discourse does not impose upon the speaker. According to Genette,

> Benveniste shows that certain grammatical forms like the pronoun "I" (and its implicit reference "thou"), the pronominal "indicators" (certain demonstrative pronouns), the adverbial indicators (like "here," "now," "yesterday," "today," "tomorrow," etc.) and, at least in French, certain verb tenses like the present, the present perfect, and the future, find themselves limited to discourse, while narrative in the strictest sense is distinguished by the exclusive use of the third person and of such forms as the preterit and the pluperfect.[4]

This distinction between discourse and narrative is, of course, based solely on an analysis of the grammatical features of two modes of discourse in which the "objectivity" of the one and the "subjectivity" of the other are definable primarily by a "linguistic order of criteria." The subjectivity of the discourse is given by the presence, explicit or implicit, of an "ego" who can be defined "only as the person who maintains the discourse." By contrast, "the objectivity of narrative is defined by the absence of all reference to the narrator." In the *narrativizing* discourse, then, we can say, with Benveniste, " 'Truly there is no longer a "narrator." The events are chronologically recorded as they appear on the horizon of the story. Here no one speaks. The events seem to tell themselves.' "[5]

4. Gérard Genette, "Boundaries of Narrative," *New Literary History* 8, no. 1 (Autumn 1976): 11. See also Jonathan Culler, *Structuralist Poetics: Structuralism, Linguistics, and the Study of Literature* (Ithaca, N.Y., 1975), chap. 9; Philip Pettit, *The Concept of Structuralism: A Critical Analysis* (Berkeley and Los Angeles, 1975); Tel Quel [Group], *Théorie d'ensemble* (Paris, 1968), esp. articles by Jean-Louis Baudry, Philippe Sollers, and Julia Kristeva; Robert Scholes, *Structuralism in Literature: An Introduction* (New Haven, Conn. and London, 1974), chaps. 4–5; Tzvetan Todorov, *Poétique de la prose* (Paris, 1971), chap. 9; and Paul Zumthor, *Langue, texte, énigme* (Paris, 1975), pt. 4.

5. Emile Benveniste as quoted by Genette, "Boundaries of Narrative," p. 9. Cf. Benveniste, *Problems in General Linguistics,* trans. Mary Elizabeth Meek (Coral Gables, Fla. 1971), p. 208.

What is involved in the production of a discourse in which "events seem to tell themselves," especially when it is a matter of events that are explicitly identified as "real" rather than "imaginary," as in the case of historical representations?[6] In a discourse having to do with manifestly imaginary events, which are the "contents" of fictional discourses, the question poses few problems. For why should not imaginary events be represented as "speaking themselves"? Why should not, in the domain of the imaginary, even the stones themselves speak—like Memnon's column when touched by the rays of the sun? But *real* events should not speak, should not tell themselves. Real events should simply be; they can perfectly well serve as the *referents* of a discourse, can be spoken about, but they should not pose as the *tellers* of a narrative. The lateness of the invention of historical discourse in human history and the difficulty of sustaining it in times of cultural breakdown (as in the early Middle Ages) suggest the *artificiality* of the notion that *real* events could "speak themselves" or be represented as "telling their own story." Such a fiction would have posed no problems before the distinction between real and imaginary events was imposed upon the storyteller; storytelling becomes a problem only *after* two orders of events dispose themselves before him as possible components of his stories and his storytelling is compelled to exfoliate under the injunction to keep the two orders unmixed in his discourse. What we call "mythic" narrative is under no obligation to keep the two orders of events distinct from one another. Narrative becomes a *problem* only when we wish to give to *real* events the *form* of story. It is because real events do not offer themselves as stories that their narrativization is so difficult.

What is involved, then, in that finding of the "true story," that discovery of the "real story" within or behind the events that come to us in the chaotic form of "historical records"? What wish is enacted, what desire is gratified, by the fantasy that *real* events are properly represented when they can be shown to display the formal coherency of a story? In the enigma of this wish, this desire, we catch a glimpse of the cultural function of narrativizing discourse in general, an intimation of the psychological impulse behind the apparently universal need not only to narrate but to give to events an aspect of narrativity.

Historiography is an especially good ground on which to consider the nature of narration and narrativity because it is here that our desire for the imaginary, the possible, must contest with the imperatives of the real, the actual. If we view narration and narrativity as the instruments by which the conflicting claims of the imaginary and the real are mediated, arbitrated, or resolved in a discourse, we begin to com-

6. See Louis O. Mink, "Narrative Form as a Cognitive Instrument," and Lionel Gossman, "History and Literature," in *The Writing of History: Literary Form and Historical Understanding,* ed. Robert H. Canary and Henry Kozicki (Madison, Wis., 1978), with complete bibliography on the problem of narrative form in historical writing.

prehend both the appeal of narrative and the grounds for refusing it. If putatively real events are represented in a non-narrative form, what kind of reality is it that offers itself, or is conceived to offer itself, to perception? What would a non-narrative representation of historical reality look like?

Fortunately, we have examples aplenty of representations of historical reality which are non-narrative in form. Indeed, the official wisdom of the modern historiographical establishment has it that there are three basic kinds of historical representation, the imperfect "historicality" of two of which is evidenced in their failure to attain to full narrativity of the events of which they treat. These three kinds are: the annals, the chronicle, and the history proper.[7] Needless to say, it is not narrativity alone which permits the distinction among the three kinds, for it is not enough that an account of events, even of past events, even of past real events, display all of the features of narrativity in order for it to count as a proper history. In addition, professional opinion has it, the account must manifest a proper concern for the judicious handling of evidence, and it must honor the chronological order of the original occurrence of the events of which it treats as a baseline that must not be transgressed in classifying any given event as either a cause or an effect. But by common consent, it is not enough that a historical account deal in real, rather than merely imaginary, events; and it is not enough that the account in its order of discourse represent events according to the chronological sequence in which they originally occurred. The events must be not only registered within the chronological framework of their original occurrence but narrated as well, that is to say, revealed as possessing a structure, an order of meaning, which they do *not* possess as mere sequence.

The annals form, needless to say, completely lacks this narrative component, consisting only of a list of events ordered in chronological sequence. The chronicle, by contrast, often seems to wish to tell a story, aspires to narrativity, but typically fails to achieve it. More specifically, the chronicle usually is marked by a failure to achieve narrative *closure*. It does not so much conclude as simply terminate. It starts out to tell a story but breaks off *in medias res*, in the chronicler's own present; it leaves things unresolved or, rather, leaves them unresolved in a story-like way. While annals represent historical reality *as if* real events did not display the form of story, the chronicle represents it *as if* real events appeared to human consciousness in the form of *unfinished* stories.

Official wisdom has it that however objective a historian might be in his reporting of events, however judicious in his assessment of evidence,

---

7. For purposes of economy, I will use as representative of the conventional view of the history of historical writing Harry Elmer Barnes, *A History of Historical Writing* (New York, 1962), chap. 3, which deals with medieval historiography in the West. See also Scholes and Robert Kellogg, *The Nature of Narrative* (Oxford, 1976), pp. 64, 211.

however punctilious in his dating of *res gestae,* his account remains something less than a proper history when he has failed to give to reality the form of a story. Where there is no narrative, Croce said, there is no history,[8] and Peter Gay, writing from a perspective that is directly opposed to the relativism of Croce, puts it just as starkly: "Historical narration without analysis is trivial, historical analysis without narration is incomplete."[9] Gay's formulation calls up the Kantian bias of the demand for narration in historical representation, for it suggests, to paraphrase Kant, that historical narratives without analysis are empty, while historical analyses without narrative are blind. So, we may ask, what kind of insight does narrative give into the nature of real events? What kind of blindness with respect to reality does narrativity dispell?

In what follows I will treat the annals and chronicle forms of historical representation not as the "imperfect" histories they are conventionally conceived to be but rather as particular products of possible conceptions of historical reality, conceptions that are alternatives to, rather than failed anticipations of, the fully realized historical discourse that the modern history form is supposed to embody. This procedure will throw light on the problems of both historiography and narration alike and will illuminate what I conceive to be the purely conventional nature of the relationship between them. What will be revealed, I think, is that the very distinction between real and imaginary events, basic to modern discussions of both history and fiction, presupposes a notion of reality in which "the true" is identified with "the real" only insofar as it can be shown to possess the character of narrativity.

*   *   *

When we moderns look at an example of a medieval annals, we cannot but be struck by the apparent naiveté of the annalist; and we are inclined to ascribe this naiveté to the annalist's apparent refusal, inability, or unwillingness to transform the set of events ordered vertically as a file of annual markers into the elements of a linear/horizontal process. In other words, we are likely to be put off by the annalist's apparent failure to see that historical events dispose themselves to the percipient eye as "stories" *waiting to be told,* waiting to be narrated. But surely a genuinely historical interest would require that we ask not how or why the annalist failed to write a "narrative" but rather what kind of notion of reality led him to represent in the *annals form* what, after all, he took to be real events. If we could answer this question, we might be able to understand why, in our own time and cultural condition, we could conceive of narrativity itself as a problem.

8. I discuss Croce in *Metahistory,* pp. 381–85.
9. Peter Gay, *Style in History* (New York, 1974), p. 189.

Volume one of the *Monumenta Germaniae Historica,* series *Scriptores,* contains the text of the *Annals of Saint Gall,* a list of events that occurred in Gaul during the eighth, ninth, and tenth centuries of our era.[10] Although this text is "referential" and contains a representation of temporality,[11] it possesses none of the attributes that we normally think of as a story: no central subject, no well-marked beginning, middle, and end, no peripeteia, and no identifiable narrative voice. In what are, for us, the theoretically most interesting segments of the text, there is no suggestion of any necessary connection between one event and another. Thus, for the period 709–734, we have the following entries:

709. Hard winter. Duke Gottfried died.
710. Hard year and deficient in crops.
711.
712. Flood everywhere.
713.
714. Pippin, Mayor of the Palace, died.
715. 716. 717.
718. Charles devastated the Saxon with great destruction.
719.
720. Charles fought against the Saxons.
721. Theudo drove the Saracens out of Aquitaine.
722. Great crops.
723.
724.
725. Saracens came for the first time.
726.
727.
728.
729.
730.
731. Blessed Bede, the presbyter, died.
732. Charles fought against the Saracens at Poitiers on Saturday.
733.
734.

This list immediately locates us in a culture hovering on the brink of dissolution, a society of radical scarcity, a world of human groups threatened by death, devastation, flood, and famine. All of the events are extreme, and the implicit criterion for their selection is their liminal nature. Basic needs—food, security from external enemies, political and

---

10. *Annales Sangallenses Maiores, dicti Hepidanni,* ed. Idlefonsus ab Arx, in *Monumenta Germaniae Historica,* series *Scriptores,* ed. George Heinrich Pertz, 32 vols. (Hanover, 1826), 1:73–85; my translation.
11. This is Oswald Ducrot and Todorov's definition of what can count as narrative. See Ducrot and Todorov, eds., *Encyclopedic Dictionary of the Sciences of Language,* trans. Catherine Porter (Baltimore, 1979), pp. 297–99.

military leadership—and the threat of their failing to be provided are the subjects of concern; but the connection between basic needs and the conditions for their possible satisfaction is not explicitly commented on. *Why* "Charles fought against the Saxons" remains as unexplained as *why* one year yielded "great crops" and another produced "flood[s] everywhere." Social events are apparently as incomprehensible as natural events. They seem to have the same order of importance or unimportance. They seem merely to have *occurred,* and their importance seems to be indistinguishable from the fact that they were recorded. In fact, it seems that their importance consists of nothing other than the fact that they were recorded.

And recorded *by whom,* we have no idea; nor any idea of *when* they were recorded. The entry for 725 ("Saracens came for the first time") suggests that this event at least was recorded *after* the Saracens had come *a second time* and sets up what we might consider to be a genuine narrativist expectation; but the coming of the Saracens and their repulsion is not the subject of this account. Charles' fight "against the Saracens at Poitiers on Saturday" is recorded, but the outcome of the battle is not told. And that "Saturday" is disturbing because the month and day of the battle are not given. There are too many loose ends—no plot in the offing; and this is frustrating, if not disturbing, to the modern reader's story expectations as well as his desire for specific information.

We note further that this account is not really inaugurated. It simply begins with the "title" (if it is a title) *Anni domini,* which stands at the head of two columns, one of dates, the other of events. Visually, at least, this title links the file of dates in the left-hand column with the file of events in the right-hand column in a promise of signification which we might be inclined to take for "mythical" were it not for the fact that *"Anni domini"* refers us both to a cosmological story given in Scripture and to a calendrical convention which historians in the West today still use to mark the units of their histories. We should not too quickly refer the meaning of the text to the mythic framework which it invokes by designating the "years" as being "of the Lord"; for these years have a regularity which the Christian mythos, with its clear hypotactic ordering of the events which make it up (Creation, Fall, Incarnation, Resurrection, Second Coming), does not possess. The regularity of the calendar signals the "realism" of the account, its intention to deal in real rather than imaginary events. The calendar locates events not in the time of eternity, not in *kairotic* time, but in chronological time, in time as it is *humanly* experienced. This time has no high points or low points; it is, we might say, paratactical and endless. It has no gaps. The list of times is full, even if the list of events is not.

Finally, the annals does not *conclude;* it simply terminates. The last entries are the following:

1045. 1046. 1047. 1048. 1049. 1050. 1051. 1052.
1053. 1054. 1055.
1056. The Emperor Henry died; and his son Henry succeeded to
   the rule.
1057. 1058. 1059. 1060. 1061. 1062. 1063. 1064.
1065. 1066. 1067. 1068. 1069. 1070. 1071. 1072.

The continuation of the list of years at the end of the account does, to be sure, suggest a continuation of the series ad infinitum or, rather, until the Second Coming. But there is no story conclusion. How could there be, since there is no central subject *about which* a story could be told?

Nonetheless, there must be a story since there is surely a plot—if by "plot" we mean a structure of relationships by which the events contained in the account are endowed with a meaning by being identified as parts of an integrated whole. By the plot of this story, however, I do not mean the myth of the Fall and Redemption (of the just parts of humankind) contained in the Bible; rather, I am referring to the list of dates given in the left-hand file of the text which confers coherence and fullness on the events by registering them under *the years in which they occurred.* To put it another way, the list of dates can be seen as the signifieds of which the events given in the right-hand column are the signifiers. The "meaning" of the events is their registration in this kind of list. This is why, I presume, the annalist would have felt little of the anxiety which the modern scholar feels when confronted with what appear to be "gaps," "discontinuities," and lack of causal connections between the events recorded in the text. The modern scholar seeks fullness and continuity in an order of events; the annalist has both in the sequence of the years. Which is the more "realistic" expectation?

Recall that we are dealing neither with oneiric nor infantile discourse. It may even be a mistake to call it "discourse" at all, but it has something discursive about it. The text summons up a "substance," operates in the domain of memory rather than of dream or fantasy, and unfolds under the sign of "the real" rather than that of the "imaginary." In fact, it seems eminently rational and, on the face of it, rather prudent in both its manifest desire to record only those events about which there could be little doubt as to their occurrence and its resolve not to interpellate facts on speculative grounds or to advance arguments about how the events are really connected to one another.

Modern commentators have remarked on the fact that the annalist recorded the Battle of Poitiers of 732 but failed to note the Battle of Tours which occurred in the same year and which, as every schoolboy knows, was one of "the ten great battles of world history." But even if the annalist had known of Tours, what principle or rule of meaning would have required him to record it? It is only from *our* knowledge of the *subsequent* history of Western Europe that we can presume to rank events in terms of their world historical significance, and even then that significance is less "world historical" than simply Western European, representing a tendency of modern historians to rank events in the record hierarchically from within a perspective that is culture-specific, not universal at all.

It is this need or impulse to rank events with respect to their significance for the culture or group that is writing its own history that makes a narrative representation of real events possible. It is surely much more "universalistic" simply to record events as they come to notice. And at the minimal level on which the annals unfolds, what gets put into the account is of much greater theoretical importance for the understanding of the nature of narrative than what gets left out. But this does raise the question of the function in this text of the recording of those years in which "nothing happened." For in fact every narrative, however seemingly "full," is constructed on the basis of a set of events which *might have been included but were left out;* and this is as true of imaginary as it is of realistic narratives. This consideration permits us to ask what kind of notion of reality authorizes construction of a narrative account of reality in which continuity rather than discontinuity governs the articulation of the discourse.

If we grant that this discourse unfolds under a sign of a desire for the real, as we must do in order to justify the inclusion of the annals form among the types of historical representation, we must conclude that it is a product of an image of reality in which *the social system,* which alone could provide the diacritical markers for ranking the importance of events, is only minimally present to the consciousness of the writer or, rather, is present as a factor in the composition of the discourse only by virtue of its absence. Everywhere it is the forces of disorder, natural and human, the forces of violence and destruction, which occupy the forefront of attention. The account deals in *qualities* rather than *agents,* figuring forth a world in which things *happen to* people rather than one in which people *do* things. It is the hardness of the winter of 709, the hardness of the year 710 and the deficiency of the crops of that year, the flooding of the waters in 712, and the imminent presence of death which recur with a frequency and regularity that are lacking in the representation of acts of human agency. Reality for this annalist wears the face of adjectives which override the capacity of the nouns they modify to resist their determinacy. Charles does manage to devastate the Saxons, to fight against them, and Theudo even manages to drive the Saracens out of Aquitaine. But these actions appear to belong to the same order of existence as the natural events which bring either "great crops" or "deficient" harvests and are as seemingly incomprehensible.

The absence of a principle for assigning importance or significance to events is signaled above all in the gaps in the list of events in the right-hand file, for example in the year 711 in which, so it seems, nothing happened. The overabundance of the waters noted for the year 712 is preceded and followed by years in which also "nothing happened." This puts one in mind of Hegel's remark that periods of human happiness and security are blank pages in history. But the presence of these blank years in the annalist's account permits us to perceive, by way of contrast, the extent to which narrative strains to produce the effect of having filled in all the gaps, to put an image of continuity, coherency, and meaning in place of the fantasies of emptiness, need, and frustrated desire that inhabit our nightmares about the destructive power of time. In fact, the annalist's account calls up a world in which need is everywhere present, in which scarcity is the rule of existence, and in which all of the possible agencies of satisfaction are lacking, absent, or exist under imminent threat of death.

The notion of possible gratification is, however, implicit in the list of dates that make up the left-hand column. The fullness of this list attests to the fullness of time or at least to the fullness of the "years of the Lord." There is no scarcity of years: they descend regularly from their origin, the year of the Incarnation, and roll relentlessly on to their potential end, the Last Judgment. What is lacking in the list of events to give it a similar regularity and fullness is a notion of a social center by which both to locate them with respect to one another and to charge them with ethical or moral significance. It is the absence of any consciousness of a *social* center that prohibits the annalist from ranking the events which he treats as elements of a historical field of occurrence. And it is the absence of such a center that precludes or undercuts any impulse he might have had to work up his discourse into the form of a narrative. Without such a center, Charles' campaigns against the Saxons remain simply "fights," the invasion of the Saracens simply a "coming," and the fact that the Battle of Poitiers was fought on a Saturday as important as the fact that the battle was even fought at all.

All this suggests to me that Hegel was right when he opined that a genuinely historical account had to display not only a certain form, that is, the narrative, but also a certain content, namely, a political-social order. In his introduction to his *Lectures on the Philosophy of History,* Hegel wrote:

> In our language the term *History* unites the objective with the subjective side, and denotes quite as much the *historia rerum gestarum,* as the *res gestae* themselves; on the other hand it comprehends not less what has *happened,* than the *narration* of what has happened. This union of the two meanings we must regard as of a higher order than mere outward accident; we must suppose historical narrations to have appeared contemporaneously with historical deeds and events. It is an internal vital principle common to both that pro-

duces them synchronously. Family memorials, patriarchal traditions, have an interest confined to the family and the clan. The
uniform course of events [my italics] which such a condition implies, is
no subject of serious remembrance; though distinct transactions or
turns of fortune, may rouse Mnemosyne to form conceptions of
them—in the same way as love and the religious emotions provoke
imagination to give shape to a previously formless impulse. But it is
the State which first presents subject-matter that is not only *adapted*
to the prose of History, but involves the production of such history
in the very progress of its own being. [12]

Hegel goes on to distinguish between the kind of "profound senti-
ments," such as "love" and "religious intuition and its conceptions," and
"that outward existence of a political constitution which is enshrined
in . . . rational laws and customs [which] is an *imperfect* Present; and cannot be thoroughly understood without a knowledge of the past." This is
why, he concludes, there are periods which, although filled with "revo-
lutions, nomadic wanderings, and the strangest mutations," are destitute
of any *objective* history. And their destitution of an objective history is
a function of the fact that they could produce "no *subjective* history, no
annals. We need not suppose," he remarks, "that the records of such
periods have accidentally perished; rather, because they were not possible, do we find them wanting." And he insists that "only in a State
cognizant of Laws, can distinct transactions take place, accompanied by
such a clear consciousness of them as supplies the ability and suggests the
necessity of an enduring record" (p. 61). When, in short, it is a matter of
providing a *narrative* of real events, we must suppose that a subject of the
sort that would provide the impulse to record its activities must exist.

Hegel insists that the proper subject of such a record is the state, but
the state is to him an abstraction. The reality which lends itself to narrative representation is the *conflict* between desire, on the one side, and the
law, on the other. Where there is no rule of law, there can be neither a
subject nor the kind of event which lends itself to narrative representation. This proposition could not be empirically verified or falsified, to be
sure; it rather enables a presupposition or hypothesis which permits us
to imagine how both "historicity" and "narrativity" are possible. It also
authorizes us to consider the proposition that neither is possible without
some notion of the legal subject which can serve as the agent, agency,
and subject of historical narrative in all of its manifestations, from the
annals through the chronicle to the historical discourse as we know it in
its modern realizations and failures.

The question of the law, legality, or legitimacy does not arise in

12. G. W. F. Hegel, *The Philosophy of History*, trans. J. Sibree (New York, 1956), pp.
60–61; all further references to Hegel's introduction will be cited parenthetically in the
text.

those parts of the *Annals of Saint Gall* which we have been considering; at least, the question of *human* law does not arise. There is no suggestion that the "coming" of the Saracens represents a transgression of any limit, that it should not have been or might have been otherwise. Since everything that happened, happened apparently in accordance with the divine will, it is sufficient simply to note its happening, to register it under the appropriate "year of the Lord" in which it occurred. The coming of the Saracens is of the same moral significance as Charles' fight against the Saxons. We have no way of knowing whether the annalist would have been impelled to flesh out his list of events and rise to the challenge of a narrative representation of those events if he had written in the consciousness of the threat to a specific social system and the possibility of anarchy against which the legal system might have been erected. But once we have been alerted to the intimate relationship that Hegel suggests exists between law, historicality, and narrativity, we cannot but be struck by the frequency with which narrativity, whether of the fictional or the factual sort, presupposes the existence of a legal system against or on behalf of which the typical agents of a narrative account militate. And this raises the suspicion that narrative in general, from the folktale to the novel, from the annals to the fully realized "history," has to do with the topics of law, legality, legitimacy, or, more generally, *authority*. And indeed, when we look at what is supposed to be the next stage in the evolution of historical representation after the annals form, that is, the chronicle, this suspicion is borne out. The more historically self-conscious the writer of any form of historiography, the more the question of the social system and the law which sustains it, the authority of this law and its justification, and threats to the law occupy his attention. If, as Hegel suggests, historicality as a distinct mode of human existence is unthinkable without the presupposition of a system of law in relation to which a specifically legal subject could be constituted, then historical self-consciousness, the kind of consciousness capable of imagining the need to represent reality as a history, is conceivable only in terms of its interest in law, legality, legitimacy, and so on.

Interest in the social system, which is nothing other than a system of human relationships governed by law, creates the possibility of conceiving the kinds of tensions, conflicts, struggles, and their various kinds of resolutions that we are accustomed to find in any representation of reality presenting itself to us as a history. Perhaps, then, the growth and development of historical consciousness which is attended by a concomitant growth and development of narrative capability (of the sort met with in the chronicle as against the annals form) has something to do with the extent to which the legal system functions as a subject of concern. If every fully realized story, however we define that familiar but conceptually elusive entity, is a kind of allegory, points to a moral, or endows events, whether real or imaginary, with a significance that they do not possess as a mere sequence, then it seems possible to conclude that every historical narrative has as its latent or manifest purpose the desire to *moralize* the events of which it treats. Where there is ambiguity or ambivalence regarding the status of the legal system, which is the form in which the subject encounters most immediately the social system in which he is enjoined to achieve a full humanity, the ground on which any closure of a story one might wish to tell about a past, whether it be a public or a private past, is lacking. And this suggests that narrativity, certainly in factual storytelling and probably in fictional storytelling as well, is intimately related to, if not a function of, the impulse to moralize reality, that is, to identify it with the social system that is the source of any morality that we can imagine.

The annalist of Saint Gall shows no concern about any system of merely human morality or law. The entry for 1056, "The Emperor Henry died; and his son Henry succeeded to the rule," contains in embryo the elements of a narrative. Indeed, it *is* a narrative, and its narrativity, in spite of the ambiguity of the connection between the first event (Henry's death) and the second (Henry's succession) suggested by the particle "and," achieves closure by its tacit invocation of the legal system: the rule of genealogical succession which the annalist takes for granted as a principle rightly governing the passing of authority from one generation to another. But this small narrative element, this "narreme," floats easily on the sea of dates which figures *succession* itself as a principle of cosmic organization. Those of us who know what was awaiting the younger Henry in his conflicts with his nobles and with the popes during the period of the investiture struggle, in which the issue of precisely *where* final authority on earth was located was fought out, may be irritated by the economy with which the annalist recorded an event so fraught with future moral and legal implications. The years 1057–72, which the annalist simply lists at the end of his record, provided more than enough "events" that prefigured the onset of this struggle, more than enough conflict to warrant a full narrative account of its inception. But the annalist simply ignored them. He apparently felt that he had done his duty solely by listing the dates themselves. What is involved, we might ask, in this refusal to narrate?

To be sure, we can conclude—as Frank Kermode suggested in his remark on this text during our discussion—that the annalist of Saint Gall was just not a very good diarist; and such a commonsensical judgment is manifestly justified. But the incapacity to keep a good diary is not theoretically different from the unwillingness to do so. From the standpoint of an interest in narrative itself, a "bad" narrative can tell us more about narrativity than a good one. If it is true that the annalist of Saint Gall was an untidy or lazy narrator, we must ask what he lacked that would have made him a competent narrator. What is absent from his account which, if it had been present, would have permitted him to transform his chronology into a historical narrative?

The vertical ordering of events itself suggests that our annalist did not want in metaphoric or paradigmatic consciousness. He does not suffer from what Roman Jakobson calls "similarity disorder." Indeed, all of the events listed in the right-hand column appear to be considered as the *same kind* of event; they are all metonymies of the general condition of scarcity or overfullness of the "reality" which the annalist is recording. *Difference,* significant variation within similitude, is figured only in the left-hand column, the list of dates. Each of these functions as a metaphor of the fullness and completion of the time of the Lord. The image of orderly succession that this column calls up has no counterpart in the events, natural and human, which are listed on the right-hand side. What the annalist lacked that would have led him to make a narrative out of the set of events he recorded was a capacity to endow *events* with the same kind of "propositionality" that is implicitly present in his representation of the sequence of dates. This lack resembles what Jakobson calls "contiguity disorder," a phenomenon represented in speech by "agrammatism" and in discourse by a dissolution of "the ties of grammatical coordination and subordination" by which "word heaps" can be aggregated into meaningful sentences.[13] Our annalist was not, of course, aphasic—as his capacity to contrive meaningful sentences amply shows. But he lacked the capacity to substitute meanings for one another in chains of semantic metonymies that would transform his list of events into a discourse about the events considered as a totality evolving in time.

Now, the capacity to envision a set of events as belonging to the same order of meaning requires a metaphysical principle by which to translate difference into similarity. In other words, it requires a "subject" common to all of the *referents* of the various sentences that register events as having occurred. If such a subject exists, it is the "Lord" whose "years" are treated as manifestations of His power to cause the events which occur in them. The subject of the account, then, does not exist *in time* and could not therefore function as the subject of a narrative. Does it follow that in order for there to be a narrative, there must be some equivalent of the Lord, some sacral being endowed with the authority and power of the Lord, existing in time? If so, what could such an equivalent be?

The nature of such a being, capable of serving as the central organizing principle of meaning of a discourse that is both realistic and narrative in structure, is called up in the mode of historical representation known as the chronicle. By common consensus among historians of historical writing, the chronicle form is a "higher" form of historical

---

13. Roman Jakobson and Morris Halle, *Fundamentals of Language* (The Hague, 1971), pp. 85–86.

conceptualization and represents a mode of historiographical representation superior to the annals form.[14] Its superiority consists, it is agreed, in its greater comprehensiveness, its organization of materials "by topics and reigns," and its greater narrative coherency. The chronicle also has a central subject, the life of an individual, town, or region, some great undertaking, such as a war or crusade, or some institution, such as a monarchy, episcopacy, or monastery. The link of the chronicle with the annals is perceived in the perseverance of the chronology as the organizing principle of the discourse, and, so we are told, this is what makes the chronicle something less than a fully realized "history." Moreover, the chronicle, like the annals but unlike the history, does not so much "conclude" as simply terminate; typically it lacks closure, that summing up of the "meaning" of the chain of events with which it deals that we normally expect from the well-made story. The chronicle typically promises closure but does not provide it—which is one of the reasons that the nineteenth-century editors of the medieval chronicles denied them the status of genuine histories.

Suppose that we look at the matter differently. Suppose that we do not grant that the chronicle is a "higher" or more sophisticated representation of reality than the annals but is merely a *different* kind of representation, marked by a desire for a kind of order and fullness in an account of reality that remains theoretically unjustified, a desire that is, until shown otherwise, purely gratuitous. What is involved in the imposition of this order and the provision of this fullness (of detail) which mark the differences between the annals and the chronicle?

I take as an example of the chronicle type of historical representation the *History of France* of Richerus of Reims, written on the eve of the year A.D. 1000 (ca. 998).[15] We have no difficulty recognizing this text as a narrative: it has a central subject ("the conflicts of the French" [1:3]); it has a proper geographical center (Gaul) and a proper social center (the archiepiscopal see of Reims, beset by a dispute over which of two claimants to the office of archbishop is the legitimate occupant of it); and it has a proper beginning in time (given in a synoptic version of the history of the world from the Incarnation down to the time and place of Richerus' own writing of his account). But the work fails as a "proper" history, at least according to the opinion of later commentators, by virtue of two considerations. First, the order of the discourse follows the order of chronology; it presents events in the order of their occurrence and cannot, therefore, offer the kind of meaning that a narratologically governed account can be said to provide. Second, and this is probably a consequence of the "annalistic" order of the discourse, the account does

14. See Barnes, *A History of Historical Writing,* pp. 65–68.
15. Richer, *Histoire de France, 888–995,* ed. and trans. Robert Latouche, 2 vols. (Paris, 1930–37); all further references to this work will be cited parenthetically in the text; my translations.

not so much *conclude* as simply *terminate;* it merely "breaks off" with the flight of one of the disputants for the office of archbishop and throws on the reader the burden of retrospectively reflecting on the linkages between the beginning of the account and its ending. The account comes down to the writer's own "yesterday," adds one more fact to the series which began with the Incarnation, and then simply ceases. As a result, all of the normal narratological expectations of the reader (this reader) remain unfulfilled. The work appears to be unfolding a plot but then belies its own appearance by merely stopping *in medias res,* with a cryptic notation: "Pope Gregory authorizes Arnulfus to assume provisionally the episcopal functions, while awaiting the legal decision that would either confer these upon him or withdraw the right to them" (2:133).

And yet Richerus is a self-conscious narrator. He explicitly says at the outset of his account that he proposes "especially to preserve in writing [ad memoriam reducere scripto specialiter propositum est]" the "wars," "troubles," and "affairs" of the French and, moreover, to write them up in a manner superior to other accounts, especially that of one Flodoard, an earlier scribe of Reims who had written an annals on which Richerus has drawn for information. Richerus notes that he has drawn freely on Flodoard's work but that he has often "put other words" in place of the original ones and "modified completely the style of the presentation [pro aliis longe diversissimo orationis scemate disposuisse]" (1:4). He also situates himself in a tradition of historical writing by citing such classics as Caesar, Orosius, Jerome, and Isidore as authorities for the early history of Gaul and suggests that his own personal observations gave him insight into the facts he is recounting that no one else could claim. All of this suggests a certain distance from his own discourse which is manifestly lacking in the writer of the *Annals of Saint Gall.* Richerus' discourse is a *fashioned* discourse, the narrativity of which, in comparison to that of the annalist, is a function of the self-consciousness with which this fashioning activity is entered upon.

Paradoxically, however, it is this self-conscious fashioning activity, an activity which gives to Richerus' work the aspect of a historical *narrative,* that decreases its "objectivity" as a *historical* account—or so the consensus of modern analysts of the text has it. For example, a modern editor of the text, Robert Latouche, indicts Richerus' pride in the originality of his style as the cause of his failure to write a proper history. "Ultimately," Latouche notes, "the *History* of Richer is not properly speaking [*proprement parler*] a history, but a work of rhetoric composed by a monk . . . who sought to imitate the techniques of Salluste." And he adds, "what interested him was not the material [*matière*] which he molded to fit his fancy, but the form" (1:xi).

Latouche is certainly right in his characterization of Richerus' failings *as a historian* supposedly interested in the "facts" of a certain period of history but is just as surely wrong in his suggestion that the work fails *as a history* because of the writer's interest in "form" rather than "matter." By *"matière,"* of course, Latouche means the referents of the discourse, the events taken individually as objects of representation. But Richerus is interested in "the conflicts of the French [Gallorum congressibus in volumine regerendis]" (1:2), especially the conflict in which his patron, Gerbert, archbishop of Reims, was currently involved for control of the see. Far from being interested primarily in form rather than matter or content, Richerus was only interested in the latter; for this conflict was one in which his own future was entailed. Where *authority* lay for the direction of affairs in the see of Reims was the question which Richerus hoped to help resolve by the composition of his narrative. We can legitimately suppose that his impulse to write a narrative of this conflict was in some way connected with a desire on his part to represent (both in the sense of writing about and in the sense of acting as an agent of) an authority whose legitimacy hinged upon the establishment of "facts" that were of a specifically historical order.

Indeed, once we note the presence of the theme of *authority* in this text, we also perceive the extent to which the truth claims of the narrative and indeed the very *right* to narrate hinges upon a certain relationship to authority per se. The first authority invoked by the author is that of his patron, Gerbert; it is by his authority that the account is composed (". . . imperii tui, pater santissime G[erbert], auctoritas seminarium dedit" [1:2]). Then there are those "authorities" represented by the classic texts on which he draws for his construction of the early history of the French (Caesar, Orosius, Jerome, etc.). There is the "authority" of his predecessor as a historian of the see of Reims, Flodoard, an authority with whom he contests as narrator and on whose style he professes to improve. It is on his own authority that Richerus effects this improvement, by putting "other words" in place of Flodoard's and modifying "completely the style of the presentation." There is, finally, not only the the authority of the Heavenly Father, who is invoked as the ultimate cause of everything that happens, but the authority of Richerus' own father (referred to throughout the manuscript as "p. m." [*pater meus*] who figures as a central subject of a segment of the work and as the witness on whose authority the account in this segment is based.

The problem of authority pervades the text written by Richerus in a way that cannot be ascribed to the text written by the annalist of Saint Gall. For the annalist, there is no need to claim the authority to narrate events since there is nothing problematical about their status as manifestations of a reality that is being contested. Since there is no "contest," there is nothing to narrativize, no need for them to "speak themselves" or be represented *as if* they could "tell their own story." It is necessary only to record them in the order that they come to notice, for since there is no contest, there is no story to tell. It is because there was a contest that there is something to narrativize for Richerus. But it is not because the contest was not resolved that the quasi narrative produced by Richerus has no closure; for the contest was in fact resolved—by the flight of Gerbert to the court of King Otto and the installation of Arnulfus as archbishop of Reims by Pope Gregory. What was lacking for a proper discursive resolution, a narrativizing resolution, was the moral principle in light of which Richerus might have judged the resolution as either just or unjust. Reality itself has judged the resolution by resolving it as it has done. To be sure, there is the suggestion that a kind of justice was provided for Gerbert by King Otto who, "having recognized Gerbert's learning and genius, installs him as bishop of Ravenna." But that justice is located at another place and is disposed by another authority, another king. The end of the discourse does not cast its light back over the events originally recorded in order to redistribute the force of a meaning that was immanent in all of the events from the beginning. There is no justice, only force; or rather only an authority that presents itself as different kinds of forces.

I wish to stress that I do not offer these reflections on the relationship between historiography and narrative as anything other than an attempt to illuminate the distinction between story elements and plot elements in the historical discourse. Common opinion has it that the plot of a narrative imposes a meaning on the events that comprise its story level by revealing at the end a structure that was immanent in the events *all along*. What I am trying to establish is the nature of this immanence in any narrative account of *real* events, the kind of events that are offered as the proper content of historical discourse. The reality of these events does not consist in the fact that they occurred but that, first of all, they were remembered and, second, that they are capable of finding a place in a chronologically ordered sequence.

In order for an account of the events to be considered a historical account, however, it is not enough that they be recorded in the order of their original occurrence. It is the fact that they *can* be recorded otherwise, in an order of narrative, that makes them at once questionable as to their authenticity and susceptible to being considered tokens of reality. In order to qualify as "historical," an event must be susceptible to at least two narrations of its occurrence. Unless at least two versions of the same set of events can be imagined, there is no reason for the historian to take upon himself the authority of giving the true account of what really happened. The authority of the historical narrative is the authority of reality itself; the historical account endows this reality with form and thereby makes it desirable, imposing upon its processes the formal coherency that only stories possess.

The history, then, belongs to the category of what might be called the "discourse of the real," as against the "discourse of the imaginary" or the "discourse of desire." The formulation is Lacanian, obviously, but I do not wish to push the Lacanian aspects of it too far. I merely wish to suggest that we can comprehend the appeal of historical discourse by recognizing the extent to which it makes the real desirable, makes the real into an object of desire, and does so by its imposition, upon events that are represented as real, of the formal coherency that stories possess. Unlike the annals, the reality that is represented in the historical narrative, in "speaking itself," speaks *to* us, summons us from afar (this "afar" is the land of forms), and displays to us a formal coherency that we ourselves lack. The historical narrative, as against the chronicle, reveals to us a world that is putatively "finished," done with, over, and yet not dissolved, not falling apart. In this world, reality wears the mask of a meaning, the completeness and fullness of which we can only *imagine,* never experience. Insofar as historical stories can be completed, can be given narrative closure, can be shown to have had a *plot* all along, they give to reality the odor of the *ideal.* This is why the plot of a historical narrative is always an embarrassment and has to be presented as "found" in the events rather than put there by narrative techniques.

The embarrassment of plot to historical narrative is reflected in the all but universal disdain with which modern historians regard the "philosophy of history," of which Hegel provides the modern paradigm. This (fourth) form of historical representation is condemned because it consists of nothing but plot; its story elements exist only as manifestations, epiphenomena, of the plot structure, in the service of which its discourse is disposed. Here reality wears a face of such regularity, order, and coherence that it leaves no room for human agency, presenting an aspect of such wholeness and completeness that it intimidates rather than invites to imaginative identification. But in the plot of the philosophy of history, the various plots of the various histories which tell us of merely regional happenings in the past are revealed for what they really are: images of that authority which summons us to participation in a moral universe that, but for its story form, would have no appeal at all.

This puts us close to a possible characterization of the demand for closure in the history, for the want of which the chronicle form is adjudged to be deficient as a narrative. The demand for closure in the historical story is a demand, I suggest, for moral meaning, a demand that sequences of real events be assessed as to their significance as elements of a *moral* drama. Has any historical narrative ever been written that was not informed not only by moral awareness but specifically by the moral authority of the narrator? It is difficult to think of any historical work produced during the nineteenth century, the classic age of historical narrative, that was not given the force of a moral judgment on the events it related.

But we do not have to prejudge the matter by looking at historical texts composed in the nineteenth century; we can perceive the operations of moral consciousness in the achievement of narrative fullness in an example of late medieval historiography, the *Cronica* of Dino Compagni, written between 1310 and 1312 and generally recognized as a proper historical narrative.[16] Dino's work not only "fills in the gaps" which might have been left in an annalistic handling of its subject matter (the struggles between the Black and White factions of the dominant Guelf party in Florence between 1280 and 1312) and organizes its story according to a well-marked ternary plot structure; it also achieves narrative fullness by explicitly invoking the idea of a social system to serve as a fixed reference point by which the flow of ephemeral events can be endowed with specifically moral meaning. In this respect, the *Cronica* clearly displays the extent to which the chronicle must approach the form of an allegory, moral or anagogical as the case may be, in order to achieve *both* narrativity and historicality.

It is interesting to observe that as the chronicle form is displaced by the proper history, certain of the features of the former disappear. First of all, no explicit patron is invoked: Dino's narrative does not unfold under the authority of a specific patron, as Richerus' does; instead, Dino simply asserts his right to recount notable events *(cose notevoli)* which he has "seen and heard" on the basis of a superior capacity of foresight. "No one saw these events in their beginnings [*principi*] more certainly than I," he says. His prospective audience is not, then, a specific ideal reader, as Gerbert was for Richerus, but rather a *group* that is conceived to share his perspective on the true nature of all events: those citizens of Florence who are capable, as he puts it, of recognizing "the benefits of God, who rules and governs for all time." At the same time, he speaks to another group, the depraved citizens of Florence, those who are responsible for the "conflicts" *(discordie)* that had wracked the city for some three decades. To the former, his narrative is intended to hold out the hope of deliverance from these conflicts; to the latter, it is intended as an admonition and a threat of retribution. The chaos of the last ten years is contrasted with more "prosperous" years to come, after the emperor Henry VII has descended on Florence in order to punish a people whose "evil customs and false profits" have "corrupted and spoiled the whole world."[17] What Kermode calls "the weight of meaning" of the events recounted is "thrown forward" onto a future just beyond the immediate present, a future fraught with moral judgment and punishment for the wicked.[18]

The jeremiad with which Dino's work closes marks it as belonging to a period before which a genuine historical "objectivity," which is to say, a secularist ideology, had been established—so the commentators tell us.

---

16. *La cronica di Dino Compagni delle cose occorrenti ne'tempi suoi e La canzone morale Del Pregio dello stesso autore,* ed. Isidoro Del Lungo, 4th ed. rev. (Florence, 1902). Cf. Barnes, pp. 80–81.

17. Ibid., p. 5; my translations.

18. See Frank Kermode, *The Sense of an Ending: Studies in the Theory of Fiction* (Oxford, 1967), chap. 1.

But it is difficult to see how the kind of narrative fullness for which Dino is praised could have been attained without the implicit invocation of the moral standard that he uses to distinguish between those real events worthy of being recorded and those unworthy of it. The events that are actually recorded in the narrative appear "real" precisely insofar as they belong to an order of moral existence, just as they derive their meaning from their placement in this order. It is because the events described conduce to the establishment of social order or fail to do so that they find a place in the narrative attesting to their reality. Only the contrast between the governance of God and the anarchy of the current social situation in Florence could justify the apocalyptical tone and narrative function of the final paragraph, with its image of the emperor who will come to chasten those "who brought evil into the world through [their] bad habits." And only a moral authority could justify the turn in the narrative which permits it to come to an *end*. Dino explicitly identifies the end of his narrative with a "turn" in the moral order of the world: "The world is beginning now to turn over once more [Ora vi si ricomincia il mondo a rivolgere addosso] . . . : the Emperor is coming to take you and despoil you, by land and by sea."[19]

It is this moralistic ending which keeps Dino's *Cronica* from meeting the standard of a modern, "objective" historical account. Yet it is this moralism which alone permits the work to end or, rather, to *conclude* in a way different from the way that the annals and the chronicle forms do. But on what other grounds could a narrative of real events *possibly* conclude? When it is a matter of recounting the concourse of real events, what other "ending" could a given sequence of such events have than a "moralizing" ending? What else could narrative closure consist of than the *passage* from one moral order to another? I confess that I cannot think of any other way of "concluding" an account of *real* events; for we cannot say, surely, that any sequence of real events actually comes to an end, that reality itself disappears, that events *of the order of the real* have ceased to happen. Such events could only have seemed to have ceased to happen when meaning is shifted, and shifted by narrative means, from one physical or social space to another. Where moral sensitivity is lacking, as it seems to be in an annalistic account of reality, or is only potentially present, as it appears to be in a chronicle, not only meaning but the means to track such shifts of meaning, that is, narrativity, appears to be lacking also. Where, in any account of reality, narrativity is present, we can be sure that morality or a moralizing impulse is present too. There is no other way that reality can be endowed with the kind of meaning that both displays itself in its consummation and withholds itself by its displacement to another story "waiting to be told" just beyond the confines of "the end."

What I have been working around to is the question of the *value*

19. Compagni, pp. 209–10.

attached to narrativity itself, especially in representations of reality of the sort which historical discourse embodies. It may be thought that I have stacked the cards in favor of my thesis (that narrativizing discourse serves the purpose of moralizing judgments) by my use of exclusively medieval materials. And perhaps I have; but it is the modern historiographical community which has distinguished between annals, chronicle, and history forms of discourse on the basis of their attainment of narrative fullness or failure to attain it. And this same scholarly establishment has yet to account for the fact that just when, by its own account, historiography was transformed into a so-called objective discipline, it was the narrativity of the historical discourse that was celebrated as one of the signs of historiography's maturation as a science—a science of a special sort, but a science nonetheless. It is the historians themselves who have transformed narrativity from a manner of speaking into a paradigm of the form which reality itself displays to a "realistic" consciousness. It is they who have made narrativity into a value, the presence of which in a discourse having to do with real events signals at once its objectivity, its seriousness, and its realism.

I have sought to suggest that this value attached to narrativity in the representation of real events arises out of a desire to have real events display the coherence, integrity, fullness, and closure of an image of life that is and can only be imaginary. The notion that sequences of real events possess the formal attributes of the stories we tell about imaginary events could only have its origin in wishes, daydreams, reveries. Does the world really present itself to perception in the form of well-made stories, with central subjects, proper beginnings, middles, and ends, and a coherence that permits us to see "the end" in every beginning? Or does it present itself more in the forms that the annals and chronicle suggest, either as mere sequence without beginning or end or as sequences of beginnings that only terminate and never conclude? And does the world, even the social world, ever really come to us as already narrativized, already "speaking itself " from beyond the horizon of our capacity to make scientific sense of it? Or is the fiction of such a world, a world capable of speaking itself and of displaying itself as a form of a story, necessary for the establishment of that moral authority without which the notion of a specifically social reality would be unthinkable? If it were only a matter of realism in representation, one could make a pretty good case for both the annals and chronicle forms as paradigms of ways that reality offers itself to perception. Is it possible that their supposed want of objectivity, manifested in their failure to narrativize reality adequately, has nothing to do with the modes of perception which they presuppose but with their failure to represent the *moral* under the aspect of the *aesthetic*? And could we answer that question without giving a narrative account of the history of objectivity itself, an account that would already prejudice the outcome of the story we would tell in favor of the *moral* in general? Could we ever narrativize *without* moralizing?

Narration in the Psychoanalytic Dialogue

Roy Schafer

1. Preface: Psychoanalytic Theories as Narratives

Freud established a tradition within which psychoanalysis is understood as an essentialist and positivist natural science. One need not be bound by this scientific commitment, however; the individual and general accounts and interpretations Freud gave of his case material can be read in another way. In this reading, psychoanalysis is an interpretive discipline whose practitioners aim to develop a particular kind of systematic account of human action. We can say, then, either that Freud was developing a set of principles for participating in, understanding, and explaining the dialogue between psychoanalyst and analysand or that he was establishing a set of codes to generate psychoanalytic meaning, recognizing this meaning in each instance to be only one of a number of kinds of meaning that might be generated.

Psychoanalytic theorists of different persuasions have employed different interpretive principles or codes—one might say different narrative structures—to develop their ways of doing analysis and telling about it.[1] These narrative structures present or imply two coordinated accounts: one, of the beginning, the course, and the ending of human

1. See my "On Becoming an Analyst of One Persuasion or Another," *Contemporary Psychoanalysis* 15 (July 1979): 345–60. I will frequently refer the reader to my own books and articles since many brief assertions and discussions here are based on more extended arguments in specialized publications not likely known to most readers of this journal. My great debt to many thinkers in psychoanalysis (especially Freud) and in other interpretive disciplines is acknowledged in these earlier publications.

development; the other, of the course of the psychoanalytic dialogue. Far from being secondary narratives about data, these structures provide primary narratives that establish what is to count as data. Once installed as leading narrative structures, they are taken as certain in order to develop coherent accounts of lives and technical practices.

It makes sense, and it may be a useful project, to present psychoanalysis in narrational terms. In order to carry through this project, one must, first of all, accept the proposition that there are no objective, autonomous, or pure psychoanalytic data which, as Freud was fond of saying, compel one to draw certain conclusions. Specifically, there is no single, necessary, definitive account of a life history and psychopathology, of biological and social influences on personality, or of the psychoanalytic method and its results. What have been presented as the plain empirical data and techniques of psychoanalysis are inseparable from the investigator's precritical and interrelated assumptions concerning the origins, coherence, totality, and intelligibility of personal action. The data and techniques exist as such by virtue of two sets of practices that embody these assumptions: first, a set of *practices of naming and interrelating* that is systematic insofar as it conforms to the initial assumptions; and second, a set of *technical practices* that is systematic insofar as it elicits and shapes phenomena that can be ordered in terms of these assumptions. No version of psychoanalysis has ever come close to being codified to this extent. The approach to such codification requires that the data of psychoanalysis be unfailingly regarded as constituted rather than simply encountered. The sharp split between subject and object must be systematically rejected.

In his formal theorizing, Freud used two primary narrative structures, and he often urged that they be taken as provisional rather than as final truths. But Freud was not always consistent in this regard, sometimes presenting dogmatically on one page what he had presented tentatively on another. One of his primary narrative structures begins with the infant and young child as a beast, otherwise known as the id, and ends with the beast domesticated, tamed by frustration in the course of development in a civilization hostile to its nature. Even though this taming leaves each person with two regulatory structures, the ego and the superego, the protagonist remains in part a beast, the carrier of the

---

Roy Schafer is clinical professor of psychology and psychiatry at Cornell University Medical College, adjunct professor of psychology at New York University, and a supervising and training analyst at Columbia University's Center for Psychoanalytic Training and Research. He is the author of *A New Language for Psychoanalysis, Language and Insight,* and *Narrative Actions in Psychoanalysis: Narratives of Space and Narratives of Time.*

indestructible id. The filling in of this narrative structure tells of a lifelong transition: if the innate potential for symbolization is there, and if all goes well, one moves from a condition of frightened and irrational helplessness, lack of self-definition, and domination by fluid or mobile instinctual drives toward a condition of stability, mastery, adaptability, self-definition, rationality, and security. If all does not go well, the inadequately tamed beast must be accommodated by the formation of pathological structures, such as symptoms and perversions.

Freud did not invent this beast, and the admixture of Darwinism in his account only gave it the appearance of having been established in a positivist scientific manner. The basic story is ancient; it has been told in many ways over the centuries, and it pervades what we consider refined common sense.[2] But Freud used the old story well. His tale of human development, suffering, defeat, and triumph was extraordinarily illuminating in its psychological content, scientifically respectable in its conceptualization and formalization, dramatically gripping in its metaphorical elaboration, and beneficial in his work with his patients.

2. Refined common sense structures the history of human thought about human action. It takes into account the emotional, wishful, fantasy-ridden features of action, its adaptive and utilitarian aspects, and the influence on it of the subject's early experiencing of intimate formative relationships and of the world at large. The repositories of common sense include mythology, folk wisdom, colloquial sayings, jokes, and literature, among other cultural products, and, as Freud showed repeatedly, there are relatively few significant psychoanalytic propositions that are not stated or implied by these products. Refined common sense serves as the source of the precritical assumptions from which the psychoanalytic narrative structures are derived, and these structures dictate conceptual and technical practices. But common sense is not fixed. The common sense presented in proverbs and maxims, for example, is replete with internal tension and ambiguity. Most generalizations have countergeneralizations (A penny saved is a penny earned, but one may be penny-wise and pound-foolish; one should look before one leaps, but he who hesitates is lost, and so on), and just as common sense may be used to reaffirm traditional orientations and conservative values (Rome wasn't built in a day), it may also be used to sanction a challenge to tradition (A new broom sweeps clean) or endorse an ironic stance (The more things change, the more they remain the same). Since generalizations of this sort allow much latitude in their application, recourse to the authority of common sense is an endless source of controversy over accounts of human action. Still, common sense is our storehouse of narrative structures, and it remains the source of intelligibility and certainty in human affairs. Controversy itself would make no sense unless the conventions of common sense were being observed by those engaged in controversy.

Psychoanalysis does not take common sense plain but rather transforms it into a comprehensive distillate, first, by selection and schematic reduction of its tensions and ambiguities and, second, by elevating only some of these factors (such as pleasure versus reality and id versus ego) to the status of overarching principles and structures. Traditionally, these elevations of common sense have been organized and presented as psychoanalytic metapsychology.

As more than one such distillation of common sense has been offered in the name of psychoanalysis, there have been phases in the development of psychoanalytic theory, and there are schools of psychoanalysis, each with a distinctive theory of its own. Each distillation (phase or school) has been elaborated and organized in terms of certain leading narrative structures that are to be taken as certain.

Because this archetypal story has been mythologically enshrined in the metaphoric language that all of us have learned to think and live by, it is more than appealing to have it authorized and apparently confirmed by psychological science. At the same time, however, it is threatening to be told persuasively how much it is the beast that pervades, empowers, or at least necessitates our most civilized achievements. Except when we are moralizing about others, human beings do not wish to think consciously of having bestial origins, continuities, and destinies, and so we develop defenses and allow ourselves to think only of certain aspects of our "natures." Through his uncompromising effort to establish a systematic psychoanalytic life story in these terms, Freud exposed our paradoxical attitude toward his fateful story of human lives.

Freud's other primary narrative structure is based on Newtonian physics as transmitted through the physiological and neuroanatomical laboratories of the nineteenth century. This account presents psychoanalysis as the study of the mind viewed as a machine—in Freud's words, as a mental apparatus. This machine is characterized by inertia; it does not work unless it is moved by force. It works as a closed system; that is, its amount of energy is fixed, with the result that storing or expending energy in one respect decreases the energy available for other operations: thus on purely quantitative grounds, love of others limits what is available for self-love, and love of the opposite sex limits what is available for love of the same sex. The machine has mechanisms, such as the automatically operating mechanisms of defense and various other checks and balances.

In the beginning, the forces that move the machine are primarily the brute organism's instinctual drives. Here the tale of the mental apparatus borrows from the tale of the brute organism and consequently becomes narratively incoherent: the mechanical mind is now said to behave like a creature with a soul—seeking, reacting, and developing. The tale continues with increasing incoherence.[3]

3. To sketch this increasing incoherence: In the beginning, the mental apparatus is primitive owing to its lack of structure and differentiated function. Over the course of time, the apparatus develops itself in response to experience and along lines laid down by its inherent nature; it becomes complex, moving on toward an ending in which, through that part of it called the ego, it can set its own aims and take over and desexualize or neutralize energies from the id. At the same time, the ego takes account of the requirements of the id, the superego, external reality, and its own internal structural problems, and it works out compromises and syntheses of remarkable complexity. When nothing untoward happens during this development, the machine functions stably and efficiently; otherwise, it is a defective apparatus, most likely weak in its ego, superego, or both. A defective apparatus cannot perform some of the functions for which it is intended, and it performs some others unreliably, inefficiently, and maladaptively, using up or wastefully discharging precious psychic energy in the process. Its effective operation depends on its mechanism's success in restricting the influence of the archaic heritage of infancy. This machine is dedicated to preserving its own structure; it guarantees its own continuity by serving as a bulwark against primal chaos and changes itself only under dire

Both of Freud's primary narrative structures assume thoroughgoing determinism: the determinism of evolutionary necessity and the determinism of Newtonian forces. No room is left for freedom and responsibility. Those actions that appear to be free and responsible must be worked into the deterministic narrative of the beast, the machine, or the incoherent mingling of the two. Freedom is a myth of conscious thought.

Freud insisted on the two narrative structures I have synopsized as the core of what he called his metapsychology, and he regarded them as indispensible. But, as I said at the outset, Freud can be read in other ways. One can construct a Freud who is a humanistic-existentialist, a man of tragic and ironic vision,[4] and one can construct a Freud who is an investigator laying the foundation for a conception of psychoanalysis as an interpretive study of human action.[5] Although we can derive these alternative readings from statements made explicitly by Freud when, as a man and a clinician, he took distance from his official account, we do not require their authority to execute this project; and these alternative readings are not discredited by quotations from Freud to the opposite effect.

That Freud's beast and machine are indeed narrative structures and are not dictated by the data is shown by the fact that other psychoanalysts have developed their own accounts, each with a more or less different beginning, course, and ending. Melanie Klein, for example, gives an account of the child or adult as being in some stage of recovery from a rageful infantile psychosis at the breast.[6] Her story starts with a universal yet pathological infantile condition that oscillates between paranoid and melancholic positions. For her, our lives begin in madness, which includes taking in the madness of others, and we continue to be more or less mad though we may be helped by fortuitous circumstances or by analysis. Certain segments of common speech, for example, the metaphors of the witch, the poisonous attitude, and the people who get under your skin or suck out your guts, or the common recognition that we can all be "crazy" under certain circumstances all support this account that emphasizes unconscious infantile fantasies of persecution, possession, and devastation.

---

necessity. This mechanistic account accords well with the ideology of the Industrial Revolution. We still tend to view the body in general and the nervous system in particular as marvelous machines, and traditional metapsychologists still ask us to view the mind in the same way.

4. See my "The Psychoanalytic Vision of Reality," *A New Language for Psychoanalysis* (New Haven, Conn., and London, 1976), pp. 22–56.

5. See *A New Language for Psychoanalysis* and my *Language and Insight* (New Haven, Conn. and London, 1978).

6. See Hanna Segal's *Introduction to the Work of Melanie Klein* (New York, 1964).

To bypass many other more or less useful narratives that over the years have been proposed in the name of psychoanalysis, we currently have one developed by Heinz Kohut. Kohut tells of a child driven in almost instinctlike fashion to actualize a cohesive self. The child is more or less hampered or damaged in the process by the empathic failures of caretakers in its intimate environment. Its growth efforts are consequently impeded by reactive and consoling grandiose fantasies, defensive splitting and repression, and affective "disintegration products" that experientially seem to act like Freud's drives or else to take the form of depressive, hypochondriacal, perverse, or addictive symptoms. In truth, however, these pathological signs are bits and pieces of the shattered self striving to protect itself, heal itself, and continue its growth. The ending in Kohut's story is for each person a point on a continuum that ranges from a frail, rageful, and poverty-stricken self to one that is healthy, happy, and wise.[7]

My schematization of Freudian narration and of Klein's and Kohut's alternatives can be useful. Schematization, when recognized as such, is not falsification. It can serve as a code for comparative reading in terms of beginnings, practices, and possible endings. It can clarify the sets of conventions that govern the constituting and selective organizing of psychoanalytic data. And in every interesting and useful case, it will help us remain attentive to certain commonsensically important events and experiences, such as the vicissitudes of the development, subjective experience, and estimation of the self or the child's struggles with a controlling, frightening, and misunderstood environment. Let us say, then, that some such code prepares us to engage in a systematic psychoanalytic dialogue.

I shall now attempt to portray this psychoanalytic dialogue in terms of two agents, each narrating or telling something to the other in a rule-governed manner. Psychoanalysis as telling and retelling along psychoanalytic lines: this is the theme and form of the present narration. It is, I think, a story worth telling. This much has been my author's

---

7. For the most part, Kohut remains aware that he is developing a narrative structure. He goes so far as to invoke a principle of complementarity, arguing that psychoanalysis needs and can tolerate a second story, namely, Freud's traditional tripartite psychic structure (id, ego, superego). On Kohut's account, this narrative of psychic structure is needed in order to give an adequate account of phases of development subsequent to the achievement, in the early years of life, of a cohesive self or a healthy narcissism. This recourse to an analogy with the complementary theory of physics fails to dispel the impression one may gain of narrative incoherence. The problem is, however, not fatal: I am inclined to think that complementarity will be dropped from Kohut's account once it becomes clear how to develop the tale of the embattled self into a comprehensive and continuous narrative—or once it becomes professionally acceptable to do so. See Kohut's *The Analysis of the Self: A Systematic Approach to the Psychoanalytic Treatment of Narcissistic Personality Disorders* (New York, 1971) and *The Restoration of the Self* (New York, 1977).

preface—if, that is, a preface can be clearly distinguished from the narration that it both foretells and retells.

2. Narration in the Psychoanalytic Dialogue

We are forever telling stories about ourselves. In telling these self-stories *to others* we may, for most purposes, be said to be performing straightforward narrative actions. In saying that we also tell them *to ourselves,* however, we are enclosing one story within another. This is the story that there is a self to tell something to, a someone else serving as audience who is oneself or one's self. When the stories we tell others about ourselves concern these other selves of ours, when we say, for example, "I am not master of myself," we are again enclosing one story within another. On this view, the self is a telling. From time to time and from person to person, this telling varies in the degree to which it is unified, stable, and acceptable to informed observers as reliable and valid.

Additionally, we are forever telling stories about others. These others, too, may be viewed as figures or other selves constituted by narrative actions. Other people are constructed in the telling about them; more exactly, we narrate others just as we narrate selves. The other person, like the self, is not something one has or encounters as such but an existence one tells. Consequently, telling "others" about "ourselves" is doubly narrative.

Often the stories we tell about ourselves are life historical or autobiographical; we locate them in the past. For example, we might say, "Until I was fifteen, I was proud of my father" or "I had a totally miserable childhood." These histories are present tellings. The same may be said of the histories we attribute to others. We change many aspects of these histories of self and others as we change, for better or worse, the implied or stated questions to which they are the answers. Personal development may be characterized as change in the questions it is urgent or essential to answer. As a project in personal development, personal analysis changes the leading questions that one addresses to the tale of one's life and the lives of important others.

People going through psychoanalysis—analysands—tell the analyst about themselves and others in the past and present. In making interpretations, the analyst retells these stories. In the retelling, certain features are accentuated while others are placed in parentheses; certain features are related to others in new ways or for the first time; some features are developed further, perhaps at great length. This retelling is done along psychoanalytic lines. What constitutes a specifically psychoanalytic retelling is a topic I shall take up later.

The analyst's retellings progressively influence the what and how of the stories told by analysands. The analyst establishes new, though often contested or resisted, questions that amount to regulated narrative possibilities. The end product of this interweaving of texts is a radically new, jointly authored work or way of working. One might say that in the course of analysis, there develops a cluster of more or less coordinated new narrations, each corresponding to periods of intensive analytic work on certain leading questions.[8] Generally, these narrations focus neither on the past, plain and simple, nor on events currently taking place outside the psychoanalytic situation. They focus much more on the place and modification of these tales within the psychoanalytic dialogue. Specifically, the narrations are considered under the aspect of transference and resistance as these are identified and analyzed at different times and in relation to different questions. The psychoanalytic dialogue is characterized most of all by its organization in terms of the here and now of the psychoanalytic relationship. It is fundamentally a dialogue concerning the present moment of transference and resistance.

But transference and resistance themselves may be viewed as narrative structures. Like all other narrative structures, they prescribe a point of view from which to tell about the events of analysis in a regulated and therefore coherent fashion. The events themselves are constituted only through one or another systematic account of them. Moreover, the analysis of resistance may be told in terms of transference and vice versa. (I will return to the analysis of resistance in section 3.)

In the traditional transference narration, one tells how the analysand is repetitively reliving or reexperiencing the past in the present relationship with the analyst. It is said that there occurs a regression within the transference to the infantile neurosis or neurotic matrix, which then lies exposed to the analyst's view. This is, however, a poor account. It tells of life history as static, archival, linear, reversible, and literally retrievable. Epistemologically, this story is highly problematic. Another and, I suggest, better account tells of change of action along certain lines; it emphasizes new experiencing and new remembering of the past that unconsciously has never become the past. More and more, the alleged past must be experienced consciously as a mutual interpenetration of the past and present, both being viewed in psychoanalytically organized and coordinated terms.[9] If analysis is a matter of moving in a direction, it is a moving forward into new modes of constructing experience. On this account, one must retell the story of regression to the infantile neurosis within the transference; for even though much of its matter may be defined in terms of the present version of the past, the

8. See my "The Appreciative Analytic Attitude and the Construction of Multiple Life Histories," *Psychoanalysis and Contemporary Thought* 2, no. 1 (1979): 3–24.

9. See my "The Interpretation of Transference and the Conditions for Loving," *Journal of the American Psychoanalytic Association* 25, no. 2 (1977): 335–62.

so-called regression is necessarily a progression. Transference, far from being a time machine by which one may travel back to see what one has been made out of, is a clarification of certain constituents of one's present psychoanalytic actions. This clarification is achieved through the circular and coordinated study of past and present.

The technical and experiential construction of personal analyses in the terms of transference and resistance has been found to be therapeutically useful. But now it must be added that viewing psychoanalysis as a therapy itself manifests a narrative choice. This choice dictates that the story of the dialogue and the events to which it gives rise be told in terms of a doctor's curing a patient's disease. From the inception of psychoanalysis, professional and ideological factors have favored this kind of account, though there are some signs today that the sickness narrative is on its way to becoming obsolete. Here I want only to emphasize that there are a number of other ways to tell what the two people in the analytic situation are doing. Each of these ways either cultivates and accentuates or neglects and minimizes certain potential features of the analysis; none is exact and comprehensive in every way. For example, psychoanalysis as therapy tells the story from the standpoint of consciousness: consciously, but only consciously, the analysand presents his/her problems as alien interferences with the good life, that is, as symptoms in the making of which he/she has had no hand; or the analyst defines as symptomatic the problems he/she consciously wishes to emphasize; or both. In many cases, this narrative facilitates undertaking the analysis; at the same time, a price is paid, at least for some time, by this initial and perhaps unavoidable collusion to justify analysis on these highly defensive and conscious grounds of patienthood.

My own attempt to remain noncommittal in this respect by speaking of analyst and analysand rather than therapist and patient is itself inexact in at least three ways. First, it does not take into account the analyst's also being subject to analysis through his/her necessarily continuous scrutiny of countertransferences. Second, during the analysis, the analysand's self is retold as constituted by a large, fragmented, and fluid cast of characters: not only are aspects of the self seen to incorporate aspects of others, they are also unconsciously imagined as having retained some or all of the essence of these others; that is, the self-constituents are experienced as introjects or incomplete identifications, indeed sometimes as shadowy presences of indeterminate location and origin. The problematic and incoherent self that is consciously told at the beginning of the analysis is sorted out, so far as possible, into that which has retained otherness to a high degree and that which has not. A similar sorting out of the constituents of others' selves is also accomplished; here the concept of projecting aspects of the self into others plays an important role. The upshot is that what the analysand initially tells as self and others undergoes considerable revision once the initial conscious account has been worked over analytically.[10] A third inexactness in my choice of terminology is that the division into analyst and analysand does not provide for the increasing extent to which the analysand becomes coanalyst of his/her own problems and, in certain respects, those of the analyst, too. The analysand, that is, becomes coauthor of the analysis as he/she becomes a more daring and reliable narrator. Here I touch on yet another topic to take up later, that of the unreliable narrator: this topic takes in analyst as well as analysand, for ideally both of them do change during analysis, if to different degrees, and it leads into questions of how, in the post-positivist scheme of things, we are to understand validity in analytic interpretation.

If we are forever telling stories about ourselves and others and to ourselves and others, it must be added that people do more than tell: like authors, they also show. As there is no hard-and-fast line between telling and showing, either in literary narrative[11] or in psychoanalysis, the competent psychoanalyst deals with telling as a form of showing and with showing as a form of telling. Everything in analysis is both communication and demonstration.

Perhaps the simplest instances of analytic showing are those non-verbal behaviors or expressive movements that include bodily rigidity, lateness to or absence from scheduled sessions, and mumbling. The analyst, using whatever he/she already knows or has prepared the way for, interprets these showings and weaves them into one of the narrations of the analysis: for example, "Your lying stiffly on the couch shows that you're identifying yourself with your dead father"; or, "Your mumbling shows how afraid you are to be heard as an independent voice on this subject." Beyond comments of this sort, however, the analyst takes these showings as communications and on this basis may say (and here I expand these improvised interpretations), "You are conveying that you feel like a corpse in relation to me, putting your life into me and playing your dead father in relation to me; you picture me now as yourself confronted by this corpse, impressing on me that I am to feel your grief for you." Or the analyst might say, "By your mumbling you are letting me know how frightened you are to assert your own views to me just in case I might feel as threatened by such presumption as your mother once felt and might retaliate as she did by being scornful and turning her back on you." In these interpretive retellings, the analyst is no longer controlled by the imaginary line between telling and showing.

Acting out as a form of remembering is a good case in point.[12] For example, by anxiously engaging in an affair with an older married man,

10. See my "Self-Control," *Language and Insight,* pp. 67–103.

11. See Wayne C. Booth's *The Rhetoric of Fiction* (Chicago, 1961).

12. See Sigmund Freud's "Remembering, Repeating and Working-Through," *The Standard Edition of the Complete Psychological Works of Sigmund Freud,* ed. James Strachey, 24 vols. (London, 1953–1974), 12:145–56.

a young woman in analysis is said to be remembering, through acting out, an infantile Oedipal wish to seduce or be sexually loved and impregnated by her father, now represented by the analyst. In one way, this acting out is showing; in another way, it is telling by a displaced showing. Once it has been retold as remembering through acting out, it may serve as a narrative context that facilitates further direct remembering and further understanding of the analytic relationship.

The competent analyst is not lulled by the dramatic rendition of life historical content into hearing this content in a simple, contextless, time-bound manner. Situated in the present, the analyst takes the telling also as a showing, noting, for example, when that content is introduced, for it might be a way of forestalling the emotional experiencing of the immediate transference relationship; noting also how that content is being told, for it might be told flatly, histrionically, in a masochistically self-pitying or a grandiosely triumphant way; noting further the story line that is being followed and many other narrative features as well. The analyst also attends to cues that the analysand, consciously or unconsciously, may be an unreliable narrator: highlighting the persecutory actions of others and minimizing the analysand's seduction of the persecutor to persecute; slanting the story in order to block out significant periods in his/her life history or to elicit pity or admiration; glossing over, by silence and euphemism, what the analysand fears will cast him/her in an unfavorable light or sometimes in too favorable a light, as when termination of analysis is in the air, and, out of a sense of danger, one feels compelled to tell and show that one is still "a sick patient." All of which is to say that the analyst takes the telling as performance as well as content. The analyst has only tellings and showings to interpret, that is, to retell along psychoanalytc lines.

What does it mean to say "along psychoanalytic lines"? Earlier I mentioned that more than one kind of psychoanalysis is practiced in this world, so let me merely summarize what conforms to my own practice, namely, the story lines that characterize Freudian retellings. The analyst slowly and patiently develops an emphasis on infantile or archaic modes of sexual and aggressive action (action being understood broadly to take in wishing, believing, perceiving, remembering, fantasizing, behaving emotionally, and other such activities that, in traditional theories of action, have been split off from motor action and discussed separately as thought, motivation, and feeling). The analyst wants to study and redescribe all of these activities from the standpoint of such questions as "What is the analysand doing?" "Why now?" "Why in this way?" and "What does this have to do with me and what the analysand fears might develop between us sexually and aggressively?"

Repeatedly the analysand's stories (experiences, memories, symptoms, selves) go through a series of transformations until finally they can be retold not only as sexual and aggressive modes of action but also as defensive measures adopted (out of anxiety, guilt, shame, and depression) to disguise, displace, deemphasize, compromise, and otherwise refrain from boldly and openly taking the actions in question. The analyst uses multiple points of view (wishful, defensive, moral, ideal, and adaptive) and expects that significant features of the analysand's life can be understood only after employing all of these points of view in working out contextual redescriptions or interpretations of actions. Single constituents are likely to require a complex definition; for example, sexual and aggressive wishing are often simultaneously ascribable to one and the same personal problem or symptom along with moral condemnation of "self" on both grounds.

The Freudian analyst also progressively organizes this retelling around bodily zones, modes, and substances, particularly the mouth, anus, and genitalia; and in conjunction with these zones, the modes of swallowing and spitting out, retaining and expelling, intruding and enclosing, and the concrete conceptions of words, feelings, ideas, and events as food, feces, urine, semen, babies, and so on. All of these constituents are given roles in the infantile drama of family life, a drama that is organized around births, losses, illnesses, abuse and neglect, the parents' real and imagined conflicts and sexuality, gender differences, sibling relations, and so on. It is essential that the infantile drama, thus conceived, be shown to be repetitively introduced by the analysand into the analytic dialogue, however subtly this may be done, and this is what is accomplished in the interpretive retelling of transference and resistance.

3. Drives, Free Association, Resistance, and Reality Testing

To illustrate and further develop my thesis on narration in the psychoanalytic dialogue, I shall next take up four concepts that are used repeatedly in narrations concerning this dialogue: drives, free association, resistance, and reality testing.

Drives

Drives appear to be incontrovertible facts of human nature. Even the most casual introspection delivers up a passive picture of the self being driven by internal forces. It might therefore seem perfectly justified to distinguish being driven from wishing, in that wishing seems clearly to be a case of personal action. The distinction is, however, untenable. It takes conscious and conventional testimony of drivenness as the last or natural word on the subject; but to do so is to ignore the proposition that introspection is itself a form of constructed experience based on a specific narration of mind.

The introspection narrative tells that each person is a container of experience fashioned by an independently operating mind and, that by the use of mental eyes located outside this container, the person may look in and see what is going on.[13] Thus the introspector stands outside his/her mind, thinking—with what? A second mind? We have no unassailable answer. The introspection narrative tells us that far from constructing or creating our lives, we witness them. It thereby sets drastic limits on discourse about human activity and responsibility. The uncritical and pervasive use of this narrative form in daily life and in psychological theories shows how appealing it is to disclaim responsibility in this way.

The drive narrative depends on this introspection narrative and so is appealing in the same way. It appeals in other ways as well. As I mentioned earlier, the drive narrative tells the partly moralistic and partly Darwinian-scientific tale that at heart we are all animals, and it sets definite guidelines for all the tales we tell about ourselves and others. By following these guidelines, we fulfill two very important functions, albeit often painfully and irrationally: we simultaneously derogate ourselves (which we do for all kinds of reasons) and disclaim responsibility for our actions. Because these functions are being served, many people find it difficult to accept the proposition that drive is a narrative structure, that is, an optional way of telling the story of human lives.

Consider, for example, a man regarding a woman lustfully. One might say, "He wishes more than anything else to take her to bed"; or one might say, "His sexual drive is overwhelming and she is its object." The wishing narrative does not preclude the recognition that physiological processes may be correlated with such urgent wishing, though it also leaves room for the fact that this correlation does not always hold. In case the physiological correlates are present, the wishing narrative also provides for the man's noticing these stimuli in the first place, for his having to give meaning to them, for his selecting just that woman, and for his organizing the situation in terms of heterosexual intercourse specifically. From our present point of view, the chief point to emphasize is that the wishing narrative allows one to raise the question, in analytic work as in everyday life, why the subject tells himself that he is passive in relation to a drive rather than that he is a sexual agent, someone who lusts after a specific woman.

A similar case for wishful action may be made in the case of aggression. In one version or theory, aggression is a drive that requires dis-

---

13. See Gilbert Ryle's *The Concept of Mind* (New York, 1965). The introspection narrative has been extensively elaborated through a spatial rendering of mental activity, perhaps most of all through the language of internalization and externalization. This spatial language includes: inner world, inwardly, internalize, projection, deep down, levels, layers, and the like. See my "Internalization: Process or Fantasy?" *A New Language for Psychoanalysis,* pp. 155–78.

charge in rages, assaults, vituperation, or something of that sort; in another version, aggression is an activity or mode of action that is given many forms by agents who variously wish to attack, destroy, hurt, or assert and in each case to do so for reasons and in contexts that may be ascertained by an observer. The observer may, of course, be the agent himself/herself.

In the course of analysis, the analysand comes to construct narratives of personal agency ever more readily, independently, convincingly, and securely, particularly in those contexts that have to do with crucially maladaptive experiences of drivenness. The important questions to be answered in the analysis concern personal agency, and the important answers reallocate the attributions of activity and passivity. Passivity also comes into question because, as in the case of unconscious infantile guilt (so-called superego guilt), agency may be ascribed to the self irrationally (for example, blame of the "self" for the accidental death of a parent).

Free Association

The fundamental rule of psychoanalysis is conveyed through the instruction to associate freely and to hold back nothing that comes to mind. This conception is controlled by the previously mentioned narrative of the introspected mind: one is to tell about thinking and feeling in passive terms; it is to be a tale of the mind's running itself, of thoughts and feelings coming and going, of thoughts and feelings pushed forward by drives or by forces or structures opposing them. Again, the analysand is to be witness to his/her own mind. The psychoanalytic model for this narration is Freud's "mental apparatus."

If, however, one chooses the narrative option of the analysand as agent, that is, as thinker and constructor of emotional action, the fundamental rule will be understood differently and in a way that accords much better with the analyst's subsequent interpretive activity. According to this second narrative structure, the instruction establishes the following guidelines: "Let's see what you will do if you just tell me everything you think and feel without my giving you any starting point, any direction or plan, any criteria of selection, coherence, or decorum. You are to continue in this way with no formal beginning, no formal middle or development, and no formal ending except as you introduce these narrative devices. And let's see what sense we can make of what you do under these conditions. That is to say, let's see how we can retell it in a way that allows you to understand the origins, meanings, and significance of your present difficulties and to do so in a way that makes change conceivable and attainable."

Once the analysand starts the telling, the analyst listens and interprets in two interrelated ways. First, the analyst retells what is told from the standpoint of its content, that is, its thematic coherence. For example, the analysand may be alluding repeatedly to envious attitudes while consciously portraying these attitudes as disinterested, objective criticism. By introducing the theme of envy, the analyst, from his/her special point of view on analytic narration, identifies the kind of narrative that is being developed. (Of course, one does not have to be an analyst to recognize envy in disguise; but this only illustrates my point that analytic narration is not sharply set off from refined common sense.) The specific content then becomes merely illustrative of an unrecognized and probably disavowed set of attitudes that are held by the analysand who is shown to be an unreliable narrator in respect to the consciously constructed account. Ultimately, the unreliability itself must be interpreted and woven into the dialogue as an aspect of resistance.

The analysand's narrative, then, is placed in a larger context, its coherence and significance are increased, and its utility for the analytic work is defined. The analyst has not listened in the ordinary way. Serving as an *analytic* reteller, he/she does not, indeed, cannot coherently, respond in the ordinary way: listening in the ordinary way, as in countertransference, results in analytic incoherence; the analyst's retellings themselves become unreliable and fashioned too much after the analyst's own "life story."

In the second mode of listening and interpreting, the analyst focuses on the action of telling itself. Telling is treated as an object of description rather than, as the analysand wishes, an indifferent or transparent medium for imparting information or thematic content. The analyst has something to say about the how, when, and why of the telling. For example, the analyst may tell that the analysand has been circling around a disturbing feeling of alienation from the analyst, the narration's circumstantial nature being intended to guarantee an interpersonally remote, emotionally arid session; and if it is envy that is in question, the analyst may tell that the analysand is trying to spoil the analyst's envied competence by presenting an opaque account of the matter at hand.

In this way, the analyst defines the complex rules that the analysand is following in seeming to "free associate."[14] There are rules of various kinds for alienated discourse, for envious discourse, and so on, some very general and well known to common sense and some very specialized or individual and requiring careful definition in the individual case, but which must still, ultimately, be in accord with common sense. The analyst treats free association as neither free nor associative, for within the strategy of analyzing narrative actions, it is not an unregulated or passive performance.

The analysand consciously experiences many phenomena in the passive mode: unexpected intrusions or unexpected trains of thought,

---

14. See my "Free Association," *Language and Insight*, pp. 29–66.

irrelevant or shameful feelings, incoherent changes of subject, blocking and helpless withholdings of thoughts, and imperative revisions of raw content. The analysand consciously regards all of these as unintentional violations of the rules he/she consciously professes to be following or wishes to believe are being followed. But what is to the analysand flawed or helpless performance is not so to the analyst. For the analyst, free associating is a no-fault activity. What is consciously unexpected or incomprehensible is seen rather as the analysand's having unconsciously introduced more complex rules to govern the narrative being developed: the analysand may have become uneasy with what is portrayed as the drift of thought and sensed that he/she was heading into danger, or perhaps the tale now being insistently foregrounded is a useful diversion from another and more troubling tale. In the interest of being "a good patient," the analysand may even insist on developing narratives in primitive terms, for instance, in terms of ruthless revenge or infantile sexual practices, when at that moment a more subjectively distressing but analytically useful account of the actions in question would have to be given in terms of assertiveness, or fun-lovingness, or ordinary sentimentality. Whatever the case may be, a new account is called for, a more complex account, one in which the analysand is portrayed as more or less unconsciously taking several parts at once—hero, victim, dodger, and stranger. These parts are not best understood as autonomous subselves having their say ("multiple selves" is itself only a narrative structure that begs the question); rather, each of these parts is one of the regulative narrative structures that one person, the analysand, has adopted and used simultaneously with the others, whether in combination, opposition, or apparent incoherence. The analyst says, in effect, "What I hear you saying is . . ." or "In other words, it's a matter of . . . ," and this is to say that a narrative is now being retold along analytic lines as *the only narrative it makes good enough sense to tell at that time.*

Resistance

Resistance can be retold so as to make it appear in an altogether different light; furthermore, it can be retold in more than one way. Before I show how this is so, I should synopsize Freud's account of resistance.[15] For Freud, "*the* resistance," as he called it, was an autonomous force analogous to the censorship in the psychology of dreams. The term refers to the many forms taken by the analysand's opposition to the analyst. The resistance, Freud said, accompanies the analysis every step of the way, and technically nothing is more important than to ferret it out and analyze it. The resistance is often sly, hidden, secretive, obdu-

15. See, for example, Freud's "The Dynamics of Transference," *Standard Edition,* 12:97–108.

rate, and so on. In the terms of Freud's theory of psychic structure, there is a split in the analysand's ego; the rational ego wants to go forward while the defensive ego wants to preserve the irrational status quo. The analysand's ego fears change toward health through self-understanding, viewing that course as too dangerous or too mortifying to bear. These accounts of resistance establish narrative structures of several pairs of antagonists in the analytic situation: one part of the ego against another, the ego against the id, the analysand against the analyst, and the analyst against the resistance. The conflict centers on noncompliance with the fundamental rule of free association, a rule that in every case can be observed by the analysand only in a highly irregular and incomplete fashion. Presenting the resistance as a force in the mind, much like a drive, further defines the form of the analytic narration: resistance is presented as animistic or anthropomorphic, a motivated natural force that the subject experiences passively.

How does the story of resistance get to be retold during an analysis? In one retelling, resistance transforms into an account of transference, both positive and negative. Positive transference is resistance attempting to transform the analysis into some repetitive version of a conflictual infantile love relationship on the basis of which one may legitimately abandon the procedures and goals of analysis itself. In the case of negative transference, the analyst is seen irrationally and often unconsciously as an authoritarian parent to be defied. Through a series of transformations, and with reference to various clues produced by the analysand, the opposition is retold by the analyst as an enactment of the oral, anal, and phallic struggles of infancy and childhood, that is, as a refusal to be fed or weaned or else as a biting; or as a refusal to defecate in the right place and at the right time, resorting instead to constipated withholding or diarrheic expelling of associations, feelings, and memories; or as furtive masturbation, primal scene voyeurism and exhibitionism, defensive or seductive changes of the self's gender, and so on. Thus the distinction between the analysis of resistance and the analysis of transference, far from being the empirical matter it is usually said to be, is a matter of narrative choice. Told in terms of transference, resistance becomes disclaimed repetitive activity rather than passive experience.[16] And it is as activity that it takes its most intelligible, coherent, and modifiable place in the developing life historical contexts.

There is another, entirely affirmative way to retell the story of resistance. In this account, the analysand is portrayed as doing something on his/her behalf, something that makes sense unconsciously though it may not yet be understood empathically by the analyst. The analyst may then press confrontations and interpretations on the analysand at the wrong time, in the wrong way, and with the wrong content. Kohut's

16. See my "The Idea of Resistance," *A New Language for Psychoanalysis,*" pp. 217–63.

account of narcissistic rage in response to such interventions presents the analysand as protecting a fragile self against further disintegration in response to the analyst's empathically deficient interventions. Or the analysand may be protecting the analyst against his/her own anticipated ruthless, destructive, or at least permanently alienating form of love. Matters of personal pride and honor may be involved. In one instance, the analysand's resistance was understood as a form of self-abortion and in another instance as a refusal to be forced into what was taken to be a phallic role.

Whatever the case and whatever the manifestly oppositional attitude, the analysand is portrayed as engaged in a project of preservation, even enhancement, of self or analyst or both. The project is one that the analysand at that moment rightly refuses to abandon despite what may be the misguided efforts of the analyst to narrate the analysis along other lines. In this affirmative narration of resisting, the analyst may be an uncomprehending brute or an unwitting saboteur. One young woman's spontaneously defiant insistence on persistently excoriating her parents had to be retold analytically in two main ways: as a turning away from the unbearable horror of her imagined inner world and as a firm assertion on her part that the problem resided in the family as a system and not merely in her infantile fantasies and wishes. On the one hand, there was a crucial strategy of self-prevention implied in her apparent resistance: as she said at one point, "If I let myself appreciate myself and see what, against all odds, I've become, it would break my heart." On the other hand, there was the analysand's search for the self-affirming truth of parental madness. To have thought of her strident analytic activity simply as resistance would have been to start telling the wrong kind of psychoanalytic story about it.

A third way to retell the story of resistance radically questions the analysand's use of ability and inability words. It is developed along the following lines. Resistance seems to go against the analysand's wishes and resolutions. The analysand pleads inability: for example, "Something stops me from coming out with it," or "My inhibitions are too strong for me to make the first move," or "I can't associate anything with that dream." The narrative structure of inability in such respects is culturally so well established that it seems to be merely an objective expression of the natural order of things. Yet it may be counted as another aspect of the analysand as unconsciously unreliable narrator. In the first example (not coming out with it), the retelling might be developed along these lines: "You *don't* come out with it, and you *don't* yet understand why you *don't* act on your resolution to do so." In the third example (inability to associate), it might be developed like this: "You *don't* think of anything that seems to you to be relevant or acceptable, anything that meets your rules of coherence, good sense, or good manners, and you dismiss what you *do* think of."

In giving these examples, I am not presenting actual or recommended analytic interventions so much as I am making their logic plain. In practice, these interventions are typically developed in ways that are tactful, tentative, circuitous, and fragmentary. For a long time, perhaps, the "don't" element is only implied in order to avoid the analysand's mishearing description as criticism and demand; *exhortation* has no place in the analyst's interventions. Nor am I suggesting that the analyst's initial descriptions are the decisive words on any important subject. They are only the first words on the subject in that they begin to establish the ground rules for another kind of story to be told and so of another kind of experience to construct. These are the rules of action language and the reclaiming of disclaimed action.

Choosing action as the suitable narrative language allows the analyst to begin to retell many inability narrations as disclaimings of action. In order to analyze resistance—now to be designated as resist*ing*—one must take many narrations presented by analysands in terms of *can* and *can't* and retell them in terms of *do* and *don't* and sometimes *will* and *won't*. Usually, the analysand is disclaiming the action unconsciously. That this is so does not make the disclaiming (defense, resistance) any the less an action; nor does it make what is being disclaimed any the less an action. In analytic narration, one is not governed by the ordinary conventions that link action to conscious intent.

So often, the analyst, after first hearing "I can't tell you" or "I can't think about that," goes on to establish through close and sustained consideration of free associations the reasons why the analysand does not or will not tell or think about whatever it is that is troublesome. It may be that the action in question would be humiliating, frightening, or apparently incoherent and therefore too mad to be tolerated. It may be that unconsciously the not telling or not thinking is an act of anal retention or Oedipal defiance that is being presented as innocent helplessness. It may be that an important contention between two events has never before been defined, so that the analysand, lacking a suitable narrative structure, simply does not take up the two in one consciously constructed context; connections and contexts might come into existence only through the analyst's interpretive activity. Interpretation may also give the reasons why the context and connections never have been developed. In all such instances, it is no longer ability that is in question, it is the proper designation of a ruled performance.

The same narrative treatments of action and inaction are common in daily life: one hears, "I couldn't control myself," "I can't concentrate on my studies," "I can't love him," and so on. Implicit in these narrations, as in the resisting narrations, is the disclaiming of the activity in what is being told. This disclaiming is accomplished by taking recourse to the terms of uncontrollable, impersonal forces. These accounts, too, may be retold analytically. For instance, after some analysis, "I can't concentrate on my studies" may become the following (synopsized) narrative: "I don't concentrate on what I resolve to work on. I think of other things instead. I think of girls, of my dead father, of all the failures of my life. These are the things that really matter to me, and I rebel against the idea that I should set them aside and just get through the reading like a machine. It's like shitting on demand. Additionally, by not working, I don't risk experiencing either frightening grandiose feelings if I succeed or the shame of mediocrity if I just pass. On top of which, really getting into the work is sexually exciting; it feels something like sexual peeping to read, as I must, between the lines, and it feels wrong to do that." Retold in this way, "I can't concentrate on my studies" becomes "I don't concentrate for certain reasons, some or all of which I did not dare to realize before now. I told myself I was trying to concentrate and couldn't when actually I was doing other things instead and doing them for other reasons." The narrative has changed from the conscious one of helplessness and failure, designed to protect the consciously distressing status quo, to a narrative of unconscious activity in another kind of reality. The new story, told now by a more reliable narrator, is a story of personal action, and as such it may serve as a basis for change.

Nothing in the immediately preceding account implies that for narrative purposes, *inability* words or, for that matter, *necessity* words are narratively ruled totally out of the analytic court. Rather, these words are now found to be useful and appropriate in a far more restricted set of circumstances than before. These sets of circumstances include unusual physical and mental ability and training and also one's inevitable confrontations with the forceful independent actions of others and with impersonal events in the world. Yet even these necessities become analytically relevant only in terms of how the analysand takes them. In any event, necessity (or happening) does not include mental forces and structures that reduce a person to impotence; much impotence is enacted rather than imposed.[17]

Thus the analyst may retell resisting to the analysand in two ways: as what the analysand *is not doing* and why and as what he/she *is doing* and why. It is a matter simply of how best to retell the actions in question. Both versions are technically useful in the analysis of resisting. Neither depends on a narration composed in terms of autonomous and antagonistic natural forces that are thwarting conscious and wholehearted resolve. Both may be encompassed in a narrative of action. There is nothing in the analysis of resistance that necessarily leads beyond this narrative framework into the one structured in terms of psychic forces or other processes of desymbolization or dehumanization.[18]

17. See my "Impotence, Frigidity, and Sexism," *Language and Insight,* pp. 139–71.
18. For a contrasting view, see, for example, Paul Ricoeur's "The Question of Proof in Psychoanalysis," *Journal of the American Psychoanalytic Association* 25, no. 4 (1977): 835–72, esp. sec. 2. Juergen Habermas, working within a purely hermeneutic orientation, has taken

Reality Testing

Traditionally, the official psychoanalytic conception of reality has been straightforwardly positivistic. Reality is "out there" or "in there" in the inner world, existing as a knowable, certifiable essence. At least for the analytic observer, the subject and object are clearly distinct. Reality is encountered and recognized innocently: in part it simply forces itself on one; in part it is discovered or uncovered by search and reason free of theory. Consequently, reality testing amounts simply to undertaking to establish what is, on the one hand, real, true, objective and, on the other hand, unreal, false, subjective. On this understanding, one may then conclude, for example, that x is fantasy (inner reality) and y is fact (external reality); that mother was not only loving as had always been thought but also hateful; that the situation is serious but not hopeless or vice versa; and so on.

But this positivistic telling is only one way of giving or arriving at an account of the subject in the world, and it is incoherent with respect to the epistemological assumptions inherent in psychoanalytic inquiry, that is, those assumptions that limit us always to dealing only with *versions* of reality. The account I am recommending necessarily limits one to constructing some version or some vision of the subject in the world. One defines situations and invests events with multiple meanings, which are all more or less adequately responsive to different questions that the narrator, who may be the subject or someone else, wants to answer and which are also responsive to the rules of context that the narrator intends to follow and to the level of abstraction that he/she wishes to maintain. Sometimes, for example, an assertive action of a certain kind in a certain situation may with equal warrant be described as sadistic *and* masochistic, regressive *and* adaptive. In this account, reality is always mediated by narration. Far from being innocently encountered or discovered, it is created in a regulated fashion.

The rules regulating creation of reality may be conventional, in which case no questions are likely to be raised about the world and how we know it; if needed, consensual validation will be readily obtained. But things can be otherwise. Once certain rules are defined, they may prove to violate convention in a way that is incoherent or at least not understandable at a given moment. In this case, the place of these rules requires further investigation and interpretation; those rules that inform truly original ideas may necessitate revision of accepted ideas about the

---

what is, from the present point of view, an intermediate position on this matter in his discussion of the contents of the unconscious as deformed, privatized, degrammaticized language. See his *Knowledge and Human Interests*, trans. Jeremy J. Shapiro (Boston, 1971), chaps. 10–12; my discussion owes much to Habermas' penetrating analysis of the linguistic and narrative aspects of psychoanalytic interpretation.

rules that "must" be followed and the kind of reality that it is desirable or interesting to construct. Freud's highly particularized, "overdetermined" accounts of the idiosyncratic systems of rules followed in dreams, neuroses, perversions, psychoses, and normal sexual development showed his real genius.

One may say that *psychoanalytic interpretation tells about a second reality.* In this reality, events or phenomena are viewed from the standpoint of repetitive re-creation of infantile, family-centered situations bearing on sex, aggression, and other such matters. Only superficially does the analytic construction of this second reality seem to be crudely reductive; it is crudely reductive only when it is performed presumptuously or stupidly, as when the analyst says, "This is what you are *really* doing." The competent analyst says in effect, "Let me show you over the course of the analysis another reality, commonsensical elements of which are already, though incoherently and eclectically, included in what you now call reality. We shall be looking at you and others in your life, past and present, in a special light, and we shall come to understand our analytic project and our relationship in this light, too. This second reality is as real as any other. In many ways it is more coherent and inclusive and more open to your activity than the reality you now vouch for and try to make do with. On this basis, it also makes the possibility of change clearer and more or less realizable, and so it may open for you a way out of your present difficulties."

From the acceptance of this new account, there follows a systematic project of constructing a psychoanalytic reality in which one retells the past and the present, the infantile and the adult, the imagined and the so-called real, and the analytic relationship and all other significant relationships. One retells all this in terms that are increasingly focused and coordinated in psychoanalytic terms of action. One achieves a narrative redescription of reality. This retelling is adapted to the clinical context and relationship, the purpose of which is to understand anew the life and the problems in question. The analysand joins in the retelling (redescribing, reinterpreting) as the analysis progresses. The second reality becomes a joint enterprise and a joint experience. And if anyone emerges as a crude reductionist it is the analysand, viewed now as having unconsciously reduced too many events simply to infantile sexual and aggressive narratives.

At this point we may return once more to the question of the unreliable narrator for it bears on the large question of validity of interpretation. To speak of the unreliable narrator, one must have some conception of a reliable narrator, that is, of validity; and yet the trend of my argument suggests that there is no single definitive account to be achieved. Validity, it seems, can only be achieved within a system that is viewed as such and that appears, after careful consideration, to have the virtues of coherence, consistency, comprehensiveness, and common sense. This is the system that establishes the second reality in psycho-analysis. The analysand is helped to become a reliable narrator in this second reality which is centered on transference and resistance. A point of view is maintained and employed that both establishes a maximum of reliability and intelligibility of the kind required and confirms, her-meneutically, that achievement. The increased possibility of change, of new and beneficial action in the world, is an essential aim of this project and an important criterion of its progress. It must be added at once that the appropriate conception of change excludes randomness or person-ally ahistorical or discontinuous consequences, such as abrupt and total reversals of values and behavior. The reallocation of activity and passiv-ity is another important aim and criterion. Finally, the analytic accounts achieved may be judged more or less valid by their ability to withstand further tough and searching questions about the story that has now been told and retold from many different, psychologically noncontradictory though often conflictual, perspectives and in relation to considerable evidence constituted and gathered up within the analytic dialogue.

4. The Normative Life History

Psychoanalytic researchers have always aimed to develop a norma-tive, continuous psychoanalytic life history that begins with day one, to be used by the psychoanalyst as a guide for his/her participation in the analytic dialogue. Freud set this pattern by laying out the psychosexual stages and defining the instinctual vicissitudes, the stage of narcissism, phase-specific orientations and conflicts (oral, anal, etc.), the origins and consolidation of the ego and superego, and other such developmental periods, problems, and achievements. Yet it is safe to say that in the main, his life histories take shape around the time of the Oedipus com-plex, that is, the time between the ages of two and five. In his account, earlier times remain shadowy prehistory or surmised constitutional in-fluences, not too accessible to subjective experience or verification.

Today the field of psychoanalysis is dominated by competing theories about these earlier, shadowy phases of mental development. These now include the phase of autism, symbiosis, and separation-individuation; the phase of basic trust and mistrust; the phase of pure narcissism, in which there are no objects which are not primarily part of the self; the mirror phase; and variations on the Kleinian paranoid-schizoid and depressive phases or "positions" of infancy. For the most part, these phases are defined and detailed by what are called con-structions or reconstructions, that is, surmises based on memories, sym-bolic readings, and subjective phenomena encountered in the analysis of adults, though some direct observation of children has also been em-ployed. These surmises concern the nature of the beginning of subjective experience and the formative impact of the environment on that experience, an impact which is estimated variously by different theorists. In all, a concerted attempt is being made to go back so far in the individual's subjective history as to eliminate its prehistory altogether.

These projects are, for the most part, conceived and presented as fact-finding. On the assumption that there is no other way to understand the present, it is considered essential to determine what in fact it was like way back when. Whatever its internal differences, this entire program is held to have heuristic as well as therapeutic value. It is not my present intention to dispute this claim. I do, however, think that from a methodological standpoint, this program has been incorrectly conceived.

The claim that these normative life historical projects are simply fact-finding expeditions is, as I argued earlier, highly problematic. At the very outset, each such expedition is prepared for what is to be found: it has its maps and compasses, its conceptual supplies, and its probable destination. This preparedness (which contradicts the empiricists' pretensions of innocence) amounts to a narrative plan, form, or set of rules. The sequential life historical narration that is then developed is no more than a second-order retelling of clinical analysis. But this retelling confusingly deletes reference to the history of the analytic dialogue. It treats that dialogue as though—to change my metaphor—it is merely the shovel used to dig up history and so is of no account, except perhaps in manuals on the technique of digging up true chronologies. The theorists have therefore committed themselves to the narrative form of the case history, which is a simplified form of traditional biography.

Is there a narrative form that is methodologically more adequate to the psychoanalytic occasion? I believe there is. It is a story that begins in the middle, which is the present: the beginning is the beginning of the analysis. The present is not the autobiographical present, which at the outset comprises what are called the analysand's presenting problems or initial complaints together with some present account of the past; the reliability and usefulness of both of these constituents of the autobiographical present remain to be determined during the analysis. Once the analysis is under way, the autobiographical present is found to be no clear point in time at all. One does not even know how properly to conceive that present; more and more it seems to be both a repetitive, crisis-perpetuating misremembering of the past and a way of living defensively with respect to a future which is, in the most disruptive way, imagined fearfully and irrationally on the model of the past.

It soon becomes evident that, interpretively, one is working in a temporal circle. One works backward from what is told about the autobiographical present in order to define, refine, correct, organize, and complete an analytically coherent and useful account of the past, and one works forward from various tellings of the past to constitute that present and that anticipated future which are most important to explain.[19] Under the provisional and dubious assumption that past, present, and future are separable, each segment of time is used to set up a series of questions about the others and to answer the questions addressed to it by the others. And all of these accounts keep changing as the analytic dialogue continues.[20]

I said that the analytic life history is a second-order history. The first-order history is that of the analytic dialogue. (This history is more like a set of histories that have been told from multiple perspectives over the course of the analysis and that do not actually lend themselves to one seamless retelling; I shall refer to it as one history, nevertheless, inasmuch as analysts typically present it in that way.) This history is situated in the present: it is always and necessarily a present account of the meanings and uses of the dialogue to date or, in other words, of the transference and resistance. The account of the origins and transformations of the life being studied is shaped, extended, and limited by what it is narratively necessary to emphasize and to assume in order to explain the turns in this dialogue. The analysand's stories of early childhood, adolescence, and other critical periods of life get to be retold in a way that both summarizes and justifies what the analyst requires in order to do the kind of psychoanalytic work that is being done.

The primary narrative problem of the analyst is, then, not how to tell a normative chronological life history; rather, it is how to tell the several histories of each analysis. From this vantage point, the event with which to start the model analytic narration is not the first occasion of thought—Freud's wish-fulfilling hallucination of the absent breast; instead, one should start from a narrative account of the psychoanalyst's retelling of something told by an analysand and the analysand's response to that narrative transformation. In the narration of this moment of dialogue lies the structure of the analytic past, present, and future. It is from this beginning that the accounts of early infantile development are constructed. Those traditional developmental accounts, over which analysts have labored so hard, may now be seen in a new light: less as positivistic sets of factual findings about mental development and more as hermeneutically filled-in narrative structures. The narrative structures that have been adopted control the telling of the events of the analysis, including the many tellings and retellings of the analysand's life history. The time is always present. The event is always an ongoing dialogue.

---

19. See my "The Psychoanalytic Life History," *Language and Insight*, pp. 3–27.

20. Freud's major case studies follow this narrative form. His report on the Rat Man is a good case in point; one has only to compare his notes on the case with his official report on it to see what different tales he told and could have told about this man, that is, *about his work with this man*. See Freud's "Notes upon a Case of Obsessional Neurosis," *Standard Edition*, 10:153–249.

The Law of Genre

Jacques Derrida

Translated by Avital Ronell

Genres are not to be mixed.

I will not mix genres.

I repeat: genres are not to be mixed. I will not mix them.

Now suppose I let these utterances resonate all by themselves.

Suppose: I abandon them to their fate, I set free their random virtualities and turn them over to my audience—or, rather, to *your* audience, to your auditory grasp, to whatever mobility they retain and you bestow upon them to engender effects of all kinds without my having to stand behind them.

I merely said, and then repeated: genres are not to be mixed; I will not mix them.

As long as I release these utterances (which others might call speech acts) in a form yet scarcely determined, given the open context out of which I have just let them be grasped from "my" language—as long as I do this, you may find it difficult to choose among several interpretative options. They are legion, as I could demonstrate. They form an open and essentially unpredictable series. But you may be tempted by *at least* two types of audience, two modes of interpretation, or, if you prefer to give these words more of a chance, then you may be tempted by two different genres of hypothesis. Which ones?

On the one hand, it could be a matter of a fragmentary discourse whose propositions would be of the descriptive, constative, and neutral genre. In such a case, I would have named the operation which consists of "genres are not to be mixed." I would have designated this operation in a neutral fashion without evaluating it, without recommending or

©1980 by The Johns Hopkins University Press. From *Glyph* 7 (Spring 1980).

advising against it, certainly without binding anyone to it. Without claiming to lay down the law or to make this an act of law, I merely would have summoned up, in a fragmentary utterance, the sense of a practice, an act or event, as you wish: which is what sometimes happens when we revert to "genres are not to be mixed." With reference to the same case, and to a hypothesis of the same type, same mode, same genre—or same order: when I said, "I will not mix genres," you may have discerned a foreshadowing description—I am not saying a prescription—the descriptive designation telling in advance what will transpire, predicting it in the constative mode or genre, that is, it will happen thus, I will not mix genres. The future tense describes, then, what will surely take place, as you yourselves can judge; but for my part it does not constitute a commitment. I am not making you a promise here, nor am I issuing myself an order or invoking the authority of some law to which I am resolved to submit myself. In this case, the future tense does not set the time of a performative speech act of a promising or ordering type.

But another hypothesis, another type of audience, and another interpretation would have been no less legitimate. "Genres are not to be mixed" could strike you as a sharp order. You might have heard it resound the elliptical but all the more authoritarian summons to a law of a "do" or "do not" which, as everyone knows, occupies the concept or constitutes the value of *genre.* As soon as the word "genre" is sounded, as soon as it is heard, as soon as one attempts to conceive it, a limit is drawn. And when a limit is established, norms and interdictions are not far behind: "Do," "Do not" says "genre," the word "genre," the figure, the voice, or the law of genre. And this can be said of genre in all genres, be it a question of a generic or a general determination of what one calls "nature" or *physis* (for example, a biological *genre* in the sense of *gender,* or the human *genre,* a genre of all that is in general), or be it a question of a typology designated as nonnatural and depending on laws or orders which were once held to be opposed to *physis* according to those values associated with *technè, thesis, nomos* (for example, an artistic, poetic, or literary genre). But the whole enigma of genre springs perhaps most closely from within this limit between the two genres of genre which, neither separable nor inseparable, form an odd couple of one without the other in which each evenly serves the other a citation to appear in the figure of the other, simultaneously and indiscernibly saying "I" and

---

Jacques Derrida is professor of the history of philosophy at L'Ecole Normale Supérieure in Paris. His greatly influential works include *Writing and Difference, Of Grammatology, Spurs: Of Nietzsche's Styles,* and the forthcoming *Positions* and *Dissemination.* **Avital Ronell** teaches German at the University of Virginia and is the author of *Poetics of Desire and Principles of Textuality in Kafka's "Das Schloss."*

"we," me the genre, we genres, without it being possible to think that the "I" is a species of the genre "we." For who would have us believe that we, we two, for example, would form a genre or belong to one? Thus, as soon as genre announces itself, one must respect a norm, one must not cross a line of demarcation, one must not risk impurity, anomaly, or monstrosity. And so it goes in all cases, whether or not this law of genre be interpreted as a determination or perhaps even as a destination of *physis,* and regardless of the weight or range imputed to *physis.* If a genre is what it is, or if it is supposed to be what it is destined to be by virtue of its *telos,* then "genres are not to be mixed"; one should not mix genres, one owes it to oneself not to get mixed up in mixing genres. Or, more rigorously: genres should not intermix. And if it should happen that they do intermix, by accident or through transgression, by mistake or through a lapse, then this should confirm, since, after all, we are speaking of "mixing," the essential purity of their identity. This purity belongs to the typical axiom: it is a law of the law of genre, whether or not the law is, as one feels justified in saying, "natural." This normative position and this evaluation are inscribed and prescribed even at the threshold of the "thing itself," if something of the genre "genre" can be so named. And so it follows that you might have taken the second sentence in the first person, "I will not mix genres," as a vow of obedience, as a docile response to the injunction emanating from the law of genre. In place of a constative description, you would then hear a promise, an oath; you would grasp the following respectful commitment: I promise you that I will not mix genres, and, through this act of pledging utter faithfulness to my commitment, I will be faithful to the law of genre, since, by its very nature, the law invites and commits me in advance not to mix genres. By publishing my response to the imperious call of the law, I would correspondingly commit myself to be responsible.

Unless, of course, I were actually implicated in a wager, a challenge, an impossible bet—in short, a situation that would exceed the matter of merely engaging a commitment from me. And suppose for a moment that it were impossible not to mix genres. What if there were, lodged within the heart of the law itself, a law of impurity or a principle of contamination? And suppose the condition for the possibility of the law were the *a priori* of a counter-law, an axiom of impossibility that would confound its sense, order, and reason?

I have just proposed an alternative between two interpretations. I did not do so, as you can imagine, in order to check myself. The line or trait that seemed to separate the two bodies of interpretation is affected *straight away* by an essential disruption that, for the time being, I shall let you name or qualify in any way you care to: as internal division of the trait, impurity, corruption, contamination, decomposition, perversion, deformation, even cancerization, generous proliferation, or degenerescence. All these disruptive "anomalies" are engendered—and this is their common law, the lot or site they share—by *repetition.* One might even say by citation or re-citation *(ré-cit),* provided that the restricted use of these two words is not a call to strict generic order. A citation in the strict sense implies all sorts of contextual conventions, precautions, and protocols in the mode of reiteration, of coded signs, such as quotation marks or other typographical devices used for writing a citation. The same holds no doubt for the *récit* as a form, mode, or genre of discourse, even—and I shall return to this—as a literary type. And yet the law that protects the usage, in *stricto sensu,* of the words "citation" and "*récit*" is threatened intimately and in advance by a counter-law that constitutes this very law, renders it possible, conditions it and thereby renders it impossible—for reasons of edges on which we shall run aground in just a moment—to edge through, to edge away from, or to hedge around the counter-law itself. The law and the counter-law serve each other citations summoning each other to appear, and each recites the other in this proceeding *(procès).* There would be no cause for concern if one were rigorously assured of being able to distinguish with rigor between a citation and a non-citation, a *récit* and a non-*récit* or a repetition within the form of one or the other.

I shall not undertake to demonstrate, assuming it is still possible, why you were unable to decide whether the sentences with which I opened this presentation and marked this context were or were not repetitions of a citational type; or whether they were or were not of the performative type; or certainly whether they were, both of them, together—and each time together—the one or the other. For perhaps someone has noticed that, from one repetition to the next, a change had insinuated itself into the relationship between the two initial utterances. The punctuation had been slightly modified, as had the content of the second independent clause. Theoretically, this barely noticeable shift could have created a mutual independency between the interpretative alternatives that might have tempted you to opt for one or the other, or for one *and* the other of these two sentences. A particularly rich combinatory of possibilities would thus ensue, which, in order not to exceed my time limit and out of respect for the law of genre and of the audience, I shall abstain from recounting. I am simply going to assume a certain relationship between what has just now happened and the origin of literature, as well as its aborigine or its abortion, to quote Philippe Lacoue-Labarthe.

Provisionally claiming for myself the authority of such an assumption, I shall let our field of vision contract as I limit myself to a sort of species of the genre "genre." I shall focus on this genre of genre which is generally supposed, and always a bit too rashly, not to be part of nature, of *physis,* but rather of *technè,* of the arts, still more narrowly of poetry, and most particularly of literature. But at the same time, I take the liberty to think that, while limiting myself thus, I exclude nothing, at least in principle and *de jure*—the relationships here no longer being those of extension, from exemplary individual to species, from species to genre as genus or from the genre of genre to genre in general; rather, as we shall see, these relationships are a whole order apart. What is at stake, in effect, is exemplarity and its whole *enigma*—in other words, as the word "enigma" indicates, exemplarity and the *récit*—which works through the logic of the example.

Before going about putting a certain example to the test, I shall attempt to formulate, in a manner as elliptical, economical, and formal as possible, what I shall call the law of the law of genre. It is precisely a principle of contamination, a law of impurity, a parasitical economy. In the code of set theories, if I may use it at least figuratively, I would speak of a sort of participation without belonging—a taking part in without being part of, without having membership in a set. With the inevitable dividing of the trait that marks membership, the boundary of the set comes to form, by invagination, an internal pocket larger than the whole; and the outcome of this division and of this abounding remains as singular as it is limitless.

To demonstrate this, I shall hold to the leanest generalities. But I should like to justify this initial indigence or asceticism as well as possible. For example, I shall not enter into the passionate debate that poetics has brought forth on the theory and the history of genre-theory, on the critical history of the concept of genre from Plato to the present. My stance is motivated by these considerations: in the first place, we now have at our disposal some remarkable and, of late, handsomely enriched works dealing either with primary texts or critical analyses. I am thinking especially of the journal *Poétique,* of its issue entitled "Genres" (32) and of Genette's opening essay, "Genres, 'Types,' Modes." From yet another point of view, *L'Absolu littéraire* [The literary absolute] has already created quite a stir in this context, and everything that I shall risk here should perhaps resolve itself in a modest annotation on the margins of this magistral work which I assume some of you have already read. I could further justify my abstention or my abstinence here simply by acknowledging the terminological luxury or rapture as well as the taxonomic exuberance which debates of this kind, in a manner by no means fortuitous, have sparked: I feel completely powerless to contain this fertile proliferation—and not only because of time constraints. I shall put forth, instead, *two* principal *motives,* hoping thereby to justify my keeping to scant preliminary generalities at the edge of this problematic.

To what do these two motives essentially relate? In its most recent phase—and this much is certainly clear in Genette's propositions—the most advanced critical axis has led to a rereading of the entire history of genre-theory. This rereading has been inspired by the perception—and it must be said, despite the initial denial, by the correction—of two types

of misconstruing or confusion. On the one hand, and this will be the first
motive or ground for my abstention, Plato and Aristotle have been subjected to considerable deformation, as Genette reminds us, insofar as
they have been viewed in terms alien to their thinking, and even in terms
that they themselves would have rejected; but this deformation has usually taken on the form of *naturalization.* Following a classical precedent,
one has deemed natural structures or typical forms whose history is
hardly natural but, rather, quite to the contrary, complex and heteroge-
neous. These forms have been treated as natural—and let us bear in
mind the entire semantic scale of this difficult word whose span is so
far-ranging and open-ended that it extends as far as the expression
"natural language," by which term everyone agrees tacitly to oppose
natural language only to a formal or artificial language without thereby
implying that this natural language is a simple physical or biological
production. Genette insists at length on this naturalization of genres:
"The history of genre-theory is strewn with these fascinating outlines
that *inform and deform reality,* a reality often heterogenous to the literary
field, and that claim to discover a natural 'system' wherein they construct
a factitious symmetry heavily reinforced by fake windows" (p. 408, italics
added). In its most efficacious and legitimate aspect, this critical reading
of the history (and) of genre-theory is based on an opposition between
nature and history and, more generally—as the allusion to an artificial
construct indicates (". . . wherein they construct a factitious symmetry. . . .")—on an opposition between nature and what can be
called the series of all its others. Such an opposition seems to go without
saying; placed within this critical perspective, it is never questioned.
Even if it has been tucked away discretely in some passage that has
escaped my attention, this barely visible suspicion clearly had no effect
on the general organization of the problematic. This does not diminish
the relevance or fecundity of a reading such as Genette's. But a place
remains open for some preliminary questions concerning his presuppositions, for some questions concerning the boundaries where it
begins to take hold or take place. The form of these boundaries will
contain me and rein me in. These general propositions whose number is
always open and indeterminable for whatever critical interpretation will
not be dealt with here. What however seems to me to require more
urgent attention is the relationship of nature to history, of nature to its
others, *precisely when genre is on the line.*

    Let us consider the most general concept of genre, from the mini-
mal trait or predicate delineating it permanently through the modula-
tions of its types and the regimens of its history: it rends and defends
itself by mustering all its energy against a simple opposition that arises
from nature and from history, as from nature and the vast lineage of its
others (*technè, nomos, thesis,* then *spirit, society, freedom, history,* etc.). Be-

tween *physis* and its others, *genos* certainly locates one of the privileged scenes of the process and, no doubt, sheds the greatest obscurity on it. One need not mobilize etymology to this end and could just as well equate *genos* with birth, and birth in turn with the generous force of engenderment or generation—*physis,* in fact—as with race, familial membership, classificatory genealogy or class, age class (generation), or social class; it comes as no surprise that, in nature and art, genre, a concept that is essentially classificatory and genealogico-taxonomic, itself engenders so many classificatory vertigines when it goes about classifying itself and situating the classificatory principle or instrument within a set. As with the class itself, the principle of genre is unclassifiable; it tolls the knell of the knell (*glas*), in other words, of classicum, of what permits one to call out (*calare*) orders and to order the manifold within a nomenclature. *Genos* thus indicates the place, the now or never of the most necessary meditation on the "fold" which is no more historical than natural in the classical sense of these two words, and which turns *phyein* over to itself across others that perhaps no longer relate to it according to that epoch-making logic which was decisory, critical, oppositional, even dialectical but rather according to the trait of an entirely different contract. *De jure,* this meditation acts as an absolute prerequisite without which any historical perspectivizing will always be difficult to legitimate. For example, the Romantic era—this powerful figure indicted by Genette (since it attempted to reinterpret the system of modes as a system of genres)—is no longer a simple era and can no longer be inscribed as a moment or a stage placeable within the trajectory of a "history" whose concept we could be certain of. Romanticism, if something of the sort can be thus identified, is also the general repetition of all the folds that in themselves gather, couple, divide *physis* as well as *genos* through the genre, and through all the genres of genre, through the mixing of genre that is "more than a genre," through the excess of genre in relation to itself, as to its abounding movement and its general assemblage which coincides, too, with its dissolution.[1] Such a "moment" is no longer a simple moment *in* the history and theory of literary genres. To treat it thus would in effect implicate one as tributary—whence the strange logic—of something that has in itself constituted a certain Romantic motif, namely, the teleological ordering of history. Romanticism simultaneously obeys naturalizing and historicizing logic, and it can be shown easily enough that we have not yet been delivered from the Romantic heritage—even though we might wish it so and assuming that such a deliverance would be of compelling interest to us—as long as we persist in drawing attention to historical concerns and the truth of historical

---

1. In this respect, the second footnote in *L'Absolu littéraire* (Paris, 1978), p. 271, seems to me, let us say, a bit too equitable in its rigorous and honest prudence.

production in order to militate against abuses or confusions of naturalization. The debate, it could be argued, remains itself a part or effect of Romanticism.

A second motive detains me at the threshold or on the edge of a possible problematic of genre (as) history and theory of history and of genre-theory—another genre, in fact. For the moment, I find it impossible to decide—impossible for reasons that I do not take to be accidental, and this, precisely, is what matters to me—I find it impossible to decide whether the possibly exemplary text which I intend to put to the test does or does not lend itself to the distinction drawn between *mode* and *genre*. Now, as you may recall, Genette demonstrates the stringent necessity of this distinction; and he rests his case on "the confusion of modes and genres" (p. 417). This implies a serious charge against Romanticism, even though "the romantic reinterpretation of the system of modes as a system of genres is neither *de facto* nor *de jure* the epilogue to this long history" (p. 415). This confusion, according to Genette, has aided and abetted the naturalization of genres by projecting onto them the "privilege of naturalness, which was *legitimately* . . . that of three modes . . ." (p. 421). Suddenly, this naturalization "makes these arch-genres into ideal or natural types which they neither are nor can be: there are no arch-genres that can totally escape historicity *while preserving a generic definition*. There are modes, for example: the *récit*. There are genres, for example: the novel; the relation of genres to modes is complex and perhaps not, as Aristotle suggests, one of simple inclusion."

If I am inclined to poise myself on *this* side of Genette's argument, it is not only because of his ready acceptance of the distinction between nature and history but also because of its implications with regard to mode and to the distinction between mode and genre. Genette's definition of mode contains this singular and interesting characteristic: it remains, in contradistinction to genre, purely formal. Reference to a content has no pertinence. This is not the case with genre. The generic criterion and the modal criterion, Genette says, are "absolutely heterogenous": "each genre defined itself essentially by a specification of content which was not prescribed by the definition of mode . . ." (p. 417). I do not believe that this recourse to the opposition of form and content, this distinction between mode and genre, need be contested, and my purpose is not to challenge isolated aspects of Genette's argument. One might just question the presuppositions for the legitimacy of such an argument. One might also question the extent to which his argument can help us read a given text when it behaves in a given way with regard to mode and genre, especially when the text does not seem to be written sensibly within their limits but rather about the very subject of those limits and with the aim of disrupting their order. The limits, for instance, of that mode which would be, according to Genette, the *récit* ("There are modes, for example: the *récit*"). Of the (possibly) exemplary text which I shall address shortly, I shall not hasten to add that it is a "*récit*," and you will soon understand why. In this text, the "*récit*" is not only a mode, and a mode put into practice or put to the test because it is deemed impossible; it is also the name of a theme. It is the nonthematizable thematic content of something of a textual form that *assumes* a point of view with respect to the genre, even though it perhaps does not come under the heading of any genre—and perhaps no longer even under the heading of literature, if it indeed wears itself out around genreless modalizations, and would confirm one of Genette's propositions: "Genres are, properly speaking, literary/or aesthetic/ categories; modes are categories that pertain to linguistics or, more precisely, to an anthropology of verbal expression" (p. 418).

In a very singular manner, the very short text which I will discuss presently makes the *récit* and the impossibility of the *récit* its theme, its impossible theme or content at once inaccessible, indeterminable, interminable, and inexhaustible; and it makes the word "*récit*," under the aegis of a certain form, its titleless title, the mentionless mention of its genre. This text, as I shall try to demonstrate, seems to be made, among other things, to make light of all the tranquil categories of genre-theory and history in order to upset their taxonomic certainties, the distribution of their classes, and the presumed stability of their classical nomenclatures. It is a text destined, at the same time, to summon up these classes by conducting their proceeding, by proceeding from the proceeding to the law of genre. For if the juridical code has frequently thrust itself upon me in order to hear this case, it has done so to call as witness a (possible) exemplary text and because I am convinced fundamental rights are bound up in all of this: the law itself is at stake.

These are the two principal reasons why I shall keep to the liminal edge of (the) history (and) of genre-theory. Here now, very quickly, is the law of abounding, of *excess*, the law of participation without membership, of contamination, etc., which I mentioned earlier. It will seem meager to you, and even of staggering abstractness. It does not particularly concern either genres, or types, or modes, or any form in the strict sense of its concept. I therefore do not know under what title the field or object submitted to this law should be placed. It is perhaps the limitless field of general textuality. I can take each word of the series (genre, type, mode, form) and decide that it will hold for all the others (all genres of genres, types, modes, forms; all types of types, genres, modes, forms; all forms of forms, etc.). The trait common to these classes of classes is precisely the identifiable recurrence of a common trait by which one recognizes, or should recognize, a membership in a class. There should be a trait upon which one could rely in order to decide that a given textual event, a given "work," corresponds to a given class (genre, type, mode, form, etc.). And there should be a code enabling one to decide questions of class-membership on the basis of this trait. For example—a

very humble axiom, but, by the same token, hardly contestable—if a
genre exists (let us say the novel, since no one seems to contest its generic
quality), then a code should provide an identifiable trait and one which is
identical to itself, authorizing us to determine, to adjudicate whether a
given text belongs to this genre or perhaps to that genre. Likewise,
outside of literature or art, if one is bent on classifying, one should
consult a set of identifiable and codifiable traits to determine whether
this or that, such a thing or such an event belongs to this set or that class.
This may seem trivial. Such a distinctive trait *qua* mark is however always
a priori remarkable. It is always possible that a set—I have compelling
reasons for calling this a text, whether it be written or oral—re-marks on
this distinctive trait within itself. This can occur in texts that do not, at a
given moment, assert themselves to be literary or poetic. A defense
speech or newspaper editorial can indicate by means of a mark, even if it
is not explicitly designated as such, "Violà! I belong, as anyone may
remark, to the type of text called a defense speech or an article of the
genre newspaper-editorial." The possibility is always there. This does
not constitute a text *ipso facto* as "literature," even though such a possibility, always left open and therefore eternally remarkable, situates perhaps
in every text the possibility of its becoming literature. But this does not
interest me at the moment. What interests me is that this re-mark—ever
possible for every text, for every corpus of traces—is absolutely necessary for and constitutive of what we call art, poetry, or literature. It
underwrites the eruption of *technè*, which is never long in coming. I
submit this axiomatic question for your consideration: Can one identify
a work of art, of whatever sort, but especially a work of discursive art, if it
does not bear the mark of a genre, if it does not signal or mention it or
make it remarkable in any way? Let me clarify two points on this subject.
First, it is possible to have several genres, an intermixing of genres or a
total genre, the genre "genre" or the poetic or literary genre as genre of
genres. Second, this re-mark can take on a great number of forms and
can itself pertain to highly diverse types. It need not be a designation or
"mention" of the type found beneath the title of certain books (novel,
récit, drama). The remark of belonging need not pass through the consciousness of the author or the reader, although it often does so. It can
also refute this consciousness or render the explicit "mention" menda-
cious, false, inadequate, or ironic according to all sorts of overdetermined figures. Finally, this remarking-trait need be neither a
theme nor a thematic component of the work—although of course this
instance of belonging to one or several genres, not to mention all the
traits that mark this belonging, often have been treated as theme, even
before the advent of what we call "modernism." If I am not mistaken in
saying that such a trait is remarkable, that is, noticeable, in every aesthetic, poetic, or literary corpus, then consider this paradox, consider the

irony (which is irreducible to a consciousness or an attitude): this supplementary and distinctive trait, a mark of belonging or inclusion, does
not properly pertain to any genre or class. The re-mark of belonging
does not belong. It belongs without belonging, and the "without" (or the
suffix "-less") which relates belonging to non-belonging appears only in
the timeless time of the blink of an eye (*Augenblick*). The eyelid closes,
but barely, an instant among instants, and what it closes is verily the eye,
the view, the light of day. But without such respite, nothing would come to
light. To formulate it in the scantiest manner—the simplest but most
apodictic—I submit for your consideration the following hypothesis: a
text cannot belong to no genre, it cannot be without or less a genre.
Every text participates in one or several genres, there is no genreless
text; there is always a genre and genres, yet such participation never
amounts to belonging. And not because of an abundant overflowing or a
free, anarchic, and unclassifiable productivity, but because of the *trait* of
participation itself, because of the effect of the code and of the generic
mark. Making genre its mark, a text demarcates itself. If remarks of
belonging belong without belonging, participate without belonging, then
genre-designations cannot be simply part of the corpus. Let us take the
designation "novel" as an example. This should be marked in one way or
another, even if it does not appear, as it often does in French and
German texts, in the explicit form of a subtitled designation, and even if
it proves deceptive or ironic. This designation is not novelistic; it does
not, in whole or in part, take part in the corpus whose denomination it
nonetheless imparts. Nor is it simply extraneous to the corpus. But this
singular topos places within and without the work, along its boundary, an
inclusion and exclusion with regard to genre in general, as to an identifiable class in general. It gathers together the corpus and, at the same
time, in the same blinking of an eye, keeps it from closing, from identifying itself with itself. This axiom of non-closure or non-fulfillment
enfolds within itself the condition for the possibility and the impossibility
of taxonomy. This inclusion and this exclusion do not remain exterior to
one another; they do not exclude each other. But neither are they immanent or identical to each other. They are neither one nor two. They
form what I shall call the *genre-clause,* a clause stating at once the juridical
utterance, the precedent-making designation and the law-text, but also
the closure, the closing that excludes itself from what it includes (one
could also speak of a floodgate [*écluse*] of genre). The clause or floodgate of genre declasses what it allows to be classed. It tolls the knell of
genealogy or of genericity, which it however also brings forth to the light
of day. Putting to death the very thing that it engenders, it cuts a strange
figure; a formless form, it remains nearly invisible, it neither sees the day
nor brings itself to light. Without it, neither genre nor literature come to
light, but as soon as there is this blinking of an eye, this clause or this

floodgate of genre, at the very moment that a genre or a literature is broached, at that very moment, degenerescence has begun, the end begins.

The end begins, this is a citation. Maybe a citation. I might have taken it from the text which seems to me to bring itself forth as an example, as an example of this unfigurable figure of clusion.

What I shall try to convey to you now will not be called by its generic or modal name. I shall not say this drama, this epic, this novel, this novella or this *récit*—certainly not this *récit*. All of these generic or modal names would be equally valid or equally invalid for something which is not even quite a book, but which was published in 1973 in the editorial form of a small volume of thirty-two pages. It bears the title *La Folie du jour* [approximately: The Madness of the Day]. The author's name: Maurice Blanchot. In order to speak about it, I shall call this thing La Folie du jour, its given name which it bears legally and which gives us the right, as of its publication date, to identify and classify it in our copyright records at the Bibliothèque Nationale. One could fashion a non-finite number of readings from *La Folie du jour*. I have attempted a few myself, and shall do so again elsewhere, from another point of view. The *topos* of view, sight, blindness, *point of view* is, moreover, inscribed and traversed in *La Folie du jour* according to a sort of permanent revolution that engenders and virtually brings to the light of day points of view, twists, versions, and reversions of which the sum remains necessarily uncountable and the account, impossible. The deductions, rationalizations, and warnings that I must inevitably propose will arise, then, from an act of unjustifiable violence. A brutal and mercilessly depleting selectivity will obtrude upon me, upon us, in the name of a law that *La Folie du jour* has, in its turn, already reviewed, and with the foresight that a certain kind of police brutality is perhaps an inevitable accomplice to our concern for professional competence.

What will I ask of *La Folie du jour*? To answer, to testify, to say what it has to say with respect to the law of mode or the law of genre and, more precisely, with respect to the law of the *récit*, which, as we have just been reminded, is a mode and not a genre.

On the cover, below the title, we find no mention of genre. In this most peculiar place that belongs neither to the title nor to the subtitle, nor even simply to the corpus of the work, the author did not affix, although he has often done so elsewhere, the designation "*récit*" or "novel," maybe (but only maybe) by erroneously subsuming both of them, Genette would say, under the unique category of the genre. About this designation which figures elsewhere and which appears to be absent here, I shall say only two things:

1. On the one hand it commits one to nothing. Neither reader nor

critic nor author are bound to believe that the text preceded by this designation conforms readily to the strict, normal, normed, or normative definition of the genre, to the law of the genre or of the mode. Confusion, irony, the shift in conventions toward a new definition (in what name should it be prohibited?), the search for a supplementary effect, any of these things could prompt one to entitle as *novel* or *récit* what in truth or according to yesterday's truth would be neither one nor the other. All the more so if the words "*récit*," "novel," "*ciné-roman*," "complete dramatic works" or, for all I know, "literature" are no longer in the place which conventionally mentions genre but, as has happened and will happen again (shortly), they are found to be holding the position and function of the title itself, of the work's given name.

2. Blanchot has often had occasion to modify the genre-designation from one version of his work to the next or from one edition to the next. Since I am unable to cover the entire spectrum of this problem, I shall simply cite the example of the "*récit-*" designation effaced between one version and the next of *Death Sentence* (trans. Lydia Davis [Barrytown, N.Y., 1978]) at the same time as a certain epilogue is removed from the end of a double *récit*, which, in a manner of speaking, constitutes this book. This effacement of "*récit*," leaving a trace that, inscribed and filed away, remains as an effect of supplementary relief which is not easily accounted for in all of its facets. I cannot arrest the course of my lecture here, no more than I can pause to consider the very scrupulous and minutely differentiated distribution of the designations "*récit*" and "novel" from one narrative work to the next, no more than I can question whether Blanchot distinguished the genre and mode designations, no more than I can discuss Blanchot's entire discourse on the difference between the narratorial voice and the narrative voice which is, to be sure, something other than a mode. I would point out only one thing: at the very moment the first version of *Death Sentence* appears, bearing mention as it does of "*récit*," the first version of *La Folie du jour* is published with another title about which I shall momentarily speak.

La Folie du jour, then, makes no mention of genre or mode. But the word "*récit*" appears at least four times in the last two pages in order to name the theme of *La Folie du jour*, its sense or its story, its content or part of its content—in any case, its decisive proceedings and stakes. It is a *récit* without a theme and without a cause entering from the outside; yet it is without interiority. It is the *récit* of an impossible *récit* whose "production" occasions what happens or, rather, what remains, but which does not relate it, nor relate to it as to an outside reference, even if everything remains foreign to it and out of bounds. It is even less feasible for me to relate to you the story of *La Folie du jour* which is staked precisely on the possibility and the impossibility of relating a story. Nonetheless, in order to create the greatest possible clarity, in the name of daylight itself, that is to say (as will become clear), in the name of the

law, I shall take the calculated risk of flattening out the unfolding or
coiling up of this text, its permanent revolution whose rounds are made
to recoil from any kind of flattening. And this is why the one who says
"I," and the one after all who speaks to us, who "recites" for us, this one
who says "I" tells his inquisitors that he cannot manage to constitute
himself as narrator (in the sense of the term that is not necessarily literary) and tells them that he cannot manage to identify with himself
sufficiently or to remember himself well enough to gather the story and
récit that are demanded of him—which the representatives of society and
the law require of him. The one who says "I" (who does not manage to
say "I") seems to relate what has happened to him or, rather, what has
nearly happened to him after presenting himself in a mode that defies all
norms of self-presentation: he nearly lost his sight (his facility for *viewing*) following a traumatic event—probably an assault. I say "probably"
because *La Folie du jour* wholly upsets, in a discrete but terribly efficient
manner, all the certainties upon which so much of discourse is constructed: the value of an event, first of all, of reality, of fiction, of appearance and so on, all this being carried away by the disseminal and
mad polysemy of "day," of the word "day," which, once again, I cannot
dwell upon here. Having nearly lost his sight (*vue*), having been taken
in by a kind of medico-social institution, he now resides under the watch-
ful eye of doctors, handed over to the authority of these specialists who
are representatives of the law as well, legist doctors who demand that he
testify—and in his own interest, or so it seems at first—about what happened to him so that remedial justice may be dispensed. His faithful
récit—(but let me borrow for the sake of simplicity, and because it conforms fairly well to this context, the English word "account")—hence, his
faithful account of events should render justice unto the law. The law
demands a narrative account.

Pronounced four times in the last three pages of *La Folie du jour*, the
word "account" does not seem to designate a literary genre but rather a
certain type or mode of discourse. That is, in effect, the appearance of it.
Everything seems to happen as if the account—the question of or rather
the demand for the account, the response, and the nonresponse to the
demand—found itself staged and figured as one of the themes, objects,
stakes in a more bountiful text, *La Folie du jour,* whose genre would be of
another order and would in any case overstep the boundaries of the
account with all its generality and all its genericity. The account itself
would of course not cover this generic generality of the literary corpus
named *La Folie du jour.* Now we might already feel inclined to consider
this appearance suspect, and we might be jolted from our certainties by
an allusion that "I" will make: the one who says "I," who is not by force of
necessity a narrator, nor necessarily always the same, notes that the
representatives of the law, those who demand of him an account in the
name of the law, consider and treat him, in his personal and civil iden-

tity, not only as an "educated" man—and an educated man, they often tell him, ought to be able to speak and recount; as a competent subject, he ought to be able to know how to piece together a story by saying "I" and "exactly" how things happened to him—they regard him not only as an "educated" man, but also as a writer. He is writer and reader, a creature of "libraries," *the* reader of this account. This is not sufficient cause, but it is, in any case, a first clue and one whose impact incites us to think that the required account does not simply remain in a relationship that is extraneous to literature or even to a literary genre. Lest we not be content with this suspicion, let us weigh the possibility of the inclusion of a modal structure within a vaster, more general corpus, whether literary or not and whether or not related to the genre. Such an inclusion raises questions concerning edge, borderline, boundary, and abounding which do not arise without a fold.

What sort of a fold? According to which fold and which figure of enfoldment?

Here are the three final paragraphs; they are of unequal length, with the last of these comprising approximately one line:

> They demanded: Tell us "exactly" how things happened.—An account? I began: I am neither learned nor ignorant. I have known some joy. This is saying too little. I related the story in its entirety, to which they listened, it seems, with great interest—at least initially. But the end was a surprise for them all. "After that beginning," they said, "you should proceed to the facts." How so? The account was over.
>
> I should have realized that I was incapable of composing an account of these events. I had lost the sense of the story; this happens in a good many illnesses. But this explanation only made them more demanding. Then I noticed, for the first time, that they were two and that this infringement on their traditional method—even though it can be explained away by the fact that one of them was an eye doctor, the other a specialist in mental illnesses—increasingly gave our conversation the character of an authoritarian interrogation, overseen and controlled by a strict set of rules. To be sure, neither of them was the chief of police. But being two, due to that, they were three, and this third one remained firmly convinced, I am sure, that a writer, a man who speaks and reasons with distinction, is always capable of recounting the facts which he remembers.
>
> An account? No, no account, nevermore.

In the first of the three paragraphs that I have just cited, he claims that something is to begin after the word "account" punctuated by a question mark (An account?—herein implied: they want an account, is it then an account that they want? "I began . . ."). This something is nothing other than the first line on the first page of *La Folie du jour*. These are the same words, in the same order, but this is not a citation in the strict sense for, stripped of quotation marks, these words commence or re-commence a quasi-account that will engender anew the entire sequence comprising this new point of departure. In this way, the first words ("I am neither learned nor ignorant . . .") that come after the word "account" and its question mark, that broach the beginning of the account extorted by the law's representatives—these first words mark a collapse that is unthinkable, irrepresentable, unsituable within a linear order of succession, within a spatial or temporal sequentiality, within an objectifiable topology or chronology. One sees, without seeing, one reads the crumbling of an upper boundary or of the initial edge in *La Folie du jour,* uncoiled according to the "normal" order, the one regulated by common law, editorial convention, positive law, the regime of competency in our logo-alphabetical culture, etc. Suddenly, this upper or initial boundary, which is commonly called the first line of a book, is forming a pocket inside the corpus. It is taking the form of an *invagination* through which the trait of the first line, the borderline, splits while remaining the same and traverses yet also bounds the corpus. The "account" which he claims is beginning at the end and, by legal requisition, is none other than the one that has begun from the beginning of *La Folie du jour* and in which, therefore, he gets around to saying that he begins, etc. And it is without beginning or end, without content and without edge. There is only content without edge—without boundary or frame—and there is only edge without content. The inclusion (or occlusion, inocclusive invagination) is interminable: it is an analysis of the account that can only turn in circles in an unarrestable, inenarrable, and insatiably recurring manner—but one terrible for those who, in the name of the law, require that order reign in the account, for those who want to know, with all the required competence, "exactly" how this happens. For if "I" or "he" continued to tell what he has told, he would end up endlessly returning to this point and beginning again to begin, that is to say, to begin with an end that precedes the beginning. And from the viewpoint of objective space and time, the point at which he stops is absolutely unascertainable ("I have told them the entire story . . ."), for there is no "entire" story except for the one that interrupts itself in this way.

A lower edge of invagination will, if one can say so, respond to this "first" invagination of the upper edge by intersecting it. The "final line" resumes the question posed *before* the "I began" (An account?) and bespeaks a resolution or promises it, tells of the commitment made no longer to give an account. As if he had already given one! And yet, yes (yes and no), an account has taken place. Hence the last word: "An account? No, no account, nevermore." It has been impossible to decide whether the recounted event and the event of the account itself ever took place. Impossible to decide whether there was an account, for the one who barely manages to say "I" and to constitute himself as narrator recounts that he has not been able to recount—but what, exactly? Well, everything, including the demand for an account. And if an assured and guaranteed decision is impossible, this is because there is nothing more to be done than to commit oneself, to perform, to wager, to allow chance its chance—to make a decision that is essentially edgeless, bordering perhaps only on madness.

Yet another impossible decision follows, one which involves the promise "No, no account, nevermore": Is this promise a part of or apart from the account? Legally speaking, it is party to *La Folie du jour,* but not necessarily to the account or to the simulacrum of the account. Its trait splits again into an internal and external edge. It repeats—without citing—the question apparently posed above (An account?) of which it can be said that, in this permanent revolution of order, it follows, doubles, or reiterates it in advance. Thus another lip or invaginating loop takes shape here. This time the lower edge creates a pocket in order to come back into the corpus and to rise again on this side of the upper or initial line's line of invagination. This would form a double chiasmatic invagination of edges:

A. "I am neither learned nor ignorant..."
B. "An account? I began:"
A'. "I am neither learned nor ignorant..."
B'. "An account? No, no account, nevermore..."

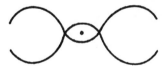

"I began..."

It is thus impossible to decide whether an event, account, account of event, or event of accounting took place. Impossible to settle upon the simple borderlines of this corpus, of this ellipse unremittingly repealing itself within its own expansion. When we fall back on the poetic consequences enfolded within this dilemma, we find that it becomes difficult indeed to speak here with conviction about an account as a determined mode included within a more general corpus or one simply related, in its determination, to other modes or, quite simply, to something other than itself. All is narrative account and nothing is; the account's outgate remains within the account in a non-inclusive mode, and this structure is itself related so remotely to a dialectical structure that it even inscribes dialectics in the account's ellipse. All is account, nothing is: and we shall not know whether the relationship between these two propositions—the strange conjunction of the account and the accountless—belongs to the account itself. What indeed happens when the edge pronounces a sentence?

Faced with this type of difficulty—the consequences or implications of which cannot be deployed here—one might be tempted to take recourse in the law or the rights which govern published texts. One might be tempted to argue as follows: all these insoluble problems of delimitation are raised "on the inside" of a book classified as a work of literature or literary fiction. Pursuant to these juridical norms, this book has a beginning and an end that leave no opening for indecision. This book has a determinable beginning and end, a title, an author, a publisher, its distinctive denomination is *La Folie du jour.* At this place, where I am pointing, on this page, right here, you can see its first word; here, its final period, perfectly situable in objective space. And all the sophisticated transgressions, all the infinitesimal subversions that may captivate you are not possible except within this enclosure for which these transgressions and subversions moreover maintain an essential need in order to take place. Furthermore, on the inside of this normed space, the word "account" does not name a literary operation or genre, but a current mode of discourse, and it does so regardless of the formidable problems of structure, edge, set theory, the part and whole, etc., that it raises in this "literary" corpus.

That is all well and good. But in its very relevance, this objection cannot be sustained—for example, it cannot save the modal determination of the account—except by referring to extra-literary and even extra-linguistic juridical norms. The objection makes an appeal to the law and calls to mind the fact that the subversion of La Folie du jour needs the law in order to take place. Whereby the objection reproduces and accomplishes its staging within *La Folie du jour:* the account, mandated and prescribed by law but also, as we shall see, commanding, requiring, and producing law in turn. In short, the whole critical scene of competence in which we are engaged is *party* to and *part* of *La Folie du jour,* in whole and in part, the whole is a part.

The whole does nothing but begin. I could have begun with what resembles the absolute beginning, with the juridico-historical order of this publication. What has been lightly termed the first version of *La Folie du jour* was not a book. Published in the journal *Empédocle* (2 May 1949), it bore another title—indeed, several other titles. On the journal's cover, here it is, one reads:

Maurice Blanchot
Un récit?
[*An Account?*]

Later, the question mark disappears twice. First, when the title is reproduced within the journal in the table of contents:

Maurice Blanchot
Un récit
[*An Account*],

then below the first line:

Un récit	[*An Account*
par	by
Maurice Blanchot	M. B.]

Could you tell whether these titles, written earlier and filed away in the archives, make up a single title, titles of the same text, titles of the account (which of course figures as an impracticable mode in the book), or the title of a genre? Even if the latter were to cause some confusion, it would be of the sort that releases questions already implemented and enacted by *La Folie du jour*. This enactment enables in turn the denaturalization and deconstitution of the oppositions nature/history and mode/genre.

Now let us turn to some of these questions. First, to what could the words "An Account" refer in their manifold occurrences and diverse punctuations? And precisely how does reference function here? In one case, the question mark can *also* serve as a supplementary remark indicating the necessity of all these questions as the insolvent character of indecision: Is this an account? Is it an account that I entitle? asks the title in entitling. Is it an account that they want? What entitles them? Is it an account as discursive mode or as literary operation, or perhaps even as literary genre whose theme would be mode or genre? Likewise, the title could excerpt, as does a metonymy, a fragment of the account without an account (to wit, the words "an account" with and without a question mark), but such an iterative excepting is not citational. For the title, guaranteed and protected by law but also making law, retains a referential structure which differs radically from the one underlying other occurrences of the "same" words in the text. Whatever the issue—title, reference, or mode and genre—the case before us always involves the law and, in particular, the relations formed around and to law. All the questions which we have just addressed can be traced to an enormous matrix that generates the non-thematizable thematic power of a simulated account: it is this inexhaustible writing which recounts without telling, and which speaks without recounting.

Account of an accountless account, an account without edge or boundary, account all of whose visible space is but some border of itself without "self," consisting of the framing edge without content, without modal or generic boundaries—such is the law of this textual event, of this text that also speaks the law, its own and that of the other as reader of this text which, speaking the law, also imposes itself as a law text, as the text of the law. What, then, is the law of the genre of this singular text? It is law, it is the figure of the law which will also be the invisible center, the themeless theme of *La Folie du jour* or, as I am now entitled to say, of "An Account?"

This law, however, as law of genre, is not exclusively binding on the genre *qua* category of art and literature. But, paradoxically, and just as impossibly, the law of genre also has a controlling influence and is binding on that which draws the genre into engendering, generations, genealogy, and degenerescence. You have already witnessed its approach often enough, with all the figures of this degenerescent self-engendering of an account, with this figure of the law which, like the day that it is, challenges the opposition between the law of nature and the law of symbolic history. The remarks that have just been made on the double chiasmatic invagination of edges should suffice to exclude any notion linking all these complications to pure form or one suggesting that they could be formalized outside the content. The question of the literary genre is not a formal one: it covers the motif of the law in general, of generation in the natural and symbolic senses, of birth in the natural and symbolic senses, of the generation difference, sexual difference between the feminine and masculine genre/gender, of the hymen between the two, of a relationless relation between the two, of an identity and difference between the feminine and masculine. The word "hymen" tells us several things. It not only points toward a paradoxical logic that is inscribed without however being formalized under this name; it should, in the first place, serve to remind the Anglo-American reader that, in French, the semantic scale of *genre* is much larger and more expansive than in English, and thus always includes within its reach the gender. Additionally, and with respect to the "hymen," let us not forget everything that Philippe Lacoue-Labarthe and Jean-Luc Nancy tell us in *L'Absolu littéraire* (especially on p. 276) about the relationship between genre *(Gattung)* and marriage, as well as about the intricate bonds of serial connections begotten by *gattieren* ("to mix," "to classify"), *gatten* ("to couple"), *Gatte/Gattin* ("husband/wife"), and so forth?

Once articulated within the precinct of Blanchot's entire discourse on the neuter, the most elliptical question would inevitably have to assume this form: What about a neutral genre/gender? Or one whose neutrality would not be *negative* (neither . . . nor), nor dialectical, but affirmative, and doubly affirmative (or . . . or)?

Here again, due to time limitations but also to more essential reasons concerning the structure of the text, I shall have to excerpt some abstract fragments. This will not occur without a supplement of violence and pain.

As first word and surely most impossible word of *La Folie du jour*, "I" presents itself as self *(moi)*, me, a man. Grammatical law leaves no doubt about this subject. The first sentence, phrased in French in the masculine ("Je ne suis ni savant ni ignorant" and not "Je ne suis ni savante ni ignorante"), says, with regard to knowledge, nothing but a double negation (neither . . . nor). Thus, no glint of self-presentation. But the double negation gives passage to a double affirmation (yes, yes) that enters into alignment or alliance with itself. Forging an alliance or marriage-bond ("hymen") with itself, this boundless double affirmation utters a measureless, excessive, immense *yes:* both to life and to death:

> I am neither learned nor ignorant. I have known some joy. This is saying too little: I am living, and this life gives me the greatest pleasure. And death? When I die (perhaps soon), I shall know an immense pleasure. I am not speaking of the foretaste of death, which is bland and often disagreeable. Suffering is debilitating. But this is the remarkable truth of which I am sure: I feel a boundless pleasure in living and shall be boundlessly content to die.

Now, seven paragraphs further along, the chance and probability of such an affirmation (one that is double and therefore boundless, limitless) is granted to woman. It returns to woman. Rather, not to woman or even to the feminine, to the female genre/gender, or to the generality of the feminine genre but—and this is why I spoke of chance and probability—"usually" to women. It is "usually" women who say yes, yes. To life to death. This "usually" avoids treating the feminine as a general and generic force; it makes an opening for the event, the performance, the uncertain contingencies, the encounter. And it is indeed from the contingent experience of the encounter that "I" will speak here. In the passage that I am about to cite, the expression "men" occurs twice. The second occurrence names the sexual genre, the sexual difference (*aner, vir*—but sexual difference does not occur between a species and a genre); in the first occurrence, "men" comes into play in an indecisive manner in order to name either the genre of human beings (the *genre humain,* named "species" in the text) or sexual difference:

> Men would like to escape death, bizarre *species* that they are. And some cry out, "die, die," because they would like to escape life. "What a life! I'll kill myself, I'll surrender!" This is pitiful and strange; it is in error.
> But I have encountered *beings* who never told life to be quiet or death to go away—usually women, beautiful creatures. As for men, terror besieges them. . . . [Italics added]

What has thus far transpired in these seven paragraphs? Usually women, beautiful creatures, relates "I." As it happens, encounter, chance, affirmation of chance do not always manage to happen. There is no natural or symbolic law, universal law, or law of a genre/gender here. Only usually, usually women, (comma of apposition) beautiful creatures. Through its highly calculated logic, the comma of apposition leaves open the possibility of thinking that these women are not beautiful and then, on the other hand, as it happens, capable of saying yes, yes to life to death, of not saying be quiet, go away to life to death. The comma of apposition lets us think that they are beautiful, women and beauties, these creatures, insofar as they affirm both life and death. Beauty, the feminine beauty of these "beings," would be bound up with this double affirmation.

Now I myself, who "am neither learned nor ignorant," "I feel a boundless pleasure in living and shall be boundlessly content to die." In this random claim that links affirmation usually to women, beautiful ones, it is then more than probable that, as long as I say yes, yes, I am a woman and beautiful. *I am a woman, and beautiful.* Grammatical sex (or anatomical as well, in any case, sex submitted to the law of objectivity): the masculine genre is thus affected by the affirmation through a random drift that could always render it other. A sort of secret coupling would take place here, forming an odd marriage ("hymen"), an odd couple, for none of this can be regulated by objective, natural, or civil law. The "usually" is a mark of this secret and odd hymen, of this coupling that is also perhaps a mixing of genres. The genres pass into each other. And we will not be barred from thinking that this mixing of genres, viewed in light of the madness of sexual difference, may bear some relation to the mixing of literary genres.

"I," then, can keep alive the chance of being a fe-male or of changing sex. His transsexuality permits him, in a more than metaphorical and transferential way, to engender. He can give birth, and many other signs which I cannot mention here bear this out, among other things the fact that on several occasions he "brings something forth to the light of day." In the rhetoric of *La Folie du jour,* the idiomatic expression "to bring forth to the light of day" ("donner le jour") is one of the players in an exceedingly powerful polysemic and disseminal game that I shall not attempt to reproduce here. I only retain its standard and dominant meaning which the spirit of linguistics gives it: *donner le jour* is to give birth—a verb whose subject is usually maternal, that is to say, generally female. At the center, closely hugging an invisible center, a primal scene could have alerted us, if we had had the time, to the *point of view* of *La Folie du jour* and to *A Primal Scene.* This is also called a "short scene."

"I" can bring forth to light, can give birth. To what? Well, precisely to law or more exactly, to begin with, to the representatives of law, to those who wield authority—and let us also understand by this the authority of the author, the rights of authorship—simply by virtue of possessing an overseer's right, the right to see, the right to have everything in sight. This panoptic and this synopsis demand nothing else, but nothing less. Now herein lies the essential paradox: from where and from whom do they derive this power, this right-to-sight that permits them to have "me" at their disposal? Well, from "me," rather, from the subject who is subjected to them. It is the "I"-less "I" of the narrative voice, the I "stripped" of itself, the one that does not take place, it is he who brings them to light, who engenders these lawmen in giving them insight into what regards them and what should not regard them.

> I liked the doctors well enough. I did not feel belittled by their doubts. The bother was that their authority grew with every hour. One isn't initially aware of it, but these men are kings. Showing me my rooms they said: Everything here belongs to us. They threw themselves upon the parings of my mind: This is ours. They interpellated my story: Speak! and it placed itself at their service. In haste, I stripped myself of myself. I distributed my blood, my privacy among them, I offered them the universe, I brought them forth to the light of day. Under their unblinking gaze, I became a water drop, an ink blot. I was shrinking into them, I was held entirely in their view and when, finally, I no longer had anything but my perfect nullity present and no longer had anything to see, they, too, ceased to see me, most annoyed, they rose, shouting: Well, where are you? Where are you hiding? Hiding is prohibited, it is a misdeed, etc.

Law, day. One believes it generally possible to oppose law to affirmation, and particularly to unlimited affirmation, to the immensity of yes, yes. Law—we often figure it as an instance of the interdictory limit, of the binding obligation, as the negativity of a boundary not to be crossed. Now the mightiest and most divided trait of *La Folie du jour* or of "An Account?" is the one relating birth to law, its genealogy, engenderment, generation, or genre—and here I ask you once more to be especially aware of gender—the one joining the very *genre* of the law to the process of the double affirmation. The excessiveness of *yes, yes* is no stranger to the genesis of law (nor to Genesis, as could be easily shown, for it also concerns an account of Genesis "in the light of seven days" [p. 20]). The double affirmation is not foreign to the genre, genius, or spirit of the law. No affirmation, and certainly no *double* affirmation without the law sighting the light of day and the daylight becoming law. Such is the madness of the day, such is an account in its "remarkable" truth, in its truthless truth.

Now the feminine, or generally affirmative gender/genre, is also the genre of this figure of law, not of its representatives, but of the law herself who, throughout an account, forms a couple with me, with the "I" of the narrative voice.

The law is in the feminine.

She is not a woman (it is only a figure, a "silhouette," and not a representative of the law) but she, *la loi,* is in the feminine, declined in the feminine; but not only as a grammatical gender/genre in my language (elsewhere Blanchot brought this genre into play for speech ["*la* parole"] and for thought ["*la* pensée"]). No, she is described as a "female element," which does not signify a female person. And the affirmative "I," the narrative voice, who has brought forth the representatives of the law to the light of day, claims to find the law seductive—sexually seductive. The law appeals to him: "The truth is that she appealed to me. In this milieu overpopulated with men, she was the only female element. One time she had me touch her knee: a bizarre impression. I declared to her: I am not the kind of man who contents himself with a knee. Her response: that would be revolting!" She pleases him and he would not like to content himself with the knee that she "had [him] touch." This contact with the knee *(genou)*, as my student and friend Pierre-François Berger brought to my notice, recalls the inflectional contiguity of the I and the we, the *je* and the *nous,* of an I/we couple of whom we shall speak again in a moment.

The law's female element has thus always appealed to: me, I, he, we. The law is appealing: "The law appealed to me . . . In order to tempt her, I called softly to the law: 'Approach, so I can see you face to face' (I wanted to take her aside for a moment). Impudent appeal; what would I have done had she responded?"

He is perhaps subjected to law, but he neither attempts to escape her, nor does he shrink before her: he wishes to seduce the law to whom he gives birth (there is a hint of incest in this) and especially—this is one of the most striking and singular traits of this scene—he inspires fear in the law. He not only troubles the representatives of the law, the lawmen who are the legist doctors and the "psy-" who demand of him, but are unable to obtain, an organized account, a testimony oriented by a sense of history or his story, ordained and ordered by reason, and by the unity of an I think, or of an originally synthetic apperception accompanying all representations. That the "I" here does not always accompany itself is by no means borne lightly by the lawmen; in fact, he alarms thus the lawmen, he radically persecutes them, and, in his manner, he conceals from them without altercation the truth they demand and without which they are nothing. But he not only alarms the lawmen, he alarms the law; one would be tempted to say the law herself, if she did not remain here a silhouette and an effect of the account. And what is more, this law whom the "I" frightens is none other than "me," than the "I," effect of his desire, child of his affirmation, of the genre "I" clasped in a specular couple with "me." They are inseparable (*je/nous* and *genou, je/toi* and *je/toit*), and so she tells him, once more, as truth: "The truth is that we can no longer be separated. I shall follow you everywhere, I shall dwell under your roof [*toit*], we shall have the same sleep." We see the law, whose silhouette stands behind her representatives, frightened by "me," by "him"; she is inclined toward and declined by *je/nous,* I/we, in front of "me," in front of him, her knees marking perhaps the articulation of a gait, the flexion of the couple and sexual difference, but also the continuity without contact of the hymen and the "mixing of genres."

> Behind their backs, I perceived the silhouette of the law. Not the familiar law, who is strict and not terribly agreeable: this one was different. Far from falling prey to her menace, I was the one who seemed to frighten her. According to her, my glance was lightning and my hands, grounds on which to perish. Moreover, she ridiculously attributed to me all kinds of power, she declared herself perpetually to be kneeling before me. But she let me demand nothing, and when she granted me the right to be in all places, that meant that I hadn't a place anywhere. [Elsewhere Blanchot designates the non-place and the atopical or hypertopical mobility of the narrative voice in this way.] When she placed me above the authorities, that meant: you are authorized to do nothing.

What game is the law, a law of this genre, playing? What is she playing up to when she has her knee touched? For if *La Folie du jour* plays down the law, plays at law, plays with law, it is also because the law herself plays. The law, in its female element, is a silhouette that plays. At what? At being . . . born, at being born like anybody and no body. She plays upon her generation and displays her genre, she plays out her nature and her history, and she makes a plaything of an account. In mock-playing herself she takes into account the account: she recites; and her birth is accountable to the account, the *récit,* one could even say to her: (to *la voix* . . .) the narrative voice, *him, her, I, we,* the neuter genre that subjects and merges itself while giving birth to her, who lets himself be captivated by the law and escapes her, whom she escapes and whom she loves. She lets herself be put in motion, she lets herself be cited by him when, in the midst of her game, she says, pursuing an idiom that her disseminal polysemy conveys to the abyss, "I see day":

> Here is one of her games. [He has just recalled that she "once had (him) touch her knee."] She showed me a section of the space between the top of the window and the ceiling: "You are there," she said. I looked at this point with intensity. "Are you there?" I looked at it with all my power. "Well?" I felt the scars of my glaze leap, my sight became a wound, my head, a gap, a gutted bull. Suddenly she cried out: "Oh! I see day! Oh God!" etc. I protested that this game tired me enormously, but she was insatiable for my glory.

For the law to see the day is her madness, is what she loves madly like the glory, the emblazed illustration, the day of the writer, of the author who says "I," and who brings forth law to the light of day. He says that she is insaturable, insatiable for his glory—he, who is, too, author of the law to which he submits himself, he, who engenders her, he, her mother who no longer knows how to say "I" or to keep memory intact. I am the mother of law, behold my daughter's madness. It is also the Madness of the Day, for day, the word "day" in its disseminal abyss, is law, the law of the law. My daughter's madness is to want to be born— like anybody, whereas she remained a "silhouette," a shadow, a profile, her face never in view. He had said to her, to the law, in order to "tempt her": "Approach, so I can see you face to face."

Such would be the "remarkable truth" that clears an opening for the madness of day—and that appeals, like law, like madness, to the one who says "I" or I/we. Let us be attentive to this syntax of truth. She, the law, says: "The truth is that we can no longer be separated. I shall follow you everywhere, I shall live under your roof . . ." He: "The truth is that she appealed to me . . . ," she, law, but also—and this is always the principal theme of these sentences—she, *la vérité*, truth. One cannot conceive truth without the madness of the law.

I have let myself be commanded by the law of our encounter, by the convention of our subject, notably the genre, the law of genre. This law, articulated as an I/we which is more or less autonomous in its move- ments, assigned us places and limits. Even though I have launched an appeal against this law, it was she who turned my appeal into a con- firmation of her own glory. But she also desires ours insatiably. Sub- mitting myself to the subject of our colloquium, as well as to its law, I sifted "An Account," *La Folie du jour.* I isolated a type, if not a genre, of reading from an infinite series of trajectories or possible courses. I have pointed out the generative principle of these courses, beginnings, and new beginnings in every sense: but from a certain point of view. Elsewhere—in accordance with other subjects, other colloquia and lec- tures, other I/we drawn together in one place—other trajectories could have, and have, come to light.

Nonetheless, it would be folly to draw any sort of general conclusion here. I could not say what exactly has happened in this scene, nor in my discourse or my account. What was perhaps seen, in the blink of time's eye, is a madness of law—and, therefore, of order, reason, sense, and meaning, of day: "But often" (said "I"), "I was dying without saying a thing. In time, I became convinced that I was seeing the madness of day face to face; such was the truth: light became mad, clarity took leave of her senses; she assailed me unreasonably, without a set of rules, without a goal. This discovery was like jaws clutching at my life." I am woman, and beautiful; my daughter, the law, is mad about me. I speculate on my daughter. My daughter is mad about me; this is law.

The law is mad, she is mad about "me." And across the madness of this day, I keep this in sight. There, this will have been my self-portrait of the genre.

The law is mad. The law is mad, is madness; but madness is not the predicate of law. There is no madness without the law; madness cannot be conceived before its relation to law. Madness is law, the law is madness. There is a general trait here: the madness of the law mad for me, the day madly in love with me, the silhouette of my daughter mad about me, her mother, etc. But *La Folie du jour, An* (accountless) *Account?*, carrying and miscarrying its titles, is not at all exemplary of this general trait. Not at all, not wholly. This is not an example of a general or generic whole. The whole, which begins by finishing and never finishes beginning apart from itself, the whole that stays at the edgeless boundary of itself, the whole greater and less than a whole and nothing, *An Account?* will not have been exemplary. Rather, with regard to the whole, it will have been wholly counter-exemplary.

The genre has always in all genres been able to play the role of order's principle: resemblance, analogy, identity and difference, taxonomic classification, organization and genealogical tree, order of reason, order of reasons, sense of sense, truth of truth, natural light and sense of history. Now, the test of *An Account?* brought to light the madness of genre. Madness has given birth to and thrown light on the genre in the most dazzling, most blinding sense of the word. And in the writing of *An Account?*, in literature, satirically practicing all genres, imbibing them but never allowing herself to be saturated with a catalog of genres, she, madness, has started spinning Peterson's genre-disc like a demented sun. And she does not only do so *in* literature, for in concealing the boundaries that sunder mode and genre, she has also inundated and divided the borders between literature and its others.

There, that is the whole of it, it is only what "I," so they say, here kneeling at the edge of literature, can see. In sum, the law. The law summoning: what "I" can sight and what "I" can say that I sight in this site of a recitation where I/we is.

Une traduction?
par
M

Secrets and Narrative Sequence

Frank Kermode

> In the conduct of an invented story there are, no doubt, certain proprieties to be observed for the sake of clearness and effect.
> —JOSEPH CONRAD, *Under Western Eyes*

> Lucinda can't read poetry. She's good,
> Sort of, at novels, though. The words, you know,
> Don't sort of get in like Lucinda's way.
> And then the story, well, you know, about
> Real people, fall in love, like that, and all.
> Sort of makes you think, Lucinda thinks.
> —GEORGE KHAIRALLAH, "Our Latest Master of the Arts"[1]

The proprieties to be observed for the sake of clearness and effect are what enable Lucinda to get on sort of better with novels than with poetry. They ensure that words don't get in the way of story and characters ("real people")—characters, for example, by falling in love, are what enable the story to continue. "And all" is sequence, also closure: plot, in short. These are the things that make Lucinda think; these are the things that are admitted (unlike words, which remain in perpetual quarantine) to Lucinda's consciousness; and what she is good at understanding is their message.

We are all rather more like Lucinda than we care to believe, always wishing words away. First we look for story—events sequentially related

---

1. From *Academe* (Beirut, 1979). My thanks to Alexander Baramki, who sent me this book.

(possessing, shall we say, an irreducible minimum of "connexity"). And sequence goes nowhere without his doppelgänger or shadow, causality. Moreover, if there are represented persons acting, we suppose them to be enacting an action, as Aristotle almost, though not quite, remarked; and we suppose them to have "certain qualities of thought and character" (*dianoia* and *ethos*), the two causes of action—as Aristotle really did remark (*Poetics* 49b36).

Hence the first questions we like to ask resemble those of Keats: "What leaf-fring'd legend . . . What men or gods are these? What maidens loth? . . . To what green altar . . .?" There seems to be a *mythos;* these persons are acting, they seem to be trying to do something or to stop somebody else from doing it (the maidens are "loth"), and they are heading somewhere. The *mythos* appears to have the usual relation to *ethos* and *dianoia*. But Keats, and we after him, are unable to discover the plot because the arrangement of the events (*synthesis tón pragmatón*) is not such as to allow us. Still, it must have some bearing upon our world, a world in which, as our experience suggests, there is evidence of sequence and cause; too much wine is followed by burning foreheads and parching tongues, sexual excitement is not perpetual and may be followed by sadness. Since matters appear to be otherwise on the urn, we are obliged to think that the contrast is the point of the story, for unless it has something to do with our normal expectations and beliefs, it can have no point. It lacks a quality we expect in imitations of our world, where heads ache and one may be disgusted. What it lacks is intelligible sequence, and this lack or absence must be the most important thing about it. That the young man will never stop singing, never kiss, implies a world in which the trees will never be bare nor maidens' beauty fade. Nothing in this sequenceless paradise has *character*—the ash, as Yeats put it, on a burnt stick. This utter eventlessness, this *nunc stans,* "teases us out of thought," which is not quite "sort of makes [us] think." We are nevertheless anxious that it should *say* something to us. What it says, we say, is that even in our world, the familiar world of chance and choice, it is an important though not self-evident fact that beauty is truth and truth beauty. The importance of the story on the urn, then, is that in its very difference it can tell us, by intruding into our sequence of scandal and outrage, in-

Frank Kermode is King Edward VII Professor of English at Cambridge University. The author of *The Sense of an Ending, Continuities,* and *Shakespeare, Spenser, Donne: Renaissance Essays,* his recent works include *The Classic* and *The Genesis of Secrecy.*

timations not obvious but comforting. We have, in the end, made it say something that suits us.[2]

I've been teasing Keats' poem into thought, into parable. Even if the *mythos* is incomplete and the characters so far above breathing human passion that we can infer very little about *ethos* or *dianoia,* we make them all relevant to a world in which we behave as if causes operated and matters came to an end. If the story on the urn does not observe the proprieties, we shall nonetheless consider it strictly in relation to those proprieties; and that will enable it to *say* something to us. Of course the poem encourages us to do these things by ending with the sort of message that seems possible and proper.

Obviously our task, and the author's, will be easier with a completed action, as Aristotle, with his talk of failure and success and of the progressive exposure of the agents' *ethos* and *pathos,* would agree. And since we are not here to talk about immobile urns, I shall hereafter consider only invented stories in which the proprieties (as to connexity, closure, and character) are better observed. The first thing to say, I think, is that stories of this kind have frequently, perhaps to all intents and purposes always, properties that are not immediately and obviously related to the proprieties I have mentioned. This might seem self-evident; we are always asking questions of well-formed narratives that are not altogether unlike those put by the poet to his urn—questions about the persons acting, questions about cause, questions about what the story *says.* And although we are all very good readers, we argue about the answers, even if we agree that the story under discussion observes the proprieties. This is partly because most of the stories we care to discuss in this way have properties not so directly under the control of propriety. Good readers may conspire to ignore these properties; but they are relevant to my main theme, which is the conflict between narrative sequence (or whatever it is that creates the "illusion of narrative sequence") and what I shall loosely, but with pregnant intention, call "secrets."

Consider first the rather obvious point that a story is always subject to interpretation. Stories as we know them begin as interpretations. They

2. After this was written, I read Jurij M. Lotman's "The Origin of Plot in the Light of Typology," *Poetics Today* 1, nos. 1–2 (1979): 161–84. Lotman speaks of two primeval kinds of plot. The first is "mythic" and has no "excesses or anomalies"; it is timeless and motionless. The second is the linear tale about incidents, news, "excesses." The two exist in dialectical interaction, and the result is a "fusion of scandal and miracle." A secret motivation arising from the "eschatological" plot intrudes into the linear plot; "mythologism penetrates into the sphere of excess." It is from such combinations that we have learnt to interpret reality as we do, plotwise. Keats' poem foreshadows this theory. The mythic event is injected into scandal and outrage; beauty subsumes a version of truth which represents it as calamity, decay, and consequence; the assurance that there is a timeless and motionless transcendent world reduces to insignificance the *faits divers* which seem to constitute the narrative of ordinary life.

grow and change on the blank of the pages. There is some truth in the theory of iconotropy; if we doubt the evidence that it happened in remote antiquity, we shall not trouble to deny that it happened in later versions of myth, in folk etymologies, in daily gossip, and perhaps even in daily newspapers. Creative distortion of this kind is indeed so familiar as to need no more words. So is the practice of deliberate, conscious narrative revision, whether in narrative midrash or by historians. There is a perpetual *aggiornamento* of the sense. Interference with the original project may begin at the beginning; as Edward Said might say, its authority is subject to primordial molestation.[3] We take this for granted in some matters, as New Testament critics assume that the parables had been distorted not only by the appended interpretations but even in their substance, before they were written down. Consequently the world divides between those who seek to restore something authentic but lost and those who conclude that the nature of parable, and perhaps of narrative in general, is to be "open"—open, that is, to penetration by interpretation. They are, in Paul Ricoeur's formula, models for the redescription of the world; they will change endlessly since the world is endlessly capable of being redescribed. And this is a way of saying that they must always have their secrets.

The capacity of narrative to submit to the desires of this or that mind without giving up secret potential may be crudely represented as a dialogue between story and interpretation. This dialogue begins when the author puts pen to paper and it continues through every reading that is not merely submissive. In this sense we can see without too much difficulty that all narrative, in the writing and the reading, has something in common with the continuous modification of text that takes place in a psychoanalytical process (which may tempt us to relate secrets to the condensations and displacements of dreams) or in the distortions induced in historical narrative by metahistorical considerations.

All that I leave to Roy Schafer[4] and Hayden White. My immediate purpose is to make acceptable a simple proposition: we may like to think, for our purposes, of narrative as the product of two intertwined processes, the presentation of a fable and its progressive interpretation (which of course alters it). The first process tends toward clarity and propriety ("refined common sense"), the second toward secrecy, toward distortions which cover secrets. The proposition is not altogether alien to the now classic *fabula/sujet* distinction. A test for connexity (an important aspect of propriety) is that one can accurately infer the fable (which is not to say it ever had an independent anterior existence). The *sujet* is what became of the fable when interpretation distorted its pristine, sequential propriety (and not only by dislocating its order of presentation,

---

3. Edward W. Said, *Beginnings* (New York, 1975), p. 83.
4. Not forever, I hope; his essay and its "refined common sense" have powerful implications for a more general narrative theory.

though the power to do so provides occasions for unobvious interpretations of a kind sequence cannot afford).

I do not know whether there is a minimum acceptable measure of
narrativity. (On whom should we conduct acceptability tests? Wyndham
Lewis' cabdriver? Philippe Sollers? The president of the the MLA?) What
seems reasonable, however, is the proposition that there will always be
some inbuilt interpretation, that it will increase as respect for propriety
decreases, and that it will produce distortions, secrets to be inquired into
by later interpretation. Even in a detective story which has the maximum
degree of specialised "hermeneutic" organisation, one can always find
significant concentrations of interpretable material that has nothing to
do with clues and solutions and that can, if we choose, be read rather
than simply discarded, though propriety recommends the latter course.[5]
In the kinds of narrative upon which we conventionally place a higher
value, the case against propriety is much stronger; there is much more
material that is less manifestly under the control of authority, less easily
subordinated to "clearness and effect," more palpably the enemy of
order, of interpretative consensus, of message. It represents a fortunate
collapse of authority (authors have authority, property rights; but they
poach their own game and thereby set a precedent to all interpreters).

Whatever the comforts of sequence, connexity (I agree that we cannot do without them), it cannot be argued that the text which exhibits
them will do nothing but contribute to them; some of it will be indifferent or even hostile to sequentiality. And although perhaps generated from some unproblematic ur-text, these nonsequential elements
may grow unruly enough to be disturbing, even to the author. Such was
the case with Conrad, to whom I shall return in a moment. He was
certainly aware of the conflict between the proprieties and the mutinous
text of interpretation. There is no doubt that sequence, *ethos,* and *dianoia*
minister to comfort and confirm our notions of what life is like (notions
that may have been derived from narrative in the first place) and
perhaps even constitute a sort of secular viaticum, bearing intimately
upon one's private eschatology, the sense of one's own life and its closure.
Such are their comforts, and sometimes we want them badly enough to
wish away what has to come with them: the treacherous text, with its
displacements and condensations, its debauched significances and un-
official complicities. Because the authors may themselves be alarmed by
these phenomena (but also because they need to please), we may enter
into collusion with them and treat all the evidence of insubordinate text
as mere disposable noise or use the evidence selectively, when it can be
adapted to strengthen the facade of propriety.

Secrets, in short, are at odds with sequence, which is considered as

5. See my "Novel and Narrative" (Glasgow, 1972); rpt. in *The Theory of the Novel,* ed.
John Halperin (New York, 1974), pp. 155–74.

an aspect of propriety; and a passion for sequence may result in the suppression of the secret. But it is there, and one way we can find the secret is to look out for evidence of suppression, which will sometimes tell us where the suppressed secret is located. It must be admitted that we rarely read in this way, for it seems unnatural; and when we do we are uncomfortably aware of the difference between what we are doing and what the *ordinary reader* not only does but seems to have been meant to do. To read a novel expecting the satisfactions of closure and the receipt of a message is what most people find enough to do; they are easier with this method because it resembles the one that works for ordinary acts of communication. In this way the gap is closed between what is sent and what is received, which is why it seems to many people perverse to deny the author possession of an authentic and normative sense of what he has said. Authors, indeed, however keenly aware of other possibilities, are often anxious to help readers behave as they wish to; they "foreground" sequence and message. This cannot be done without backgrounding something, and indeed it is not uncommon for large parts of a novel to go virtually unread; the less manifest portions of its text (its secrets) remain secret, resisting all but abnormally attentive scrutiny, reading so minute, intense, and slow that it seems to run counter to one's "natural" sense of what a novel is, a sense which one feels to have behind it the history and sociology of the genre. That history has ensured that most readers underread, and the authors in turn tend to encourage underreading because success depends upon it; there is public demand for narrative statements that can be agreed with, for problems rationally soluble. By the same token the authors are suspicious of overreaders, usually members of a special academic class that has the time to pry into secrets. Joyce said he had written a book to keep the professors busy; but James would not have said so, nor would Conrad, in whom the struggle between propriety and secrecy is especially intense, nor Robbe-Grillet, who claims to write for the man in the street. This measure of collusion between novelist and public (his de facto contract or gentleman's agreement is with *la cour et la ville* not with *l'école*) helps one to see why the secrets are so easily overlooked and why—given that the problems only begin when the secrets are noticed—we have hardly, even now, found decent ways to speak of these matters.

If anybody thinks this is an exaggerated account of the matter, let him reflect that Forster's *A Passage to India* had a very unusual success on publication and gave rise to lively arguments about its account of Indian life and politics; yet it was a good many years before anybody noticed that it had secrets. What is more, I spend much of my time among learned men who were devoted colleagues and friends of Forster and who know *Passage* well, but they never seem to talk about its secrets, only about its message and what, in their view, is wrong with it.

2

It is time, however, to consider a single text in more detail, and I shall henceforth be talking about *Under Western Eyes*. This novel was not, in 1911 or I think since, what could be called a popular success, though it offers a decent measure of connexity and closure (falling off a little, it must be allowed, from the highest standards of propriety). Its political and psychological messages are gratifyingly complex; one can engage in an enlightened critical conversation about *ethos* and *dianoia* without talking about much else and so pass for an intelligent professional giving an effective "reading." Indeed that, until recently at any rate, was what the normal institutional game consisted of. Nor is it without interest; but the game is conducted within a very limited set of rules, in the establishment of which the author as well as the institution has played a part. Under these rules it is not obligatory to talk of secrets. There are handier, more tangible or manageable mysteries.

Under Western Eyes wants to allow this game to be played, but it also gives due notice that a different game is possible; it indicates, by various signs, that there are other matters that might be considered and that, though ignorable, they are detectable, given the right kind of attention. So it is a suitable text for my purpose, which is to consider the survival of secrecy in a narrative that pays a lot of attention to the proprieties which, according to its narrator, should be observed "for the sake of clearness and effect." Conrad took a high view of art and a low view of his public, which is why writing fiction seems to have been a continual cause of misery to him. It forced him into a situation sometimes reflected in his characters, a *dédoublement*. There is one writer who labours to save the "dense" reader (one equipped, so to speak, with only Western eyes) from confusion, disappointment, and worry; and another dedicated to interpretation, to secrets, though at the same time he fears them as enemies of order, sequence, and message. There must be a strict repression of all that contests their supremacy, "else novel-writing becomes a mere debauch of the imagination," as Conrad told Mrs. Garnett, who was worried about the "self-imposed limitation" of the method employed in *Under Western Eyes*.[6]

I am already operating, and will continue to operate, a crude distinction in the readership, actual or potential, of *Under Western Eyes*. There is a larger public which Conrad, although he rather despised it, wanted to read his book. To some extent he abrogates authority (which the common reader values highly) by interfering as usual with the "normal" sequence of the story and by installing an unreliable narrator; all

6. Conrad, *Letters from Joseph Conrad, 1895–1924*, ed. Edward Garnett (Indianapolis, 1928), p. 234.

narrators are unreliable, but some are more expressly so than others;[7] the more unreliable they are, the more they can say that seems irrelevant to, or destructive of, the proprieties. They break down the conventional relationship between sequential narrative and history-likeness, with its arbitrary imposition of truth; they complicate the message. They are more or less bound to bore or antagonize the simpler reader, who feels that he has been left outside and cannot, without pains he is unwilling to take, gain access on his own terms, a due sequaciousness being one, and another authority, so that he need not reason why. Some such explanation will suffice for the cold public reception of *Under Western Eyes;* it has not grown much warmer in these days, for all that the book is now regarded as a classic.

Saying what is a classic is the business of a second group of readers, the professionally initiate. They perform other tasks, of course. One is finding things out, in the manner of Eloise Knapp Hay and Norman Sherry. And I hope we should all rather know than be ignorant of what they tell us; it is a first principle of literary criticism that no principle should stand which prevents our being concerned with what stimulates our unaffected interest—for example, in what Conrad, when he was not writing *Under Western Eyes,* thought about Russia, Slav "mysticism," and Dostoevsky; or what Conrad originally planned to write, what he took to be the point of what he did write, and what, having written it, he cut. What he saw with his Eastern eyes is a legitimate subject of concern, though at present we are concerned with what he wrote in *Under Western Eyes.* And other members of this group assume the responsibility of saying what that was and how it is most profitable for us to think about it.

There are a great many books on Conrad, and I shall mention few of them. Albert Guerard's *Conrad the Novelist,* though it appeared in 1958, still seems to be a standard work, and not surprisingly, for it is a perceptive and resourceful book.[8] But it is characteristically uninterested in secrets. On *Under Western Eyes* it makes plain that the author's first interest is in the psychopathology of Razumov; and it would have been possible to quote Conrad in defence of this preference. Razumov, the loner, the man of independent reason undermined by the shocks of Russian despotism and anarcy, is "psychologically . . . fuller" than Lord Jim (p. 232). The design of the story (*synthesis tón pragmatón*) is commended because Razumov is enabled to keep quiet during his long period on the rack of guilt and fear, but to confess when every threat to his security has been removed. "It would be hard to conceive a plot more successfully combining dramatic suspense and psycho-moral significance." *Mythos, ethos, dianoia:* all present and sound.

7. The trouble is not that there are unreliable narrators but that we have endorsed the fiction of the "reliable" narrator.

8. Albert J. Guerard, *Conrad the Novelist* (Cambridge, Mass., 1958); all references to this work will be cited in the text.

Even the dislocated narrative sequence is said to have some advantages: by concealing what a more straightforward rendering of the fable would have revealed, it enables us to observe Razumov in Geneva before we find out that he has accepted employment as a spy for Mikulin. Such are the rewards of entrusting the narration to an observer who is not only limited and prejudiced but pretends to neither omniscience nor omnicommunicativeness. But such rewards are obtained at a cost, for the old language teacher "creates unnecessary obstacles by raising the question of authority" (p. 248). He is a clumsy device for ensuring fair play to the Russians by reminding us that their actions are being reported through a rather "dense" medium. On the other hand, first person narration, in the extended form here employed, gives "eyewitness credibility and the authority of spoken voice" (p. 249).

Here is a contradiction, interesting though perhaps only apparent. Authority doesn't normally "raise the question of authority." They have it very oft that have it not. Yet there is a sense in which Conrad does both claim and renounce authority. Having it makes for clearness and effect; Conrad admired Trollope.[9] Not having it is to risk a debauch of the imagination. The contradiction of the critic replicates a conflict in the author. Writing under conditions even more agonizing than usual, Conrad said that "following the psychology of Mr. Razumov" was "like working in hell." The point to remember is that following the psychology required him to do many other things at the same time, or it would not have been so hellish. When a critic devoted to clearness and effect argued that *Chance* should be cut by half, Conrad replied sarcastically that yes, given a certain method, it "might have been written out on a cigarette paper."[10] Clearness and effect he sought, out of need, and desire too; but there was also the pursuit of interpretations. Hence the doubling I spoke of. In the hell of composition we see one writer committed to authority, another involved in debauch.

What is the critic to say when confronted with the evidence of debauch committed behind the back of authority? Guerard is not like Lucinda, the words do get in his way to some extent. Early in the book Razumov sees the phantom of Haldin lying in the snow. He tramples over it. Gaining from this act an intuition of Russia's "sacred inertia," he decides to give Haldin up to the police. The phantom crops up from time to time in the course of the novel but can always be disposed of by reference to the psychological difficulties arising from this first hallucination. Or can it? When Razumov and Sophia Antonovna, in the garden of the exiles' villa at Geneva, are discussing whether there will be any tea left for her indoors, Razumov remarks that she might be lucky enough to find there "the cold ghost of tea." Guerard finds this odd and de-

---

9. See Frederick R. Karl, *Joseph Conrad: The Three Lives* (London, 1979), p. 68 n.
10. Conrad, preface to *Chance* (London, 1920), p. viii.

scribes it as "mildly obsessive." So it is, but fortunately it can be got rid of, psychologized as "hallucination, psychic symbol, or shorthand notice of anxiety." In such ways are the ghosts and phantoms subjected to the needs of clearness and effect, buried in the psychology. I shall dig them out in a minute or two.

There are other ways of exorcizing secrets. Near the end of the book Razumov says he had been in a position to steal Natalia's soul. Guerard speaks of the Dostoevskian power of this moment of diabolism but is anxious to be rid of it, for it does not comply with what Roy Schafer might call his "guiding fiction," his interpretation principle. Guerard dismisses Razumov's remark by arguing that Conrad, here writing for the first time in Razumov's person, "returned imaginatively" to his original plan for the novel, in which Razumov was to marry Natalia, so stealing her soul. The diabolism is, therefore, an irrelevant intrusion, a fault, a vestigial survival. Also near the end of the book, Razumov has the notion that the old language teacher is the devil. Of this second diabolistic conjecture Guerard says nothing, which is the more usual way of dealing with these awkwardnesses.

To attend to what complies with the proprieties, and by one means or another to eliminate from consideration whatever does not, is a time-honoured and perfectly respectable way of reading novels, especially when it is quite a task (as it often is in Conrad) to establish within proper bounds all the tricks and deviations which interfere with one's view of the fable. It is therefore not surprising that good readers, sensing that there is more going on than they have accounted for, show signs of strain. Guerard admires *Under Western Eyes* but admits that, having such a narrator, it lacks "the rich connotative effects and subtly disturbing rhythms of *Lord Jim*" (p. 252). On the other hand, this "self-effacing and more rational prose has the great merit of not interfering with the drama of ideas or with the drama of betrayal and redemption." *Under Western Eyes,* that is to say, is unsubtle but clear and effective.

This is an extraordinary notion, and for a good critic to hold it is evidence of a strong though uneasy desire not to let the words get in the way—it is, after all, a refined version of Lucinda's view of the matter. To an eye undimmed by, or awakened from, the proprieties, this novel positively flaunts the "irrationality" of its prose. It becomes "readable" in the way Guerard wants it to be only when, by every possible means, attention to its secrets is repressed. Guerard's psychologizing of the phantom and his exorcism of the devil are of a piece with his decision that the prose is self-effacing and rational, lacking in resonance and connotation.

If you're looking out for this kind of thing, you find it almost anywhere. Eloise Knapp Hay, for example, rightly asks why Razumov's cover story, during the preparations for his visit to Geneva, should include an eye disease and a visit to an oculist (so far as simple plotting goes, any nonocular meeting-place would have done just as well; indeed, no specification of this sort was, strictly, needed at all).[11] What Hay, having noticed this, makes of it is that Razumov, during these visits, is being commissioned "to use his own eyes to spy for the state" (p. 294), and she mentions the young man's earlier discomfort at the stares of the goggle-eyed general who interviewed him on the night he betrayed Haldin. But to leave it at that simple allegorical level is precisely to refuse the kind of covert invitation of which this text has so many. Another of Hay's interesting observations is that behind the description of Russia as "a monstrous blank page awaiting the record of an inconceivable history," there may lie an observation of Mickiewicz's to the effect that Russia was "a page prepared for writing"—an alarming thought, since one could not know that the devil would not cover the page before God did (pp. 287–88). But she is content to observe that in Conrad "the question is posed differently," without allusion to God and the devil. Here again, properly interested in the relation of Conrad's figure to its presumable source, she omits to ask what the relation is doing in the book and how it may be related to the elements of diabolism. So too, she quotes the famous letter to Cunninghame Graham, in which Conrad says that to serve a national ideal, however much suffering it may cause, is better than to serve the shadow of an eloquence that is dead, a mere phantom (p. 20). We may think of Conrad as painfully finding out in the writing of *Under Western Eyes* what the novel was; he did so by writing it, black on white, as if it were Russia, and by meditating on eyes, phantoms, and devils, as surely as by deciding to cut all the American material from the final version; it was Russia he was writing on.

The secrets to which these words and ideas are an index have no direct relation to the main business of the plot; as some analysts would say, they are not kernels but catalysts or, as Seymour Chatman calls them, "satellites." But they form associations of their own, nonsequential, secret invitations to interpretation rather than appeals to a consensus. They inhabit a misty world in which relationships are not arranged according to some agreed system but remain occult or of questionable shape. There is a relatively clean, well-lighted plot—rectangular like the room in which its climax occurs, almost without shadow, having, like Switzerland, no horizons, for they are cut off by crude and impassable barriers like the Jura, by conventional closure.

Such a plot may be suitable for the citizens of a tedious democracy, either Switzerland, where they sit colourlessly uncouth, drinking beer out of glittering glasses, obvious in an obvious light, or England, which has made its bargain with fate, so much liberty for so much cash, know-

11. Eloise Knapp Hay, *The Political Novels of Joseph Conrad* (Chicago, 1963); all references to this work will be cited in the text. See also D. C. Yelton's *Mimesis and Metaphor* (The Hague, 1967) which sees a connection between the "motif of vision" and the phantom but treats it only psychologically.

ing also that it is entitled to the obvious. Such a nation deserves novels like the view of Geneva on which Razumov turns his back in contempt, finding it "odious—oppressively odious—in its unsuggestive finish; the very perfection of mediocrity attained at last after centuries of toil and culture." But this novel contains another plot, misty, full of phantoms, of which the passage about the blank page of Russia forms a part, as would be manifest if anybody considered it in relation to the large number of allusions (they even look, when one is looking for them, obtrusive) to blackness and whiteness, paper and ink, snow and shadow—and to writing itself.

These are secrets from which, by a curious process of collusion, we avert our attention. It was a welcome surprise to find in an excellent paper by Avrom Fleishman proof that an effort of attention is after all possible.[12] Fleishman observes that the "artlessness" of the narrator is not a guarantee of factuality so much as a hint that the text is extremely artful; he sorts out the interrelations between the various documentary sources the old man is supposed to be using, notes the hints of falsification and omission, and emphasizes the abnormal interest of the novel in the acts and arts of writing, as when Razumov, prompted to write by Laspara, composes his first (Russian) spy report in the shadow of the statue of the (Genevan) writer Rousseau. He also argues that the novel moves out of writing into speech, as indeed it does: the inspiration mentioned in the last off-key conversation between the narrator and Sophia is drawn in with the breath, Razumov is no longer a writer but a beloved speaker. Fleishman draws back finally (perhaps needlessly) from his own proposal that the book suggests an "ultimate despair of written language, and of the art of fiction. . . ."

And indeed it is obvious that *Under Western Eyes* (rather than any character in it) is obsessed with writing and also with deafness—deafness not only of the ears but of the eyes (Ivanovich seems to speak from his eyes; Sophia Antonovna seems to receive "the sound of his voice into her pupils instead of her ears"; at the grand climax the narrator is blinded by his own amazement, but the slamming of a door restores his sight). There is a hint that we may, though we probably won't, read for more than mere evidence of Razumov's psychological condition. If we are willing to do so, we shall find over the plot the shadow of a secret that has defied being made altogether otherwise than it is for the sake of readers who want the work to be throughout like beer in a glittering glass. I have

---

12. Avrom Fleishman, "Speech and Writing in *Under Western Eyes,*" in *Conrad: A Commemoration,* ed. Norman Sherry (London, 1976), pp. 119–28. After this paper was written, there appeared Jeremy Hawthorn's *Joseph Conrad: Language and Fictional Self-Consciousness* (London, 1979) which contains interesting remarks on Conrad's play with English tenses and argues that when the language teacher tells Miss Haldin that he has understood "all the words" but without understanding, he is speaking for the reader as Conrad imagined him (see pp. 102–28).

been giving instances of subtler, more learned modes of inattention; even good readers find means to dispose of the evidence rather than work upon it. It would be easy to give more: for example, the explanation of all the souls and phantoms of the text as part of a refutation, or parody, of *Crime and Punishment*. This can be used to sterilize large portions of Conrad's text. I do not mean to argue that no such observations ought to be made. Like the psychological and political readings, they belong squarely to a tradition of ordinary reading that may be perfectly intelligent; a person might run his life in accordance with what he concluded from such readings, as Lawrence did from his reading of *Anna Karenina*. I object only to their use as means to exclude secrets from the text.

Let me now give one or two more detailed instances of the way in which this novel advertises and conceals its secrets. As the story of Razumov's treachery reaches its crisis, the narrator pauses to note that his job is "not in truth the writing in the narrative form a précis of a strange human document, but the rendering . . . of the moral conditions ruling over a large portion of this earth's surface; conditions not easily to be understood, much less discovered in the limits of a story, till some key-word is found; a word that could stand at the back of all the words covering the pages, a word which, if not truth itself, may perchance hold truth enough to help the moral discovery which should be the object of every tale." He stops, scans Razumov's journal, then takes up his pen again, ready to set down "black on white." Then he says that the key word is "cynicism."

Even in a novel so benignly disingenuous from the preface on (or is it benign; in a sense it hates its readers), this passage is remarkable. Playing the role of straight narrator, the old man repeatedly veers close to the position of his occult double. "A large portion of the earth's surface" is a periphrasis easily divested of its originating notion, Russia; the case is more general. He sees that the point of the narrative is not solely or primarily psychological but wanders away from the insight to speak of "moral conditions." He speaks of a key word; pauses, as it were, unwittingly speaks one of the key words of the book he is in ("black on white"), then lapses into the obvious or irrelevant "cynicism." For a real secret he substitutes a pseudosecret, though in doing so he cannot help telling the attentive reader that there is a secret there. Readers as "dense" as he himself is will be happy with "cynicism." They will get on with sequence while the double busies himself with secrets and key words such as "soul," "eyes," and "black and white." Indications that these words have a special function are various. They occur with quite abnormal frequency; they are used in such a way as to distort the plausibility of narrative and especially of dialogue. Some instances may be explained away as evidence of Razumov's stressed condition ("what I need is not a lot of haunting phantoms that I could walk through" is the kind of remark that certainly suggests stress of some kind). But in others it is simply astonishing that anybody capable of reading could fail to observe the gross distortions in what they think of as "self-effacing and rational prose."

Let us look at a continuous passage; it is ripped from the midst of a longer one, so one must allow for an even greater measure of eccentric insistence in the context of the whole: "We shall get some tea," says Ivanovitch, leading Razumov to his mistress' drawing-room. They cross a black-and-white tessellated floor. Ivanovitch's hat, black but shiny, stands outside the drawing-room which is "haunted, it is said, by evoked ghosts, and frequented, it is supposed, by fugitive revolutionists." (We may remember that the villa itself "might well have been haunted in traditional style by some doleful, groaning, futile ghost of a middle-class order.") The white paint of the panels is cracked. Ivanovitch, from behind his dark spectacles, speaks of the true light of femininity. His mistress has brilliant eyes in a death's-head face, they gleam white but their pupils are black. Ivanovitch speaks as if from his invisible eyes. The lady "ghoulishly" eats the cakes Ivanovitch brought in his hat. Razumov gives a moment's thought to Tekla, the *dame de compagnie:* "Have they terrified her out of her senses with ghosts, or simply have they only been beating her?" He is aware of having to come to terms with phantoms, with the ghastly. His interlocutors appear to understand nothing of what he says; Ivanovitch is as if deaf. The purpose of the revolutionary movement, it seems, is to "spiritualise discontent," and the lady declares herself, in matters of politics, a "supernaturalist." She can see Razumov's soul with her "shiny eyes." What does she see? asks Razumov. "Some sort of phantom in my image? . . . For, I suppose, a soul when it is seen is just that. A vain thing. There are phantoms of the living as well as of the dead." He then tells them he has seen a phantom. Soon he leaves, passing the top hat, "black and glossy in all that crude whiteness," and looks at the chequered floor below.

I'll pause there and admit that this is a very partial account of Razumov's visit, meant to bring out what a "normal" reading largely ignores. The easiest thing to notice is the unidiomatic quality of the writing. "Haunted . . . by evoked ghosts"; "Have they terrified her out of her senses with ghosts, or simply have they only been beating her?"; "Some sort of phantom in my image?" How are we to explain these oddities? I suppose the "evoked ghosts" might be put down to Conrad thinking in French, as can "simply have they only been beating her"; but however they got there we are, I think, obliged to read them, not wish them away. Both the remark about Tekla's scared appearance (was it caused by evoked ghosts?) and the character of the phantom the second-sighted lady might see in Razumov are, one would have thought, almost intolerably odd if one is reading this as a sequence-advancing, psychology-investigating dialogue. Conrad helps us to psychologize it

out of the way by making Razumov enter into a dangerous, though cen-
sored, account of his encounter with Haldin's phantom. But only our
recollections of anarchists of the period, their flirting with the occult and
with feminism, can explain the interest in seeing souls coming to terms
with phantoms; unless we decide, as we ought, that the emphasis on eyes
and seeing is otherwise, and occultly, related to the virtually un-
controlled dispersion of souls, spirits, phantoms, ghosts, ghouls, and so
forth. Here, against the repetitive black and white (against ink on paper,
against the page we are *seeing*) are crowded the evidences of things
unseen and the huge variety of eyes that may or may not see them. It is
not an easy thing to talk about such a constellation of irrational figures,
but it must somehow be done if we are to read secrets as well as
sequence—to avoid attributing all these phenomena to Razumov's "nervous exhaustion."

What I ask you to believe is that such oddities are not merely local;
they are, perhaps, the very "spirit" of the novel. If one follows Razumov
a little way from the encounter just described, one finds him talking to
Tekla with her striped cat and terrified eyes and then with Sophia
Antonovna, whose black eyes and white hair are mentioned almost as
often as she is. It is in this interview that the ghost of tea occurs.
Razumov has just mentioned that his mind is a murky medium in which
Haldin appears as a featureless shadow. He adds that Haldin is now
beyond the reach of feminine influence, except possibly that of the spiritualist lady. "Formerly the dead were allowed to rest, but now it seems
they are at the beck and call of a crazy old harridan." "Let us hope," says
Sophia humorously, "that she will make an effort and conjure up some
tea for us." The figure arises naturally from the talk about the spiritualist
lady. But it continues. "There has been tea up there. . . . If you hurry . . .
instead of wasting your time with such an unsatisfactory sceptical person
as myself, you may find the ghost of it—the cold ghost of it—still lingering. . . ." And two pages later Razumov again tells her that she risks
missing "the mere ghost of that tea." In her reply Sophia uses the figure
yet again. Then they speak of ghouls, ogres, vampires. She denies that
she is a materialist; she is described as Mephistophelian. Finally Razumov
tells the story of his escape; it is in truth the story of Haldin, gliding from
Razumov's room as if he were a phantom, at midnight; the flame gutters
as he passes. She listens but as if with her eyes not her ears—with her
black impenetrable eyes glowing under the white hair. At one point
Sophia tells him to "wait until you have trodden every particle of yourself under your own feet . . . you've got to trample down every particle of
your own feelings." These are words private to Razumov, not possible to
her; only he, and perhaps Councillor Mikulin, knows about that tram-
pling. Are we inclined to seek, in the body of the plot, a reason why
Sophia should use such an expression? No, for any notion that she had
access to secret police information about Razumov would extravagantly

spoil the plot. No; here an expression private to Razumov (if we stick to conventional characterisation)—evidence as to his peculiar psychological state—has bled into the texture of the book and attached itself to Sophia. I wonder if anything quite like it can be found in the English novel till Virginia Woolf. Note, too, the repetition ("trodden" . . . "trample"): it is an indication that we are to pause and take note of it.

I have mentioned elsewhere the oddity of Natalia Haldin's remark—that when she went to the villa she didn't at first see a soul, but then Tekla came in, and she *did* see a soul. Perhaps Conrad was not aware that the idiomatic expression "I didn't see a soul" is incapable of a positive transformation. That doesn't matter; "seeing a soul" is another important key word. The oddity of the expression is a way of directing attention to it; it must not be swept away by talk of Conrad's English. So with the other key words, the repetitions—four ghosts of tea are surely beyond a joke. The frequency with which "soul," "ghost," and related words are used has not altogether escaped attention; but if one reflects that they occur (if one allows not only "spirit" but "inspired") well over a hundred times in the novel (sometimes in grotesquely thick concentrations), besides several ghostly appearances, people appearing as if they had risen from the ground, and so on, it becomes obvious that the attention has not been very sustained. Of course, all these usages are somehow related to the appearance of Haldin's phantom in the plots of action and psychology; but they must not be totally subsumed in them. Indeed, on any reasonably minute and careful reading they cannot be, for they distort the dialogue and are incompatible with any psychology that could be thought appropriate to Razumov, who is always sane. Nor should one forget the frequency of associated key words. I have counted well over sixty references to eyes—the eyes of all the principal characters are incessantly mentioned or described—and to seeing. Black on white occurs twenty-four times expressly and many more less directly—in references to snow and darkness, light in dark rooms, and, as I have said, ink on paper. All this adds up to a quantitatively quite large body of text which on the face of it contributes nothing to sequence—clogs it, indeed.

It would be to inflict even more laborious reports on you to specify at any greater length the character of the "secret" material in *Under Western Eyes.* My purpose is to supplement the "straight" reading, which irons out such considerable quantities of text. Conrad, when he began the book, called it *Razumov;* but when it was done (on the last page of the manuscript, in fact) he changed the title to *Under Western Eyes.* He had found out what he was doing. Most readers silently restore the old title, being readier to think about Razumov than about eyes. They want something clearly seen, a message to be apprehended with civilised ease. Let us look at the underside of one more scene, Razumov's confession to Natalia.

Razumov's face is pale, his eyes dark. The inner room is dark by

contrast with the well-lit anteroom; Mrs. Haldin's face is white against
the undefined dark mass of her chair. Razumov has been writing and
stopped to come and talk, so entering the writing, the black on white, of
the narrator. He is safe; the phantom on the snow has been walked over,
though the phantom's mother is white as a ghost. Natalia enters, like a
ghost ("her presence . . . was as unforeseen as the apparition of her
brother had been," with a pun on two senses of "apparition").[13] She had
done the same in the garden of the villa; she "had been haunting him."
They stand in the rectangular box of a room with its white paper and
lack of shadows. They are trapped, we might say, in a rational plot—the
narrator has them captive "within the boundaries of his eyes." Razumov
says that he was born clear-eyed but has seen apparitions. Natalia's eyes
are trustful, as always. She says that her brother's soul is in Razumov,
reason benignly possessed by spirit. There they stand, boxed in a Western room, brought out of a "confused immensity" for the benefit of
Western eyes. They do not see the old man. Natalia removes her veil.
Her eyes are lustrous; he listens, as if to music rather than speech. She
explains that her mother expects to *see* her dead son. "It will end by her
seeing him." "That is very possible," says Razumov. "That will be the
end. Her spirit will depart." He speaks of the phantoms of the dead.
Natalia's veil lies on the floor between them. "Why are you looking at me
like this . . . ? I need . . . to see. . . ." He begins the confession: more
phantoms. The old man intervenes; Razumov stands with the veil at his
feet, "intensely black in the white crudity of the light." He seems to
vanish. He goes home and writes more in his journal. In its pages, we are
told of eyes, phantoms, his temptation to steal Natalia's soul. Was the old
Englishman the devil ("I was possessed")? Natalia has saved him; she is an
apparition ("suddenly you stood before me"), and the old man a "dis-
appointed devil." He wraps the writing in the veil.

At midnight (when spirits walk) he runs down the stairs into the
storm, the rain enveloping him like a veil. Later, deafened, he again runs
into the storm, which has transformed the dull civility of Geneva. Light-
ning blinds him; he "puts his arm over his eyes to recover his sight"; he
wanders into a drift of mist, walking "in a phantom world."

This is of course psychological disclosure, but if it is *only* that it is full
of irrelevant information, of redundancies, of what, if its business consists of sequence and psychology, is a feebly bloated rhetoric. I have
spoken of secrets; but they are all but blatantly advertised. The book has
a semblance of Geneva, but in the end it yields to Russia, misty, spiritual,
its significance occulted; it is without horizon, only by trickery and collusion got into a square, well-lighted box. The writing of the book, the
covering of the monstrous blank page, is a work of "strange mystic

13. The pun is actually French, since English "apparition" = "appearance" is virtually
obsolete.

arrogance"; it gives the western eye its box, its civilised mediocrity, but keeps its secrets also. It is a controlled "debauch"; we may ignore this aspect if we choose and read it as Genevans or Englishmen would read it. It is a question of the form of attention we choose to bestow; of our willingness to see that in reading according to restricted codes we disregard as noise what, if read differently, patiently, would make another and rarer kind of sense. And the text, almost with "cynicism," tells us what is there, confident that we shall ignore it.

"The illogicality of its attitude, the arbitrariness of its conclusions, the frequency of the exceptional, should present no difficulty to the student of many grammars. . . . There is a generosity in its ardour of speech which removes it as far as possible from common loquacity; and it is ever too disconnected to be classed as eloquence." I adapt these words from the passage near the beginning of the book in which the old language teacher speaks of the Russian character and the Russian use of language. He apologizes for the digression, which we should know is not a digression, exactly as we know it is not "idle to inquire" why Razumov should have left his written record. He is telling us (or rather the double is telling us, ventriloquially) that a large part of what he says is precisely what we are not willing to attend to. He, who claims a professional mistrust of words, is talking about the book he is in, the black on white. He is necessary; for, as Razumov remarks, "there may be truth in every manner of speaking. What if that absurd saying [that he himself might be a "chosen instrument of Providence"] were true in its essence?" What if the old Englishman should be the father of lies?

The truth is that there is in this book a "manner of speaking" that is horizonless, misty. Is there some great idea that unites all the key words, the language with which the text is obsessed? One could make shift to discover such a truth, perhaps. Black on white is the manuscript or the book; the reading of black on white (including the seeing into its soul or spirit) is a hearing with the eyes of what is said rather than written, since it is not seen. It is in the veil that covered Natalia's eyes that the manuscript is wrapped. The secrets of the book are phantoms, inexplicably appearing, ignored, trampled down, turned into lies by the father of lies, a diabolical narrator. For the reading of such a book we have the wrong kind of eyes. It despises its Genevan readers, with their requirements of brightness and obvious structure, their detached, informed interest in alien psychology, alien "mystery."

And at this point why should we not add some biographical evidence; Conrad was in one of his greatest crises as he turned *Razumov* into *Under Western Eyes* and had a severe breakdown when he finished the book. Part of the trouble was poverty; not enough people read his books. They were not sufficiently obvious. So this book provides an accurate prophecy of its own reception which is the reception of all such works;

like the language teacher, like Lucinda, we distrust words, think it better to ignore them if they seem wild or misty. And like the language teacher, we are surprised at the book's end, which is the ending of another story than the one he had seemed to be in charge of. The actual black on white defeats the narrator's attempt to achieve parsimony of sequence, squareness, limit. It seems that a god and a devil wrote simultaneously, another *dédoublement* if you like, and one that, somehow, the good reader must emulate; for if he does not he will, by concurring in the illusions of limit and authority, deny the god (the hidden god of secrets) his due. Thus may a novel complain against the commonsense way we read it, though that is the kind of reading it seems also to solicit by appearing to respect the proprieties and to aim at "clearness and effect."

Twisted Tales; or, Story, Study, and Symphony

Nelson Goodman

The eighth race at Rockingham the other day was reported in the newspaper as follows:

> Excalibur broke last from the gate, took the lead by the far turn, then dropped back to fourth coming into the stretch, but rallied to win by a nose.

My own report that evening to a friend who had bet on Excalibur went:

> Excalibur won by a nose, though he was fourth coming into the stretch after leading at the far turn despite having broken last from the gate.

Nothing strikes us as unusual here even though the order of telling completely reverses the order of occurrence. Indeed, to have withheld the result of the race to the end would have been inconsiderate under the circumstances. In other reports the telling may jump back and forth; for example:

> Excalibur, though he broke last from the gate, won by a nose after having dropped back to fourth, coming into the stretch, from the lead he had taken by the far turn.

or

> Excalibur won by a nose although, after breaking last from the gate and taking the lead at the far turn, he had dropped back to fourth coming into the stretch.

And the twenty other sequences of telling are equally admissible.

A series of snapshots taken at the four stages of the race in question and showing enough of the surroundings would, presented in any order, tell the same story. Even without such helpful verbal devices as tenses and words like "before" and "then", the order of occurrence can be readily determined. Again, a film of the race can be cut and spliced to conform to any of the different orderings possible in a verbal report. Cinema and literature alike would be severely handicapped if required always to report incidents in the order of their occurrence.

In sum, flashbacks and foreflashes are commonplace in narrative, and such rearrangements in the telling of a story seem to leave us not only with a story but with very much the same story.[1] In the reports of the race, for example, no time twisting will leave us without a story or with an altogether different story. But is this true in general? Will no disparity between the order of telling and the order of occurrence destroy either the basic identity or the narrative status of any story? An exception seems ready at hand: suppose we simply run our film of the race backward. The result, though indeed a story, seems hardly to be the same story in any usual sense but rather to be a story of the horse running *backward* from finish line to starting gate. Does cinematic narrative actually differ this sharply from narrative in a series of snapshots or in words? I think not. Our first impulse with any tale when the order of telling is clear is to take the order of occurrence to be the same as the order of telling; we then make any needed corrections in accord with temporal indications given in the narrative and with our antecedent knowledge both of what happened and of causal processes in general. But discrepancy between order of telling and order of occurrence cannot always be discovered instantaneously—or at all. If our series of snapshots is shown in reverse order at normal speed, we readily detect the reversal; for we know that a race begins at the starting gate, ends at the finish line, and so on. Even if the pictures do not show the starting gate or finish line or other identifiable parts of the track, we are not deceived; for we know that horses do not run backward. But when the *film* is run backward, such clues and considerations usually cannot be brought to

1. In an obvious and important sense. Of course, whether two versions are properly said to be of the same story—or of the same world—depends upon which of many permissible interpretations of sameness is understood; but that need not trouble us here.

Nelson Goodman is emeritus professor of philosophy at Harvard and the founder of both Project Zero and the Harvard Dance Center. His works include *The Structure of Appearance; Fact, Fiction, and Forecast;* and *Ways of Worldmaking.*

bear soon enough, and we momentarily mistake the direction of the actions filmed. A little time is needed to make the correction. What seemed like a drastic difference between film and other forms of narrative amounts to nothing more than this lag.

Suppose, though, our film is of an automobile moving slowly along an otherwise empty street. Since automobiles can go forward or backward, I cannot tell whether I am seeing a film run backward of an automobile going forward or a film run forward of an automobile going backward. Such ambiguity is not an exclusive property of film either. A series of snapshots of the automobile would be equally ambiguous; so also would a narrative in words where neither verbal indications nor knowledge of the particular event or of causal process determines order of occurrence. In all these cases, the order of occurrence is indeterminate and remains so under any transformation of the order of telling.

In other cases, the order of occurrence is determinate but vacuous. *The Conversion of Saint Paul* by Pieter Bruegel (fig. 1) tells a story and tells it so compellingly that we tend to forget that nothing in the picture literally moves, that no part of the picture precedes any other in time, and that what is explicitly shown is not actions taking place but a momentary state. Neither the telling nor what is explicitly told takes time; the picture is a timeless tale, without sequence of occurrence and also without sequence of telling; for there is no one mandatory or even preferred order of reading the picture—of translating its spatial relationships into temporal ones. And since the order of telling and the order of occurrence are both vacuous, no question arises of varying the relationship between the two. Reversing the picture reverses the spatial relationships in both picture and pictured but has no temporal effect.

Implicitly, of course, such a picture as the Bruegel tells a story of events before and after—and inferred from—the state explicitly depicted. What is thus implicitly told takes time, though its telling does not. The vacuous order of telling differs drastically from the order of occurrence but is still invariable.

Jacopo del Sellaio tells the story of Psyche in quite another way (fig. 2). Here what is explicitly told takes time, and the telling has a definite order. Several incidents, with Psyche appearing in each, are shown strung across a landscape. The impossibility of the same person being in different places at the same time notifies us that difference in spatial position among scenes is to be interpreted as difference in temporal position among the events depicted. And, as with a written tale, although the whole story is presented at once, an order of telling is plainly established. The main sequence here conforms to linguistic convention. In the West, pictorial narratives including comic strips tend to go from left to right; in the East, from right to left. This is clear when pictures of a series are on successive pages of a book or on a hand scroll, where the

Fig. 1.—Pieter Bruegel the Elder, *The Conversion of Saint Paul*. Kunsthistorische Museum, Vienna.

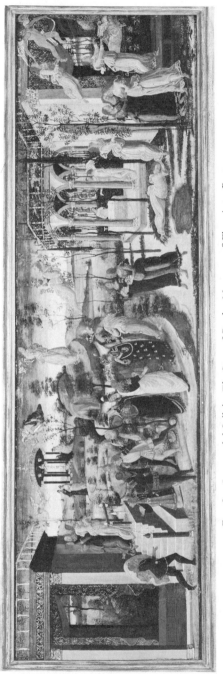

Fɪɢ. 2.—Jacopo del Sellaio, *The Story of Psyche*. Museum of Fine Arts, Boston.

order of telling is plainly established. In many other cases, the influence of linguistic connection on pictorial narrative is weak and easily overruled. In the Sellaio, the main direction of telling is fixed by the orientation of the larger figures of Psyche: five of the eight face right, and two of these, moreover, slant to the right; a sixth shows Psyche lying prone with head to the right; only one, near the right end, faces left—for the sake of design. Two slight deviations from left-to-right sequence of telling occur: in the background at the left is a sort of prologue with Psyche and companions facing left; and in the center, Psyche is shown as standing, with head turned back, at the bottom of a path that winds upward and directs attention to the next scene, at the top of the path and just left of the preceding lower scene. How much more the orientation of the figures counts for in effecting the order of telling in this picture can be seen by simply reversing the whole picture, which then reads the opposite way.

Where the order of telling is evident but the order of occurrence is not known and cannot be inferred, we sometimes assume that the order of occurrence follows the order of telling; but even when, as in the case of the Sellaio, we happen to be right, our guess is groundless. Nothing dictates agreement between the two orders. The painter might have chosen to flash forward to depict the last incident first, at the left end of the picture; or he might, keeping the orientation of each scene unchanged, have reversed their order completely, thus telling his story backward. Altogether different is the result of reversing the picture as a whole: the telling is then from right to left, but the match between order of telling and order of occurrence is unaffected, so that the story is still told not backward but from beginning to end.

In Piero di Cosimo's *Discovery of Honey,* which depicts three incidents in the legend of Silenus, what is told takes time but the order of telling is unclear (fig. 3).[2] If we take it to be from left to right, we have an example of foreflash; for in order of occurrence, the incident depicted in the center (Silenus falling off his mount) comes first, that at the right (the attempt to lift him onto his feet) second, and that at the left (boys rubbing mud on his stings) last. Thus from left to right the order of occurrence is 3, 1, 2—the last event being shown first. But direction of telling can no more be inferred from order of occurrence than conversely; and the direction of telling in this picture is not unmistakably from left to right. The scenes are not on a level line or on the same pictured plane and, what matters more, there are no such indications as the repeated left-right orientation of scenes in the Sellaio. Even thus lacking direction, though, the spatial arrangement of telling departs from the order of occurrence in that an event that does not occur between two others is

2. For help in finding many of my examples of pictorial narrative, I am grateful to Sydney Freedberg, George Hanfmann, Marianne Martin, Ann Milstein, and John Rosenfield.

FIG. 3.—Piero di Cosimo, *The Discovery of Honey* (or *Misfortunes of Silenus*). Courtesy of the Fogg Art Museum, Harvard University, Cambridge, Mass.

depicted between them. Thus we have not a foreflash or a flashback but a flashbetween.

More often than not no time order of telling is indicated in a picture; but the spatial distribution of the incidents depicted often varies in many and remarkable ways in relation to the order of occurrence. In a painting of the legend of Marsyas,[3] from Pompeii, any indications of a sequence of telling are negligible. In order of occurrence, the scenes begin at the upper left and proceed counterclockwise to the upper right. In Ghiberti's bronze *Gates of Paradise,* the east doors of the Baptistry in Florence, the sequence of occurrence is from left to right in each line and from each line to the next below it; but in the same sculptor's earlier north doors, the sequence, though also from left to right in each line, is from each line to the next above it—perhaps for the convenience of observers standing on the ground. But here again we must be careful not to assume that this is also the order of telling, which—where there is one—must be determinable quite independently of order of occurrence.

Incidentally, even in the east doors the scenes within some individual panels are arranged otherwise than from left to right. For example, in the panel of *The Garden of Eden* at the upper left corner, although the three larger scenes are indeed arranged left to right in order of occurrence, the Temptation is reduced in size and shoved into the background at the left rather than being placed between the center and right-hand scenes (fig. 4).

Memling's *Life of Christ,* like the Sellaio, depicts many incidents in a single landscape but provides little indication—by consistent orientation or winding paths or other means—of any order of telling (fig. 5). In order of occurrence the scenes follow a tortuous course from lower left to upper right (fig. 6), but nothing in the picture looked at apart from the subject makes this evident. The arrangement is two-dimensional (virtually, even three-dimensional) without beginning or end or marked route. This pictorial organization of events of a lifetime is spatial, atemporal, motivated perhaps both by considerations of design and by regarding these events as eternal and emblematic rather than as episodic or transient.

In pictures like these, foreflashes and flashbacks and even flashbetweens, which are all departures in the telling from the sequence of occurrence, are of course out of the question; for here there is not only no direction but no order of telling at all. Rearranging scenes can result merely in different patterns being marked out by the sequence of occurrence. For example, if the first two scenes in the Pompeian picture are interchanged, the pattern will be as in figure 7b rather than as in 7a, but neither constitutes order of telling. Interchanging the second and third scenes in the Memling gives the pattern in 7d rather than that in

3. See Christopher M. Dawson's *Romano-Campanian Mythological Landscape Painting,* Yale Classical Studies, vol. 9 (New Haven, Conn., 1944), p. 90.

FIG. 4.—Lorenzo Ghiberti, *The Garden of Eden,* from the east doors. Baptistry, Florence.

7c. In such cases we have no different orders of telling or different degrees of deviation from order of occurrence but only different spatial patterns and, at most, different degrees of convolution relative to order of occurrence.

Even more complex than the organization of the Memling is that of a much older work: a "picture biography" of the Japanese Buddhist Prince Shōtoku Taishi, painted by Hata no Chitei in 1069.[4] It consists of five large screens, making up one continuous picture, for hanging on three walls in the Hōryū-ji Temple. The landscape setting is Nara and the surrounding country; some of the buildings shown still survive and others are identifiable by documents. At the left end, across the water, is

4. For much information concerning this work, I am grateful to John Rosenfield and to Aya Louisa McDonald, who has made available to me the results of her intensive but as yet unpublished study of it.

FIG. 5.—Hans Memling, *The Life of Christ*. Pinacoteca, Turin.

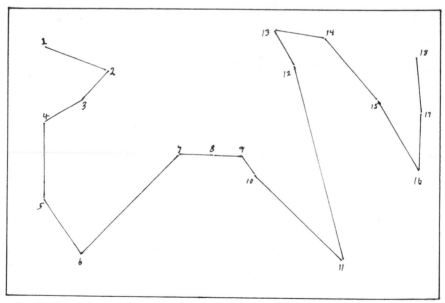

FIG. 6.—Plan of scenes in Memling's *Life of Christ*, numbered in order of occurrence.

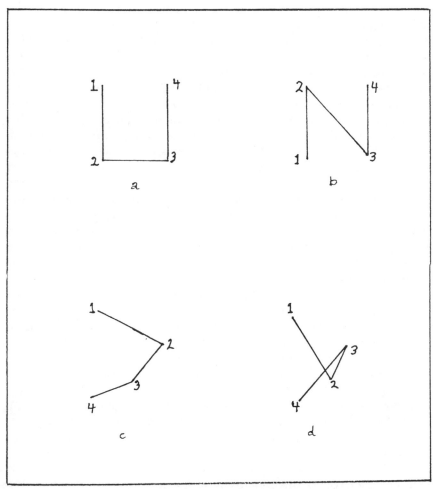

Fɪɢ. 7.—Diagram of effect of interchanges of scenes.

China. Against this background are some sixty scenes from the prince's life—or lives.

That the order of telling proceeds from right to left here is pretty definitely established by the Oriental convention, reinforced (as nearly as can be judged from available reproductions of the damaged paintings) by such internal indications as the way most figures and scenes face. But this differs drastically from the order of occurrence. Scenes from all periods of the prince's career appear on each screen: on screen one (fig. 8) the incidents date from conception to age twenty-seven; on two, from age six to forty-three; on three, from seventeen to forty-nine; on four, from sixteen to fifty, when Shōtoku died; and on the right half of five, from nine to thirty-seven. Furthermore, the scenes on each screen are not arranged in any simple chronological order, as may be seen from the diagrams in figures 9 and 10; and were we to number the scenes consecutively over the whole series and connect each next pair with a line, the resulting diagram would be a terrible tangle. At the end—on the left side of the leftmost screen (fig. 11)—are scenes from the prince's previous incarnations. Here is a notable and venerable example of flashback—of earlier events being told later.

What principles govern this arrangement? The disadvantages of keeping to the chronological order and thus, for example, putting all childhood scenes on the first screen are obvious. Considerations of design combined with spiritual detachment from the temporal override any concern for chronological order. It has been suggested that the disposition of scenes in these paintings may be according to the place where the event occurred; for example, some of the first scenes show the prince being conceived in one room, born in another, and playing in the backyard. In the flashback, incidents from the prince's earlier incarnations are depicted as in China—'out of the country', apparently signifying 'out of this life'.

On this account, the organization is geographical rather than chronological, so that scene x appears to the right of scene y not because incident x occurred before but because it occurred east of incident y.[5] If so, the paintings constitute as much a map as a story of the prince's career. We do find maps—for example, a National Geographical Society pictorial map of England and Wales—with historical events depicted and even labeled at the map positions in question.[6] But the idea that the arrangement of scenes in the Shōtoku paintings is geographical seems on the face of it highly implausible. Could the events in the prince's life have been so happily distributed over the landscape? Indeed, examination shows conclusively that the arrangement in the paintings is not geographical in any usual sense; for example, pictures of a temple at different stages of completion are in different places, and there are two separate pictures of the prince's birth. Relative geographical position cannot be inferred from relative pictorial position according to any consistent plan. Furthermore, in another series of paintings of the prince's life, pictures of the same events are arranged in a quite different way.

If there is some factor at work here other than an unworldly and atemporal or even antitemporal outlook along with a concern for all aspects of design, I have yet to discover it; but that after all is the business of scholars in the field.

These varied verbal and pictorial examples show that in a narrative

5. Curiously, although Oriental texts read from right to left, the opposite way from ours, Oriental maps normally, I am told, have the west at the left and the east at the right just as ours do, the territory being mapped as if seen from south of it.

6. But the Shōtoku paintings differ from such maps in having a well-established, and contrasting, right-to-left overall order of telling.

neither the telling nor what is explicitly told need take time, and they suggest furthermore that narrative reordered in any way at all is still narrative. That poses a problem, for although we think of narrative as the peculiarly temporal species of discourse, distinguished from description or exposition through meeting some time condition or other, we have so far discovered no such condition. That what is implicitly or explicitly told must take time hardly distinguishes narrative, for even description or depiction of a momentary and static situation implies something of what went before and will come afterward. A picture of a forest tells implicitly of trees growing from seedlings and shedding leaves; and a picture of a house implies that trees were cut for it and that its roof will soon leak.

How has the distinguishing feature of narrative escaped us? Perhaps by our concluding too hastily from the evidence considered that narrative under any transformation whatsoever of the order of telling is always still narrative. Actually, although every narrative will survive some reordering, and some narratives will survive any reordering, not every narrative will survive every reordering. Some stories when reordered in certain ways are no longer stories but studies. Consider, for example, a psychologist's report that recounts a patient's behavior chronologically. It is a story, a history. But rearranged to group the incidents according to their significance as symptoms—of, say, first suicidal tendencies, then claustrophobia, then psychopathic disregard of consequences—it is no longer a story but an analysis, a case study. Reordering of the telling here turns a narrative into something else.

Literature provides many a more notable example. Aldous Huxley's brilliant short piece on the abominable British painter Benjamin Robert Haydon contains enough reports of events in Haydon's life from childhood to death to constitute a brief biography;[7] but the arrangement of these reports is strikingly at variance with chronology. Incidents from several widely spaced periods of Haydon's life are often reported in a single paragraph. His suicide is mentioned in the middle of the paper, followed by descriptions of his marital and family life (including the straight-faced statement that one stepson "had a promising career in the navy cut short, in the Indian Ocean, by the bite of a sea-serpent"). An account of Haydon's late work and disappointments is followed by mention of the early mistake that led to his study of art. Now displacements in order of telling, as we have seen, are not in general incompatible with narrative; but here, rather than heightening the story, they work against it, being guided by how the reported incidents document and illuminate various aspects of Haydon's character, among them vanity, self-dramatization, snobbery, romanticism, dishonesty, piety, literary skill, and wit. The result is no biography but a character study, no story but an

---

7. See Aldous Huxley's "B. R. Haydon," *The Olive Tree* (London, 1936), pp. 239–61.

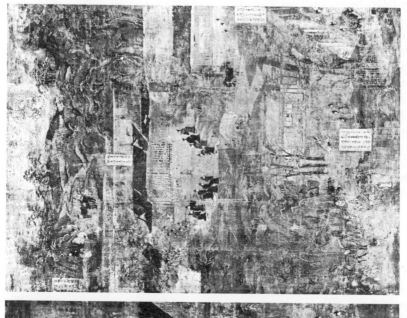

FIG. 8.—First screen of painted biography of Prince Shōtoku Taishi by Hata no Chitei for the Hōryū-ji Temple, Nara. Tokyo National Museum.

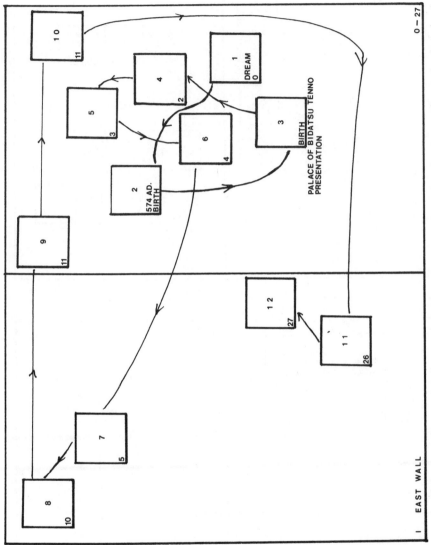

I EAST WALL

Fig. 9.—Plan of screen in figure 8. The number in the lower left corner of each square stands for the prince's age at the time of the incident depicted. The number in the center of each square indicates the chronological position of the incident relative to the others depicted on this same screen.

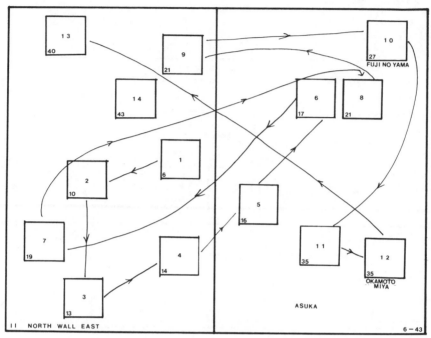

Within the figure: 13 / 40, 9 / 21, 10 / 27 FUJI NO YAMA, 14 / 43, 6 / 17, 8 / 21, 1 / 6, 2 / 10, 5 / 16, 7 / 19, 4 / 14, 11 / 35, 12 / 35 OKAMOTO MIYA, 3 / 13, ASUKA, 6 – 43

Fɪɢ. 10.—Plan of second screen of the same series.

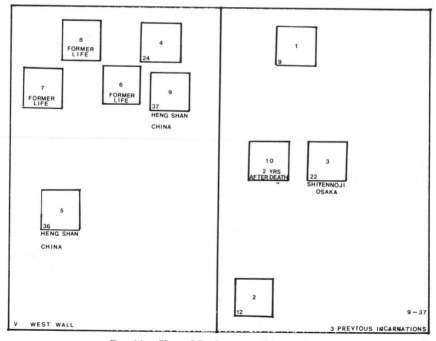

Within the figure: 8 FORMER LIFE, 4 / 24, 1 / 9, 7 FORMER LIFE, 6 FORMER LIFE, 9 / 37 HENG SHAN CHINA, 10 2 YRS AFTER DEATH, 3 / 22 SHITENNOJI OSAKA, 5 / 36 HENG SHAN CHINA, 2 / 12, 9 – 37

3 PREVIOUS INCARNATIONS

Fɪɢ. 11.—Plan of final screen of the series.

essay on self-deception and other matters. The order of the telling so groups incidents reported as to bring out kinships and contrasts that cut across and obliterate—or at least blur—the story line. Narrative gives way to exposition.

While I have at hand no actual pictorial example where the organization of scenes according to themes or characteristics makes it a study rather than a story, such a picture could easily be produced. Scenes from the life of a saint, for instance, might be grouped into those of temptations resisted, persecutions suffered, miracles performed, and so on, so that the chronicle would be dispersed and denatured under a classification of events into religiously significant kinds.

The classification that supersedes or subordinates chronology is not always in terms of topical features. Sometimes, rather, it is in terms of expressive or other aesthetically relevant qualities, as in a theatre piece that organizes its version of incidents in a hockey game, on the basis of dynamic and rhythmic properties, into movements like those of a musical work.[8] In such cases, a story becomes more a symphony than a study.

In all these examples, of course, what nullifies narrative is not the order of telling itself but the resultant alignment with certain categories that are—or are to be made—highly relevant in the context and for the purpose at hand. World structure is heavily dependent on order of elements and· on comparative weight of kinds; and reordering and weight shifting are among the most powerful processes used in making and remaking facts and worlds.[9] Although in the psychologist's report and the Huxley, the status as study rather than story is reinforced by interspersed discursive passages, the reorganization alone would I think suffice. So also would a reordering that emphasizes significant features otherwise than by a simple sorting of incidents. In other cases, narrative status rather than being nullified is merely subdued. And where order of occurrence itself happens to yield a sorting into prominent categories, we may have what is both a story and a study or symphony. These types of discourse, though distinct, are not mutually exclusive.

The general lesson, then, is that while narrative will normally survive all sorts of contortion, still sometimes when we start with a tale, enough twisting may leave us without one.

8. The reference here is to *Hockey Seen,* a theatre piece by the present writer, presented at Harvard University and the University of Pennsylvania from 1972 to 1974 and produced in August 1980, live and on television, in conjunction with the conference Art in Culture in Ghent and Knokke, Belgium.

9. See my *Ways of Worldmaking* (Indianapolis, 1978).

What Novels Can Do That Films Can't (and Vice Versa)

Seymour Chatman

The study of narrative has become so popular that the French have honored it with a term—*la narratologie*. Given the escalating and sophisticated literature on the subject, its English counterpart, "narratology," may not be as risible as it sounds. Modern narratology combines two powerful intellectual trends: the Anglo-American inheritance of Henry James, Percy Lubbock, E. M. Forster, and Wayne Booth; and the mingling of Russian formalist (Viktor Shklovsky, Boris Eichenbaum, Roman Jakobson, and Vladimir Propp) with French structuralist approaches (Claude Lévi-Strauss, Roland Barthes, Gérard Genette, and Tzvetan Todorov). It's not accidental that narratology has developed during a period in which linguistics and cinema theory have also flourished. Linguistics, of course, is one basis for the field now called semiotics—the study of all meaning systems, not only natural language. Another basis is the work of the philosopher Charles S. Peirce and his continuator, Charles W. Morris. These trees have borne elegant fruit: we read fascinating semiotic analyses of facial communication, body language, fashion, the circus, architecture, and gastronomy. The most vigorous, if controversial, branch of cinema studies, the work of Christian Metz, is also semiotically based.

One of the most important observations to come out of narratology is that narrative itself is a deep structure quite independent of its medium. In other words, narrative is basically a kind of text organization, and that organization, that schema, needs to be actualized: in written words, as in stories and novels; in spoken words combined with the movements of actors imitating characters against sets which imitate places, as in plays and films; in drawings; in comic strips; in dance movements, as in narrative ballet and in mime; and even in music, at least in program music of the order of *Till Eulenspiegel* and *Peter and the Wolf*.

A salient property of narrative is double time structuring. That is, all narratives, in whatever medium, combine the time sequence of plot events, the time of the *histoire* ("story-time") with the time of the presentation of those events in the text, which we call "discourse-time." What is fundamental to narrative, regardless of medium, is that these two time orders are independent. In realistic narratives, the time of the story is fixed, following the ordinary course of a life: a person is born, grows from childhood to maturity and old age, and then dies. But the discourse-time order may be completely different: it may start with the person's deathbed, then "flashback" to childhood; or it may start with childhood, "flashforward" to death, then end with adult life. This independence of discourse-time is precisely and only possible because of the subsumed story-time. Now of course *all* texts pass through time: it takes x number of hours to read an essay, a legal brief, or a sermon. But the internal structures of these *non*-narrative texts are not temporal but logical, so that their discourse-time is irrelevant, just as the viewing time of a painting is irrelevant. We may spend half an hour in front of a Titian, but the aesthetic effect is as if we were taking in the whole painting at a glance. In narratives, on the other hand, the dual time orders function independently. This is true in any medium: flashbacks are just as possible in ballet or mime or opera as they are in a film or novel. Thus, in theory at least, any narrative can be actualized by any medium which can communicate the two time orders.

Narratologists immediately observed an important consequence of this property of narrative texts, namely, the translatability of a given narrative from one medium to another: *Cinderella* as verbal tale, as ballet, as opera, as film, as comic strip, as pantomime, and so on. This observation was so interesting, so much in keeping with structuralist theory, and so productive of further work in narrative analysis that it tended to concentrate attention exclusively on the constancies in narrative structure across the different media at the expense of interesting differences. But now the study of narrative has reached a point where the differences can emerge as objects of independent interest.

In the course of studying and teaching film, I have been struck by the sorts of changes typically introduced by screen adaptation (and vice versa in that strange new process "novelization," which transforms

---

Seymour Chatman, professor in the department of rhetoric at the University of California, Berkeley, is the author of *The Later Style of Henry James* and *Story and Discourse: Narrative Structure in Fiction and Film*.

already exhibited films into novels). Close study of film and novel versions of the same narrative reveals with great clarity the peculiar powers of the two media. Once we grasp those peculiarities, the reasons for the differences in form, content, and impact of the two versions strikingly emerge. Many features of these narratives could be chosen for comparison, but I will limit myself to only two: description and point of view.

Critics have long recognized that descriptive passages in novels are different somehow in textual *kind* from the narrative proper. They have spoken of "blocks" or "islands" or "chunks" of description in early fiction and have noted that modern novels shy away from blatantly purple descriptive passages. Joseph Conrad and Ford Madox Ford formulated theories of what they called "distributed" exposition and description, in which the described elements were insinuated, so to speak, into the running narrative line. What has not emerged very clearly until recently, however, is a genuine theoretical explanation of novelistic description. The emphasis has been on the pictorial, the imaged. We read in typical handbooks like Thrall and Hibbard: "Description . . . has as its purpose the picturing of a scene or setting." But that is only part of the story; such a definition eliminates *inter alia* the description of an abstract state of affairs, or of a character's mental posture, or, indeed, of anything not strictly visual or visualizable. Narratologists argue that a more correct and comprehensive account of description rests on temporal structure. As we have already noted, narrative proper requires a double and independent time ordering, that of the time line of the story and that of the time line of the discourse. Now what happens in description is that the time line of the story is interrupted and frozen. Events are stopped, though our reading- or discourse-time continues, and we look at the characters and the setting elements as at a *tableau vivant.*

As an example of this process, consider a bit of the short story which underlies a film by Jean Renoir, Maupassant's "Une Partie de campagne" [A Country Excursion].[1] The story opens with a summary of events which clearly establishes story-time: "For five months they had been talking of going to lunch at some country restaurant. . . . They had risen very early that morning. Monsieur Dufour had borrowed the milkman's cart, and drove himself [on avait projeté depuis cinq mois d'aller déjeuner aux environs de Paris. . . . Aussi . . . s'était-on levé de fort bonne heure ce matin-là. M. Dufour, ayant emprunté la voiture du latier, conduisait lui-même]" (p. 63). There are three events, and, as we note from the use of the past perfect with "had," they predate the opening moment of the story proper, the moment of story-now, so to speak, which is the moment named by the expression "and drove himself." The story proper begins with the family *en voyage,* already in the midst of

---

1. Guy de Maupassant, "Une Partie de campagne," *Boule de Suif* (Paris, n.d.), pp. 63–78; all further references will be cited parenthetically in the text; my translations.

their excursion. The story sequence is *naturally* ordered: at some point in that past before the story proper began, someone first mentioned going to lunch in the country (let's call that event A); the family continued this discussion, thus event A was iterated (let's call that A sub-n since we don't know how many times the topic came up during those five months); next, Monsieur Dufour borrowed the milkman's cart, presumably the Saturday night before the trip (event B); then they arose early on Sunday morning (event C); and finally, here they are, driving along the road (event D). Notice, incidentally, the disparity between the story order and discourse order: story order is A, B, C, D; discourse order is A, C, B, D.

This first sentence, then, is straight narration which takes us out of the expository past into the narrative present. Now the very next sentence is clearly of a different order: ". . . it [the cart] had a roof supported by four iron posts to which were attached curtains, which had been raised so that they could see the countryside [. . . elle avait un toit supporté par quatre montants de fer où s'attachaient les rideaux qu'on avait relevés pour voir le paysage]" (p. 63). This is, of course, unadulterated description. Story-time stops as the narrator characterizes a story object, a prop. The sentence reflects the static character of the passage. The verb "to have" is clearly equivalent to the typical copula of description: it is not a verb of action and communicates no sense of an event but simply evokes the quality of an object or state of affairs. Maupassant could have—and more recent writers probably would have—avoided direct description by writing something like "The cart, its roof supported by four iron posts, rolled merrily down the road." This active syntax would have kept story-time going and would have eased in the characterization of the cart. Maupassant's prose provokes, rather, the start-and-stop effect customary to early fiction, a fashion now somewhat dated. Not that the surface verb, the verb in the actual verbal medium, *needs* to be the copula "to be." It could be a perfectly active verb in the strict grammatical sense and still evoke the descriptive copula at the deep narrative level, as in the sentence that immediately follows: "The curtain at the back . . . fluttered in the breeze like a flag [celui de derrière, seul, flottait au vent, comme un drapeau]." "Fluttered" is an active verb, but from the textual point of view, the sentence is pure description; it is not tied into the event chain. The sentence could as easily be phrased, "In the back there *was* a curtain fluttering in the breeze like a flag."

The paragraph continues with a brief description of Mme Dufour and makes references to the grandmother, to Henriette, and to a yellow-haired youth who later becomes Henriette's husband. Paragraphs immediately thereafter continue the narrative by citing events: the passing of the fortifications at Porte Maillot; the reaching of the bridge of Neuilly; the pronouncement by M. Dufour that at last they have reached the country, and so on.

Let's consider the opening scene of Jean Renoir's 1936 film version of this story, also entitled *Une Partie de campagne*. (Ideally, you would watch the film as you read this essay, but something of the effect, I hope, can be communicated by the following illustrations.) The whole sequence introducing the Dufours takes only a minute of viewing time, so we don't have much time to remark the details of their borrowed cart. But looking at a single frame enables us to examine it at our leisure (fig. 1).

FIG. 1

We note, for instance, that the cart is absurdly small, has only two wheels, bears the name of the owner, "Ch. Gervais," painted on the side, and has a railing on the roof. There is no flapping curtain at the back but instead some kind of sun shield, and so on. Now these details are apparently of the same order as those in the story—remember the reference to the roof, the four iron posts, and the rolled up curtains. But there are some vital differences. For one thing, the number of details in Maupassant's sentence is limited to three. In other words, the selection among the possible number of details evoked was absolutely determined: the author, through his narrator, "selected" and named precisely three. Thus the reader learns only those three and can only expand the picture imaginatively. But in the film representation, the number of details is indeterminate, since what this version gives us is a simulacrum of a French carriage of a certain era, provenance, and so on. Thus the number of details that we could note is potentially large, even vast. In practice, however, we do not register many details. The film is going by too fast, and we are too preoccupied with the meaning of this cart, with what is going to happen next, to dwell upon its physical details. We simply label: we say to ourselves, "Aha, a cart with some people in it." We react that way because of a technical property of film texts: the details are not asserted as such by a narrator but simply presented, so we tend, in a pragmatic way, to contemplate only those that seem salient to the plot as it unrolls in our minds (in what Roland Barthes calls a "hermeneutic" inquiry). Now if you think about it, this is a rather odd aesthetic situation. Film narrative possesses a plenitude of visual details, an excessive particularity compared to the verbal version, a plenitude aptly called by certain aestheticians visual "over-specification" (*überbestimmtheit*), a property that it shares, of course, with the other visual arts. But unlike those arts, unlike painting or sculpture, narrative films do not usually allow us time to dwell on plenteous details. Pressure from the narrative component is too great. Events move too fast. The contemplation of beautiful framing or color or lighting is a pleasure limited to those who can see the film many times or who are fortunate enough to have access to equipment which will allow them to stop the frame. But watching a movie under normal circumstances in a cinema is not at all like being in a gallery or art museum. The management wants us up and out of the theater so that the 10:30 patrons can take our seats. And even sophisticated moviegoers who call a film "beautiful" are more likely to be referring to literary than to visual components. Indeed, there are movies (like Terence Malick's recent *Days of Heaven*) which are criticized because their visual effects are too striking for the narrative line to support. Narrative pressure is so great that the interpretation of even non-narrative films is sometimes affected by it—at least for a time, until the audience gets its bearings. For example, there is a film which presents a sequence of frozen frames, on the basis of which the audience is prompted to construct a story. Then, after the last frame, the camera pulls away to reveal that the frames were all merely part of a collage of photographs organized randomly. This last shot "denarrativizes" the film.

Narrative pressure similarly affects the genre of film that André Bazin writes about in his essay "Painting and Cinema," the kind in which the camera moves around close-up details of a single painting. An example of this genre is Alain Resnais' film on Picasso's *Guernica* (fig. 2). No less a personage than the Inspector General of Drawing of the French Department of Education complained: "However you look at it the film is not true to the painting. Its dramatic and logical unity establishes relationships that are chronologically false." The inspector was speaking about the relationships and chronology in the implied narrative of Picasso's development as an artist, but he might as well have been speaking of the relationships and chronology implicit in a narrative hypothecated on the visual details of *Guernica* itself. By controlling the viewer's order and duration of perceiving, a film scanning a painting might imply the double time structure of narrative texts. For example, if the camera wandering over *Guernica* were first focused on the head and lantern-bearing arm sweeping in through the window, then shifted to the screaming horse, then to the body on the ground with the broken sword and flower in its hand, the audience might read into the painting a

Fig. 2.—Pablo Picasso, *Guernica*. Museum of Modern Art, New York.

story sequence which Picasso did not intend: first the alarm was heard, then the horse whinnied as the bombs fell, then one victim died.

The key word in my account of the different ways that visual details are presented by novels and films is "assert." I wish to communicate by that word the force it has in ordinary rhetoric: an "assertion" is a state- ment, usually an independent sentence or clause, that something is in fact the case, that it is a certain sort of thing, that it does in fact have certain properties or enter into certain relations, namely, those listed. Opposed to asserting there is mere "naming." When I say, "The cart was tiny; it came onto the bridge," I am asserting that certain property of the cart of being small in size and that certain relation of arriving at the bridge. However, when I say "The green cart came onto the bridge," I am asserting nothing more than its arrival at the bridge; the greenness of the cart is not asserted but slipped in without syntactic fuss. It is only named. Textually, it emerges by the way. Now, most film narratives seem to be of the latter textual order: it requires special effort for films to assert a property or relation. The dominant mode is presentational, not assertive. A film doesn't say, "This *is* the state of affairs," it merely shows you that state of affairs. Of course, there could be a character or a voice-over commentator asserting a property or relation; but then the film would be using its sound track in much the same way as fiction uses assertive syntax. It is not cinematic description but merely description by literary assertion transferred to film. Filmmakers and critics traditionally show disdain for verbal commentary because it explicates what, they feel, should be implicated visually. So in its essential visual mode, film does not describe at all but merely presents; or better, it *depicts,* in the original etymological sense of that word: renders in pictorial form. I don't think that this is mere purism or a die-hard adherence to silent films. Film attracts that component of our perceptual apparatus which we tend to favor over the other senses. Seeing is, after all, believing.

That the camera depicts but does not describe seems confirmed by a term often used by literary critics to characterize neutral, "non-narrated" Hemingwayesque fiction—the *camera eye* style. The implication of "cam- era eye" is that no one recounts the events of, for example, "The Killers": they are just *revealed,* as if some instrument—some cross between a video tape recorder and speech synthesizer—had recorded visually and then translated those visuals into the most neutral kind of language.

Now, someone might counterargue: "You're forgetting obvious cinematic devices whose intention is arguably descriptive. What about the telling close-up? What about establishing shots?" But the close-ups that come immediately to mind seem introduced for plot unravelling, for hermeneutic purposes. Think of Hitchcock's famous close-ups: the villain's amputated little finger in *The Thirty-Nine Steps;* the poisoned coffee cup in *Notorious;* Janet Leigh's horribly open eye in the bloody shower in *Psycho.* For all their capacity to arrest our attention, these close-ups in no way invite aesthetic contemplation; on the contrary, they function as extremely powerful components in the structure of the suspense. They present, in the most dramatic fashion, that abiding narrative-hermeneutic question: "My God," they cry out, "what next?" Of course, a real description in a novel may also serve to build suspense. We curse Dickens for stopping the action at a critical moment to describe something. "Keep still," shouts the sudden, terrifying figure to Pip at the beginning of *Great Expectations,* "or I'll cut your throat." And then, as we dangle in suspense, a whole paragraph describes the man: the iron on his leg, his broken shoes, the rag tied around his head, and so on. Yes, we curse Dickens—and love every second of it. But in the movie version, the sense of continuing action could not stop. Even if there were a long pause to give us a chance to take in the fearsome details of Magwitch's person, we would still feel that the clock of story-time was ticking away, that that pause was *included* in the story and not just an interval as we perused the discourse. We might very well infer that the delay means something, perhaps that Magwitch was trying to decide what to do with Pip, or, in a supersophisticated "psychological" version, that Pip's own time scale had somehow been stretched out because of his great terror. In either case, the feeling that we were sharing time passage with a character would be a sure clue that not only our discourse-time but their story-time was continuing to roll. And if it is the case that story-time necessarily continues to roll in films, and if description entails precisely the arrest of story-time, then it is reasonable to argue that films do not and cannot describe.

Then what about establishing shots? An establishing shot, if you're not up on movie jargon, is defined as follows (in Ernest Lindgren's *The Art of the Film*): "A long shot introduced at the beginning of a scene to establish the interrelationship of details to be shown subsequently in nearer shots." Standard examples are the bird's-eye shots that open *The Lady Vanishes* and *Psycho.* In *The Lady Vanishes,* the camera starts high above a Swiss ski resort, then moves down, and in the next shot we're inside the crowded hotel; in *Psycho,* the camera starts high above Phoenix, then glides down into a room where a couple are making love. It is true that both of these shots are in a certain sense descriptive or at least evocative of place; but they seem to enjoy that status only because they occur at the very beginning of the films, that is to say, before any characters have been introduced. Now narrative in its usual definition is a causal chain of events, and since "narrative event" means an "action performed by or at least of some relevance to a character," we can see why precisely the absence of characters endows establishing shots with a descriptive quality. It is not that story-time has been arrested. It is just that it has not yet begun. For when the same kind of shot occurs in the middle of a film, it does not seem to entail an arrest or abeyance of story-time. For example, recall the scene in the middle of *Notorious* just at the moment when Cary Grant and Ingrid Bergman are flying into Rio de Janeiro. We see shots of the city from the air, typical street scenes, and so on. Yet our sense is not of a hiatus in the story-time but rather that Rio is down there waiting for Cary and Ingrid to arrive. All that street activity is felt to be transpiring while the two go about their business, the business of the plot, which because of its momentarily mundane character—landing, clearing customs, and so on—is allowed to happen off screen.

Even the literal arrest of the picture, the so-called freeze-frame, where the image is reduced to a projected still photograph, does not automatically convey a description. It was popular a dozen years ago to end films that way, *in medias res.* Remember how Truffaut's young hero Antoine Doinel was frozen on the beach in *The Four Hundred Blows?* Truffaut has continued to follow the Doinel character in an interesting way, as the actor Jean-Pierre Léaud has himself aged, but I for one had no idea when I originally saw *The Four Hundred Blows* that there would be sequels; for me the sense of the frozen ending was that Doinel was trapped in a fugitive way of life. I perceived not a description but a kind of congealed iteration of future behavior.

Why is it that the force of plot, with its ongoing march of events, its ticking away of story-time, is so hard to dispel in the movies? That's an interesting question, but a psychologist or psychologically oriented aes-thetician will have to answer it. I can only hazard a guess. The answer may have something to do with the medium itself. Whereas in novels, movements and hence events are at best constructions imaged by the reader out of words, that is, abstract symbols which are different from them in kind, the movements on the screen are so iconic, so like the real life movements they imitate, that the illusion of time passage simply cannot be divorced from them. Once that illusory story-time is established in a film, even dead moments, moments when nothing moves, will be felt to be part of the temporal whole, just as the taxi meter continues to run as we sit fidgeting in a traffic jam.

Let's try these ideas out on a longer and more challenging passage of Maupassant's story, the third paragraph:

> [1] Mademoiselle Dufour was trying to swing herself standing up, but she could not succeed in getting a start. [2] She was a pretty girl of about eighteen; [3] one of those women who suddenly excite your desire when you meet them in the street, and who leave you with a vague feeling of uneasiness and of excited senses. [4] She was tall, had a small waist and large hips, with a dark skin, very large eyes, and very black hair. [5] Her dress clearly marked the outlines of her firm, full figure, which was accentuated by the motion of her hips as she tried to swing herself higher. [6] Her arms were stretched over her head to hold the rope, so that her bosom rose at every movement she made. Her hat, which a gust of wind had

blown off, was hanging behind her, [7] and as the swing gradually rose higher and higher, she showed her delicate limbs up to the knees at each time. . . . [P. 66][2]

The first narrative unit, "Mademoiselle Dufour was trying to swing herself " and so on, refers to an event. The second, "She was a pretty girl of about eighteen," seems on the face of it a straightforward description; but look at it from the point of view of a filmmaker. For one thing, "pretty" is not only descriptive but evaluative: one person's "pretty" may be another person's "beautiful" and still a third person's "plain." There will be some interesting variations in the faces selected by directors across cultures and even across time periods: Mary Pickford might be just the face for the teens and twenties, while Tuesday Weld may best represent the sixties. Renoir chose the face of Sylvie Bataille. The interesting theoretical point to be made about evaluative descriptions in verbal narrative is that they can invoke visual elaboration in the reader's mind. If he or she requires one, each reader will provide just the mental image to suit his or her own notions of prettiness. But the best a film (or theater) director can hope for is some degree of consensus with the spectator's ideal of prettiness. Even with the luckiest choice, some patrons will mutter, "I didn't think she was pretty at all." A similar point could be made about age; Sylvie Bataille's Henriette seems closer to thirty than eighteen, but that may be because of the costume she's wearing. The more serious point is that visual appearance is only a rough sign of age. Again the author's task is easier: correct attribution can be insured by simply naming the attribute. The filmmaker, on the other hand, has to depend on the audience's agreement to the justice of the visual clues.

Still another point to be made about this piece of description concerns the word "about" and the whole of the next descriptive bit in the third unit. These not only refine and add to the description but also make salient the voice of a narrator. "*About* eighteen" stresses that the narrator himself is guessing. And, "one of those women who suddenly excite your desire" tells us even more: the narrator is a man responsive to female charms, perhaps a *roué*, at least a man-about-town. Such is the

---

2. "Mlle Dufour essayait de se balancer debout, toute seule, sans parvenir à se donner un élan suffisant. C'était une belle fille de dix-huit à vingt ans; une de ces femmes dont la rencontre dans la rue vous fouette d'un désir subit, et vous laisse jusqu'à la nuit une inquiétude vague et un soulèvement des sens. Grande, mince de taille et large des hanches, elle avait la peau très brune, les yeux très grands, les cheveux très noirs. Sa robe dessinait nettement les plénitudes fermes de sa chair qu'accentuaient encore les efforts des reins qu'elle faisait pour s'enlever. Ses bras tendus tenaient les cordes au-dessus de sa tête, de sorte que sa poitrine se dressait, sans une secousse, à chaque impulsion qu'elle donnait. Son chapeau, emporté par un coup de vent, était tombé derrière elle; et l'escarpolette peu à peu se lançait, montrant à chaque retour ses jambes fines jusqu'au genou. . . ."

character of speech: it usually tells us something about the speaker. Long ago I. A. Richards labeled this function "tone." The camera, poor thing, is powerless to invoke tone, though it can present some alternatives to it. In this case, as we shall see, Renoir's sense of the need to show Henriette's innocent seductiveness seems to have prompted several amusing reaction shots which compensate for the camera's sexless objectivity.

The adjectives in our fourth segment are easier for film to handle: height, girth, skin, and hair color are features that film can communicate reliably. (The communication, of course, is always comparative, scalar: a character is tall relative to other people and objects in the film.) The motion of her hips bears a double function: the movement itself is an event, but it also contributes to the description of a part of Henriette's anatomy that the narrator finds quite absorbing. The same double role is played by the bosom and falling hat in segment six. As movements, these of course are simple for the film to convey; Henriette's voluptuousness, however, is not asserted but only suggestively depicted.

In the seventh segment, an odd ambiguity is introduced. The text says that as the swing rose, "she showed her delicate limbs up to the knees [montrant à chaque retour ses jambes fines jusqu'au genou]." The camera is certainly capable of presenting the requisite portion of anatomy. But what about the implications of "showed"? In both story and film, Henriette is generally represented as innocent; conscious exhibitionism does not go with her character, her family situation, or the times. The answer is perhaps an equivoque on the verb "to show": the definition of that word neither excludes nor includes conscious intention. And it is precisely an ambiguity that would go with the coquetry of a nineteenth-century maiden: to show but not *necessarily* to be conscious of showing. The camera, again, would seem unable to translate that verbal innuendo.

But see what Renoir makes of this problem. He elects to present Henriette first from the point of view of one of the two young boat men—not Henri, who is later to fall in love with her, but his comrade, Rodolphe. The term "point of view" means several things, but here I am using it in the strictly perceptual sense. Because the camera is behind Rodolphe's back as he looks out onto the garden through the window he's just opened, the camera, and hence the narrative point of view, identifies with him. It conspires, and invites us to conspire, with his voyeurism. Point of view is a complex matter worthy of a whole other discussion, but one theoretical observation is worth making here. The fact that most novels and short stories come to us through the voice of a narrator gives authors a greater range and flexibility than filmmakers. For one thing, the visual point of view in a film is always *there:* it is fixed and determinate precisely because the camera always needs to be placed *somewhere.* But in verbal fiction, the narrator may or may not give us a visual bearing. He may let us peer over a character's shoulder, or he may

represent something from a generalized perspective, commenting indifferently on the front, sides, and back of the object, disregarding how
it is possible to see all these parts in the same glance. He doesn't have to
account for his physical position at all. Further, he can enter solid bodies
and tell what things are like inside, and so on. In the present case,
Maupassant's narrator gives us a largely frontal view of Henriette on the
swing, but he also casually makes observations about her posterior. And,
of course, he could as easily have described the secret contents of her
heart. The filmmaker, with his bulky camera, lights, tracks, and other
machinery, suffers restrictions. But the very limitations, as Rudolf
Arnheim has shown so eloquently, encourage interesting artistic solutions. Renoir uses precisely the camera's need for placement to engage
the problem of communicating the innocent yet seductive quality of
Henriette's charms. Since seductiveness, like beauty, is in the eye of a
beholder, Renoir requisitions Rodolphe's point of view to convey it. It is
not Henriette so much as Rodolphe's reaction to Henriette, even on first
seeing her, that shall establish her seductiveness and not only in his mind
but in ours, because we cannot help but look on with him. Small plot
changes help to make the scene plausible. Henri, disgusted with the
Parisians invading his fishing sanctuary, does not even care to see what
this latest horde looks like. It is Rodolphe who opens the window,
flooding sunlight into the gloomy dining room and making a little stage
in the deep background against which Henriette and her mother move
like cute white puppets (fig. 3).

Fig. 3

At this range, we can't see anything very clearly except the waving of
Henriette's skirt in the wind, but the way that Rodolphe lowers his back
and settles his body clearly communicates his intention to gaze, and we
become his accomplices. After all, what is a stage except a space to gaze
at? (Renoir often used stagelike frames in his films to suggest several
planes of action; one of his more delightful later films is called *Le Petit*

Théâtre de Jean Renoir.) Notice that the swing is so placed that Henriette's to-and-fro movement is toward Rodolphe's window, quite as if she were performing for him, although, of course, she is quite innocent of his existence. Here we begin to get something equivalent to the ambiguity of the word "show" that we found in the story: Henriette will display herself without being aware of it, she will reveal, yet *malgré elle*. And as if clearly to establish her innocence in the matter, Renoir's next shot (fig. 4) is very different: it is a homely, mundane view of her *en famille,* the black figure of her granny on the right and her father and fiancé, Anatole, talking to each other on the left. This is followed by a discussion with the *patron* M. Poulain (played by Renoir himself) about what and where to eat. The whole effect of this shot is to background Henriette, to make her again just a bourgeois daughter and not the inducer of vague feelings of uneasiness and excited senses.

FIG. 4

There follows a shot of Henriette's joyous face (fig. 5). The shot is from below, and it wonderfully communicates her lightheartedness and euphoria at being aloft. Suddenly we are very much identified with Henriette's feelings: Rodolphe's voyeurism is forgotten. This identification also entails "point of view" but now in a transferred or even metaphorical sense of the term: it is not Henriette's perceptual point of view that the camera identifies with, since she is looking toward it. Rather, her movements and the infectious joy on her face incite us to share her emotional point of view; we empathize with her. For this effect I offer the term "interest" point of view.[3] We become identified with the fate of a character, and even if we don't see things or even think about them from his or her literal perspective, it still makes sense to say that we share the character's point of view. Renoir brilliantly communicates the effect by swaying the camera to and fro in rhythm with the to-and-fro motions of the swing.

The contrast with the banalities of the previous and following shots

3. See my *Story and Discourse: Narrative Structure in Fiction and Film* (Ithaca, N.Y. and London, 1978).

FIG. 5

enhances the difference between the buoyant fresh girl, a product of nature, and the ponderous and torpid family, especially the father, who seems rooted to the ground by his heavy black jacket, absurd tie, and gross belly bulging out of checkered trousers (fig. 6). It would be ludicrous to see such a man swinging aloft among the trees. The mother is in a middle position: though a woman of some beauty, she has become too heavy and maladroit to get her swing going on her own. She has lost the young girl's powers to fly, though she still has inclinations (which she later ends up showing in a delicious bacchanal with Rodolphe).

FIG. 6

Now we get one of my favorite shots in the film (fig. 7). It starts out as another and rather uninteresting view of mother and daughter on the swings. But then there is a long pan over the apparently empty space of the garden, past granny and some trees. Suddenly, completely unexpected figures appear—a column of young seminarians shepherded by their teachers. Heads are down until one of them spots Henriette and alerts his friend (fig. 8). Momentarily we're in their perceptual point of view, watching Henriette from their angle and distance. The shepherd prods the black sheep to cast his eyes down again to avoid the sins of the

FIG. 7

FIG. 8

flesh but manages to sneak a glance of his own (fig. 9). There follows another shot of exhilarated Henriette, enjoying her swing and totally oblivious to this new set of eyes watching her. To clinch the point, Renoir then points the camera at a third set of voyeurs (fig. 10), five precocious boys behind a hedge who exchange knowing glances. Another shot to and fro of Henriette swinging up and down, and we cut back to the boat men, but now seen from *outside* their window (fig. 11). By this time, Henriette's innocent movements have been clearly established as the provocation for Rodolphe's libidinous thoughts.

Rodolphe's voyeurism becomes explicit in an intercut sequence. First there is a shot of Henriette from Rodolphe's angle and distance; the comment in the subtitle, "Wonderful invention—swings!," is, of course, Rodolphe's (fig. 12). The distance preserves the illusion that it is through Rodolphe's vantage that we see Henriette. She unconsciously grants his wish that she sit down so that he can see her legs better (fig. 13). So the camera moves in for a closer view (fig. 14), as if Rodolphe's erotic imagination has given him extra optical magnification. We are carried along and risk being implicated further in his gaze at that wondrous flurry of

Fig. 9

Fig. 10

Fig. 11

Fig. 12

Fig. 13

Fig. 14

petticoats, though Henri comments that nothing really can be seen. At this flourish, Rodolphe is shown in an amusing reaction close-up, stroking his mustache and looking rather sheepish (fig. 15).

Fig. 15

So even though Renoir had no direct way of communicating the ambivalences in the expression "showed her legs," he created a sequence in which it can be argued that Henriette is at once innocent and seductive. The sequence is a little masterpiece of reaction editing, not only communicating the essential plot information but also providing a light commentary on French mores and the joys of youth and life, on the birth, amid sunshine and trees, of the sexual impulse. But notice that the sequence illustrates the point I was trying to make at the outset. No member of the audience will formulate in so many words that Henriette was tall, had a small waist and large hips, and so on. We may have a profound sense of Henriette's presence as incarnated by Sylvie Bataille but not of the *assertion* of those details as such. The erotic effect of her appearance explicitly described by the narrator of Maupassant's story is only implicitly depicted in the film by the reaction shots. Something of her appeal is caught by the looks on the faces of four ages of gazing men—the pubescent peekers in the hedge, the seminarians, Rodolphe, and the older priest leading his students.

One final difference between the film and the story: the features of Henriette's appearance that Maupassant's narrator asserts are given an order. First he mentions her height, then her shape, her skin, eyes, hair, then her shape again, her arms, her bosom, her hat, and finally her legs. The order itself seems at once clinical and caressing, going up and down her body, confirming our impression of the narrator as a sensualist. There is no such implication in Renoir's shots. The camera *could* have scanned her body in a cliché shot in the Hollywood mode accompanied by an offscreen wolf whistle. Renoir elected not to compromise the camera: it would have spoiled the whole effect of unconsciously seductive innocence. The camera is not required to share its viewpoint with Rodolphe and the three other groups of voyeurs. It maintains a clear distinction between shots from Rodolphe's point of view and those from a neutral point of view.[4]

4. Several participants in the narrative conference objected to my analysis of the point of view situation at this moment in Renoir's film. I hope I am correct in reporting their complaints: the chief objection was to the assumption that female members of the audience would identify with Rodolphe's voyeurism. Such identification, it was contended, would have to be limited to men—and only sexist men at that. The objection seemed to be not about the voyeurism itself but about the willingness of members of an audience to go along with it. (I hope I'm not simplifying the issue by using terms like "identify" and "going along with it"; if I am, I would welcome further clarification from interested readers.)

My response appeals largely and familiarly to the distinction, crucial to interpretation, as I see it, between aesthetics and ethics. The kind of identification that I was discussing is of course purely aesthetic. A reader must obviously be able to participate imaginatively in a character's set of mind, even if that character is a nineteenth-century lecher. One would think the days long gone in which we needed to apologize for donning the perceptual and conceptual clothing of objectionable fictional characters or unreliable narrators—Raskolnikovs or Verlocs or Jason Compsons or one of Celine's "hero" narrators. Imaginative participation in the point of view of fictional characters (need one say again?) in no way

So writer, filmmaker, comic strip artist, choreographer—each finds his or her own ways to evoke the sense of what the objects of the narrative look like. Each medium has its own properties, for better and worse usage, and intelligent film viewing and criticism, like intelligent reading, needs to understand and respect both the limitations these create and also the triumphs they invite.

---

implies moral endorsement. It is simply the way we make sense—the way implied authors enable us to become implied readers who make sense—out of unusual or even downright alien viewpoints. We don't compromise our right thinking by engaging in that kind of participation; we don't condone the character's outlook. Why should female members of Renoir's audience have any more difficulty participating in Rodolphe's lecherous point of view than male members have in participating in the point of view of Molly Bloom? How responsible is an ideology which accuses critics of promulgating characters' viewpoints which they merely wish to analyze? Does a herpetologist become a snake by dissecting a snake? I cannot see how it can be denied that Renoir's presentation of four ages of voyeurs establishes a textual intention to show Henriette as a woman eminently worth looking at, albeit with lust in some men's hearts. For a woman to participate in a male character's doing so requires no greater act of imagination than for a man to participate in Scarlett O'Hara's lust for Rhett Butler. To deny that Renoir intended to communicate voyeurism (because that would make a classic film sexist) seems critically naive. Of course Maupassant and Renoir—or more properly the implied authors of these works—are sexist by modern standards. That doesn't mean that we become sexist by reading, studying, and, yes, even enjoying them.

A comment by Roy Schafer was more useful. Schafer argued that the close-up of Henriette on the swing conveyed to him something of *her* sexual pleasure. It is not difficult to agree that swinging is easily allied to sexuality. The attribution goes along perfectly with other motifs of innocent, preconscious sexuality, of "showing her limbs," and of the vague feelings of longing for even the tiny things that move under the leaves and grass that Henriette expresses to her mother a bit later in the film. I think Schafer is right: the point of view could also be attributed to Henriette. But that causes no theoretical problem. Two points of view can exist concurrently in a single shot. It is an interesting property of cinematic narrative that we can see through one character's eyes and feel through another's heart. The camera adopts a position, an angle, and a distance which by convention associates itself with the position, angle, and distance of a character's vision. But so great is its capacity to inspire identification with characters' thinking, feeling, and general situation that we tend to identify even when the character appears to us in a completely frontal view. This sympathetic or "interest" point of view (as I call it) is particularly strong in film narratives and can easily combine with the more conventionally marked perceptual point of view.

Social Dramas and Stories about Them

Victor Turner

Anthropologists count and measure what they can in order to establish general features of the sociocultural fields they study. Although these activities have their irritating side, on the whole I found it eminently soothing, during my two and a half years of fieldwork among the Ndembu of northwestern Zambia, a west-central Bantu-speaking people, to sit in villages before a calabash of millet or honey beer and collect numerical data—on village membership, divorce frequency, bride wealth, labor migration rates, individual cash budgets, birth and homicide rates—and, more strenuously, to measure the acreage of gardens and the dimensions of ritual enclosures. These figures told me if not a story at least where to go to find stories.

I was able to infer from statistics based on censuses and genealogies of some seventy villages that these residential units consisted of cores of closely related male matrilineal kin; wives and sisters, as a result of frequent divorce, had returned to their natal villages bringing their children with them. This was, of course, only the thin end of a massive wedge. I soon discovered that Ndembu marry *virilocally,* that is, after marriage a woman resides in her husband's village. Consequently, in the long run, village continuity depends upon marital discontinuity, since one's right to reside in a given village is primarily determined by matrilineal affiliation, though one may reside in one's father's village during the father's lifetime. Clearly a sort of structural turbulence is built into these normative arrangements. For a village can only persist by recruiting widows, divorcées, and their children. There is also a propensity for men, who reside in their own matrilineal village, to persuade their sisters to leave their husbands, bringing with them the children who "properly belong" to that village. Political authority, chieftainship, headmanship, and other offices are in male hands, even in this matrilineal society; a man, however, cannot be succeeded by his own son but only by his uterine brother or his sister's son. The chain of authority, therefore, demands that, sooner or later, a headman's sister's sons will leave their paternal villages and dwell with their maternal uncle. It is easier to do this if a young man is residing with his stepfather, not the father who begat him. Thus divorce works in various ways to reassert the ultimate paramountcy of the maternal line, despite the masculine attempt to pre-empt the present through virilocal marriage.

It is my purpose to show here how certain entrenched features of a given society's social structure influence both the course of conduct in observable social events and the scenarios of its genres of cultural performance—ranging from ritual to märchen. To complete the simplified picture of Ndembu social structure I should mention, however, that in several books[1] I have tried to work out how stresses between matrilineal succession and other principles and the processes to which they give rise have affected various mundane and ritual phenomena, processes, and institutions of Ndembu society—such as village size, composition, mobility, fission, marital stability, relations between and within genealogical generations, the role of the many cult associations in counterbalancing village cleavages, lineages and families, the strong masculine stress on complex hunting and circumcision rites in a system ultimately dependent on women's agricultural and food-processing activities, and the patterning of witchcraft accusations, which are often directed against matrilineal rivals for office or prestige.

I suppose that if I had confined myself to the analysis of numerical data, guided by knowledge of salient kinship principles and political, legal, and economic contexts, I would have construed an anthropological narrative informed by what Hayden White in *Metahistory* surely would

---

1. See my *Schism and Continuity in an African Society: A Study of Ndembu Village Life* (Manchester, 1957); *The Forest of Symbols: Aspects of Ndembu Society* (Ithaca, N.Y., 1967); *The Drums of Affliction: A Study of Religious Processes among the Ndembu of Zambia* (Oxford, 1968); and *The Ritual Process: Structure and Anti-Structure* (Chicago, 1969).

Victor Turner is professor of anthropology and a member of the Center for Advanced Studies at the University of Virginia. His many publications include *Schism and Continuity in an African Society, The Forest of Symbols, The Ritual Process,* and, with Edith Turner, *Image and Pilgrimage in Christian Culture.*

have called "mechanistic" presuppositions.[2] Indeed, this was standard
practice in the British school of structuralist-functionalist anthropology
in which I was nurtured in the late forties and early fifties. One of its
main aims was to exhibit the laws of structure and process which, in a
given preliterate society, determine the specific configurations of relationships and institutions detectable by trained observation. The ultimate intent of this school, as formulated by Radcliffe-Brown, was to seek
out by the comparative method general laws by successive approximation. Each specific ethnography sought for general principles that appeared in the study of a single society. In other words, idiographic procedures, detailed descriptions of what I actually observed or learned
from informants, were pressed into the service of the development of
laws. Hypotheses developing out of idiographic research were tested
nomothetically, that is, for the purpose of formulating general sociologi-
cal laws.

   There are, of course, many virtues in this approach. My figures *did*
give me some measure of the relative importance of the principles on
which Ndembu villages are socially constructed. They pointed to trends
of individual and corporate spatial mobility. They indicated how in some
areas particularly exposed to the modern cash economy a smaller type of
residential unit based on the polygynous family, called a "farm," was
replacing the traditional circular village whose nucleus was a sibling
group of matrilineal kin. The method I used was also employed by
colleagues working from the Rhodes-Livingstone Institute and facili-
tated controlled comparison of village structures belonging to different
central African societies. Differences of kinship and local structures were
compared with differences in such variables as the divorce rate, the
amount of bride wealth, the mode of subsistence, and so forth.

   Nevertheless, this approach has its limitations. As George Spindler
has argued, "the idiography of ethnography may be distorted by the
nomethetic orientation of the ethnographer."[3] In other words, the general theory you take into the field leads you to select certain data for
attention but blinds you to other, perhaps more important, data for the
understanding of the people studied. As I came to know Ndembu well
both in stressful and uneventful times as "men and women alive" (to
paraphrase D. H. Lawrence), I became increasingly aware of this limitation. Long before I had read a word of Wilhelm Dilthey's I had shared
his notion that "structures of experience" are fundamental units in the
study of human action. Such structures are irrefrangibly threefold,

   2. See Hayden White's *Metahistory: The Historical Imagination in Nineteenth-Century
Europe* (Baltimore, 1973), p. 16; all further references to this work will be cited in the text.
   3. George D. Spindler, introduction to *The Making of Psychological Anthropology,* ed.
Spindler (Berkeley, 1978), p. 31.

being at once cognitive, conative, and affective. Each of these terms is itself, of course, a shorthand for a range of processes and capacities.

Perhaps this view was influenced by Edward Sapir's celebrated essay "The Emergence of the Concept of Personality in a Study of Cultures," in which he wrote: "In spite of the oft asserted impersonality of culture, a humble truth remains that vast reaches of culture, far from being 'carried' by a community or group . . . are discoverable only as the peculiar property of certain individuals, who cannot but give these cultural goods the impress of their own personality."[4] Not only that but persons will, desire, and feel, as well as think, and their desires and feelings impregnate their thoughts and influence their intentions. Sapir assailed cultural overdeterminism as a reified cognitive construct of the anthropologist, whose "impersonalized" culture is hardly more than "an assembly or mass of loosely overlapping idea[s] and action systems which, through verbal habit, can be made to assume the appearance of a closed system of behavior" (p. 412), a position corresponding to some extent with White's organicist paradigm—as prestigious among American anthropologists as functionalism was among their British contemporaries. It became clear to me that an "anthropology of experience" would have to take into account the psychological properties of individuals as well as the culture which, as Sapir insists, is *"never given"* to each individual but, rather, "gropingly discovered," and, I would add, some parts of it quite late in life. We never cease to learn our *own* culture, which is always changing, let alone other cultures.

It also became clear that among the many tasks of the anthropologist lay the duty not only to make structuralist and functionalist analyses of statistical and textual data (censuses and myths) but also to prehend experiential structures in the actual processes of social life. Here my own approach, and that of many other anthropologists, conforms to some extent with White's contextualist model. White, using Stephen Pepper's term, sees contextualism as the isolation of some element of the historical field (or, in the anthropological instance, the sociocultural field) as the subject of study, "whether the element be as large as 'the French Revolution' or as small as one day in the life of a specific person." The investigator "then proceeds to pick out the 'threads' that link the event to be explained to different areas of the context. The threads are identified and traced outward, into the circumambient natural and social space within which the event occurred, and both backward in time, in order to determine the 'origins' of the event, and forward in time, in order to determine its 'impact' and 'influence' on sub-

---

4. Edward Sapir, "The Emergence of the Concept of Personality in a Study of Cultures," *Journal of Social Psychology* 5 (1934): 412; all further references to this work will be cited in the text.

sequent events. This tracing operation ends at the point at which the 'threads' either disappear into the 'context' of some other 'event' or 'converge' to cause the occurrence of some new 'event.' The impulse is not to integrate all the events and trends that might be identified in the whole historical field, but rather to link them together in a chain of provisional and restricted characterizations of finite provinces of manifestly 'significant' occurrence" (White, pp. 18–19).

It is interesting to pause here for a moment and compare how Sapir and White use the metaphor of "thread." For Sapir points out that the "purely formalized and logically developed schemes" we call ethnographies do not explain behavior until "the *threads* of symbolism or implication [that] connect patterns or parts of patterns with others of an entirely different formal aspect" are discovered (p. 412; my emphasis). For Sapir these threads are *internal* to the sociocultural space studied and relate to the personality and temperament of individuals, while for White and Pepper threads describe the nature of connections between an "element" or "event" and its significant *environing* sociocultural field viewed, according to White, "synchronically" or "structurally" (p. 19). I find fascinating Sapir's notion that his threads are symbolic and implicative; for symbols, the spawn of such tropes as arise in the interaction of men and women alive, metaphors, synechdoches, metonymies new minted in crises, so to speak, really do come to serve as semiotic connectives among the levels and parts of a system of action and between that system and its significant environment. We have been neglecting the role of symbols in establishing connexity between the different levels of a narrative structure.

But I am anticipating. I shall shortly call attention to a kind or species of "element of the historical field" or "event," in White's terminology, which is cross-culturally isolable and which exhibits, if it is allowed to come to full term, a characteristic processual structure, a structure that holds firm whether one is considering a macro- or micro-historical event of this type. Before I discuss this unit, which I consider to be the social ground of many types of "narrative" and which I call "social drama," I must first mention for the benefit of my nonanthropological readers another useful distinction made by anthropologists, that between "emic" and "etic" perspectives; these terms are derived from the distinction made by linguists between "phonemic" and "phonetic," the former being the study of sounds recognized as distinct *within* a specific language, the latter being the cross-lingual study of distinguishable human sound units. Kenneth Pike, who propounded this dichotomy, should be allowed to formulate it: "Descriptions of analyses from the etic standpoint are 'alien,' with criteria external to the system. Emic descriptions provide an internal view [or an "inside view" in Hockett's terms], with criteria chosen from within the system. They represent to us the view of one familiar with this system and who knows how to function within it himself."[5] From this standpoint all four of the strategies of explanation proposed by White drawing on Pepper—formism, organicism, mechanism, and contextualism—would produce etic narratives if they were used to provide accounts of societies outside that Western cultural tradition generatively triangulated by the thinking of Jerusalem, Athens, and Rome and continued in the philosophical, literary, and social-scientific traditions of Europe, North America, and their cultural offshoots. Indeed, members of such societies (the so-called Third World) have protested, as recently as 1973,[6] that Western attempts to "explain" their cultures amount to no more than "cognitive ethnocentrism," diminishing their contribution to the global human reflexivity which modern communicational and informational systems are now making possible, if hardly easy. In other words, what we in the West consider etic, that is, "nomothetic," "non-culture-bound," "scientific," "objective," they are coming to regard as emic.

There are then *both* etic and emic ways of regarding narrative. An anthropologist, embedded in the life of an at-first-wholly-other culture and separated, save in memory, from his own, has to come to terms with that which invests and invades him. The situation is odd enough. He is tossed into the ongoing life of a parcel of people who not only speak a different language but also classify what we would call "social reality" in ways that are at first quite unexpected. He is compelled to learn, however haltingly, the criteria which provide the "inside view."

I am aware of White's "theory of the historical work" and that it bears importantly upon how to write ethnographies as well as histories; but I am also aware that any discussion of the role of narrative in other cultures requires that an emic description of narrative be made. For the anthropologist's work is deeply involved in what *we* might call "tales," "stories," "folktales," "histories," "gossip," and "informants' accounts"—types of narrative for which there may be many native names, not all of which coincide with our terms. Indeed, Max Gluckman has commented that the very term "anthropologist" means in Greek "one who talks about men," in other words, a "gossip." In our culture we have many ways of talking about men, descriptive and analytical, formal and informal, traditional and open-ended. Since ours is a literate culture, characterized by a refined division of cultural labor, we have devised numerous specialized genres by means of which we scan, describe, and interpret our behavior toward one another. But the impulse to talk about one another in different ways, in terms of different qualities and levels of mutual consciousness, precedes literacy in all human com-

5. Kenneth L. Pike, *Language in Relation to a Unified Theory of the Structure of Human Behavior* (Glendale, Cal., 1954), p. 8.

6. See Asmarom Legesse's *Gada: Three Approaches to the Study of African Society* (New York, 1973), p. 283.

munities. All human acts and institutions are enveloped, as Clifford Geertz might say, in webs of interpretive words. Also, of course, we mime and dance with one another—we have webs of interpretive non-verbal symbols. And we play one another—beginning as children—and continue through life to learn new roles and the subcultures of higher statuses to which we aspire, partly seriously, partly ironically.

Ndembu make a distinction, akin to White's division between "chronicle" and "story" as levels of conceptualization in Western culture, between *nsang'u* and *kaheka*. *Nsang'u*, chronicle, may refer, for example, to a purportedly factual record of the migration of the Lunda chiefs and their followers from the Katanga region of Zaire on the Nkalanyi River, to their encounter with the autochthonous Mbwela or Lukolwe peoples in Mwinilunga District, to battles and marriages between Lunda and Mbwela, to the establishment of Ndembu-Lunda chiefdoms, to the order of chiefly incumbents down to the present, to the raids of Luvale and Tchokwe in the nineteenth century to secure indentured labor for the Portuguese in San Tome long after the formal abolition of the slave trade, to the coming of the missionaries, followed by the British South Africa Company, and finally to British colonial rule. *Nsang'u* may also denote an autobiographical account, a personal reminiscence, or an eyewitness report of yesterday's interesting happening. *Nsang'u*, like chronicle, in White's words, arranges "the events to be dealt with in the temporal order of their occurrence" (p. 5). Just as a chronicle becomes a "story," in White's usage, "by the further arrangement of the events into the components of a 'spectacle' or process of happening, which is thought to possess a discernible beginning, middle, and end . . . in terms of inaugural motifs . . . terminating motifs . . . and transitional motifs," so *nsang'u* becomes *kaheka*.

The term *kaheka* covers a range of tales which our folklorists would no doubt sort out into a number of etic types: myth, folktale, märchen, legend, ballad, folk epic, and the like. Their distinctive feature is that they are partly told, partly sung. At key points in the narration the audience joins in a sung refrain, breaking the spoken sequence. It depends on the context of the situation and the mode of framing whether a given set of events is regarded as *nsang'u* or *kaheka*. Take, for example, the series of tales about the ancient Lunda chief Yala Mwaku, his daughter Lweji Ankonde, her lover the Luban hunter-prince Chibinda Ilung'a, and her brothers Ching'uli and Chinyama: their loves, hates, conflicts, and rec-onciliations led, on the one hand, to the establishment of the Lunda nation and, on the other, to the secession and diaspora of dissident Lunda groups, thereby spreading knowledge of centralized political or-ganization over a wide territory. This sequence may be told by a chief of putative Lunda origin to politically influential visitors as a *nsang'u*, a chronicle, perhaps to justify his title to his office. But episodes from this chronicle may be transformed into stories, that is, *tuheka* (plural of *kaheka*), and told by old women to groups of children huddled near the kitchen fire during the cold season.

A particular favorite story, analyzed recently by the distinguished Belgian structuralist Luc de Heusch,[7] relates how the drunken king Yala Mwaku was derided and beaten by his sons but cared for tenderly by his daughter Lweji Ankonde, whom he rewarded by passing on to her, on his death, the royal bracelet, the *lukanu* (made of human genitalia for the magical maintenance of the fertility of humans, animals, and crops in the whole kingdom), thus rendering her the legitimate monarch of the Lunda. Another story tells how the young queen is informed by her maidens that a handsome young hunter, Chibinda, having slain a water-buck, had camped with his companions on the far side of the Nkalanye River. She summons him to her presence, and the two fall in love at once and talk for many hours in a grove of trees (where today a sacred fire, the center of an extensive pilgrimage, burns constantly). She learns that he is the youngest son of a great Luba chief but that he prefers the free life of a forest hunter to the court. Nevertheless, he marries Lweji out of love and, in time, receives from her the *lukanu*—she has to go into seclusion during menstruation and hands Chibinda the bracelet lest it become polluted—making him the ruler of the Lunda nation. Lweji's turbulent brothers refuse to recognize him and lead their people away to carve out new kingdoms for themselves and consequently spread the format of political centralization among stateless societies.

Jan Vansina, the noted Belgian ethnohistorian, has discussed the relationship between this foundation narrative and the political structures of the many central African societies who claim that they "came from Mwantiyanvwa," as the new dynasty came to call itself.[8] He finds in this corpus of stories more than myth, although Heusch has illuminatingly treated it as such; Vansina finds clues to historical affinities between the scattered societies who assert Lunda origin—indications corroborated by other types of evidence, linguistic, archaeological, and cultural. As in other cultures, the same events may be framed as *nsang'u* or *kaheka,* chronicle or story, often according to their nodal location in the life process of the group or community that recounts them. It all depends where and when and by whom they are told. Thus, for some purposes the foundation tales of Yala Mwaku and Lweji are treated as chronicle to advance a political claim, for example, a claim to "Lundahood," as Ian Cunnison calls their assertion of descent from prestigious migrants. For the purpose of entertainment, the same tales are defined as stories, with many rhetorical touches and flourishes as well as songs inserted as evocative embellishment. Incidents may even be cited during

---

7. See Luc de Heusch's *Le Roi ivre; ou, L'Origine de l'état* (Paris, 1972).
8. See Jan Vansina's *Kingdoms of the Savannah* (Madison, Wis., 1966).

processes of litigation to legitimate or reinforce the claims of a plaintiff in a dispute over boundaries or succession to office.

For the anthropologist, however, who is concerned with the study of social action and social process, it is not these formal genres of taletelling and talebearing that most grip his attention but, rather, as we have seen, what we would call gossip, talk and rumors about the private affairs of others, what the Ndembu and their neighbors, the Luvale, call *kudiyong'ola,* related to the verb *kuyong'a,* "to crowd together," for much gossip takes place in the central, unwalled shelter of traditional villages, where the circumcised, hence socially "mature," males gather to discuss community affairs and hear the "news" from wayfarers of other communities. Frank Kermode once defined the novel as consisting of two components: scandal and myth. Certainly gossip, which includes scandal, is one of the perennial sources of cultural genres. Gossip does not occur in a vacuum among the Ndembu; it is almost always "plugged in" to social drama.

Although it might be argued that the social drama is a story in White's sense, in that it has discernible inaugural, transitional, and terminal motifs, that is, a beginning, a middle, and an end, my observations convince me that it is, indeed, a spontaneous unit of social process and a fact of everyone's experience in every human society. My hypothesis, based on repeated observations of such processual units in a range of sociocultural systems and on my reading in ethnography and history, is that social dramas, "dramas of living," as Kenneth Burke calls them, can be aptly studied as having four phases. These I label breach, crisis, redress, and *either* reintegration *or* recognition of schism. Social dramas occur within groups of persons who share values and interests and who have a real or alleged common history. The main actors are persons for whom the group has a high value priority. Most of us have what I call our "star" group or groups to which we owe our deepest loyalty and whose fate is for us of the greatest personal concern. It is the one with which a person identifies most deeply and in which he finds fulfillment of his major social and personal desires. We are all members of many groups, formal or informal, from the family to the nation or some international religious or political institution. Each person makes his/her own subjective evaluation of the group's respective worth: some are "dear" to one, others it is one's "duty to defend," and so on. Some tragic situations arise from conflicts of loyalty to different star groups.

There is no *objective* rank order in any culture for such groups. I have known academic colleagues whose supreme star group, believe it or not, was a particular faculty administrative committee and whose families and recreational groups ranked much lower, others whose love and loyalty were toward the local philatelic society. In every culture one is *obliged* to belong to certain groups, usually institutionalized ones—

family, age-set, school, firm, professional association, and the like. But such groups are not necessarily one's beloved star groups. It is in one's star group that one looks most for love, recognition, prestige, office, and other tangible and intangible benefits and rewards. In it one achieves self-respect and a sense of belonging with others for whom one has respect. Now every objective group has some members who see it as their star group, while others may regard it with indifference, even dislike. Relations among the star groupers are often highly ambivalent, re-sembling those among members of an elementary family for which, perhaps, the star group is an adult substitute. They recognize one another's common attachment to the group but are jealous of one another over the relative intensity of that attachment or the esteem in which another member is held by the group as a whole. They may contend with each other for the incumbency of high office in the group, not merely to seek power but out of the conviction that they, and they alone, really understand the nature and value of the group and can altruistically advance its interests. In other words, we find symbolic equivalents of sibling rivalry and parent-child competition among star groupers.

In several books I have discussed social dramas at some length,[9] both in small-scale societies, such as Ndembu, at the village level and in complex nations, as in the power struggle between Henry II of England and Archbishop Thomas Becket. Whether it is a large affair, like the Dreyfus affair or Watergate, or a struggle for village headmanship, a social drama first manifests itself as the breach of a norm, the infraction of a rule of morality, law, custom, or etiquette, in some public arena. This breach is seen as the expression of a deeper division of interests and loyalties than appears on the surface. The incident of breach may be deliberately, even calculatedly, contrived by a person or party disposed to demonstrate or challenge entrenched authority—for example, the Boston Tea Party—or emerge from a scene of heated feelings. Once visible, it can hardly be revoked. Whatever may be the case, a mounting crisis follows, a momentous juncture or turning point in the relations between components of a social field—at which seeming peace becomes overt conflict and covert antagonisms become visible. Sides are taken, factions are formed, and unless the conflict can be sealed off quickly within a limited area of social interaction, there is a tendency for the breach to widen and spread until it coincides with some dominant cleav-age in the widest set of relevant social relations to which the parties in conflict belong. We have seen this process at work in the Iranian crisis following the breach precipitated by the seizure of the U.S. embassy in Teheran. During the phase of crisis, the pattern of current factional

9. See my *Schism and Continuity in an African Society; The Forest of Symbols; The Drums of Affliction;* and *Dramas, Fields, and Metaphors: Symbolic Action in Human Society* (Ithaca, N.Y., 1974).

struggle within the relevant social group—be it village or world community—is exposed; and beneath it there becomes slowly visible the less plastic, more durable, but nevertheless gradually changing basic social structure, made up of relations which are relatively constant and consistent.

I found that among the Ndembu, for example, prolonged social dramas always revealed the related sets of oppositions that give Ndembu social structure its tensile character: matriliny versus virilocality; the ambitious individual versus the wider interlinking of matrilineal kin; the elementary family versus the uterine sibling group (children of one mother); the forwardness of youth versus the domineering elders; status-seeking versus responsibility; sorcerism *(wuloji)*—that is, hostile feelings, grudges, and intrigues—versus friendly respect and generosity toward others. In the Iranian crisis the divisions and coalitions of interests have become publicly visible, some of which are surprising and revelatory. Crisis constitutes many levels in all cultures. In social dramas, false friendship is winnowed from true communality of interests; the limits of consensus are reached and realized; real power emerges from behind the facade of authority.

In order to limit the contagious spread of breach, certain adjustive and redressive mechanisms, informal and formal, are brought into operation by leading members of the disturbed group. These mechanisms vary in character with such factors as the depth and significance of the breach, the social inclusiveness of the crisis, the nature of the social group within which the breach took place, and the group's degree of autonomy in regard to wider systems of social relations. The mechanisms may range from personal advice and informal arbitration to formal juridical and legal machinery and, to resolve certain kinds of crises, to the performance of public ritual. Such ritual involves a literal or moral "sacrifice," that is, a victim as scapegoat is offered for the group's "sin" of redressive violence.

The final phase consists either in the reintegration of the disturbed social group—though the scope and range of its relational field will have altered, the number of its parts will be different, and their size and influence will have changed—or the social recognition of irreparable breach between the contesting parties, sometimes leading to their spatial separation. This may be on the scale of the many exoduses of history or merely a move of disgruntled villagers to a spot a few miles away. This phase, too, may be registered by a public ceremony or ritual, indicating reconciliation or permanent cleavage between the involved parties.

I am well aware that the social drama is an agonistic model drawn after a recurrent agonistic situation, and I make no claim that there are no other types of processual units. Philip Gulliver, for example, studying another central African society, the Ndendeuli of Tanzania, directs attention to the cumulative effect of an endless series of minor incidents, cases, and events that might be quite as significant in affecting and changing social relationships as the more overtly dramatic encounters. Raymond Firth discusses "harmonic" processual units—which I call "social enterprises" that also have recognizable phase structure—which stress "the process of ordering of action and of relations in reference to given social ends" and are often economic in type. Quite often, though, such enterprises—as in the case of urban renewal in America—become social dramas if there is resistance to the aims of their instigators. The resisters perceive the inauguration of the enterprise as breach, not progress. Nor does the course of a social drama, like "true love," always "run smooth." Redressive procedures may break down, with reversion to crisis. Traditional machinery of conciliation or coercion may prove inadequate to cope with new types of issues and problems and new roles and statuses. And, of course, reconciliation may only seem to have been achieved in phase four, with real conflicts glossed over but not resolved. Moreover, at certain historical junctures, in large-scale complex societies, redress may be through rebellion, or even revolution, if the societal value-consensus has broken down and new unprecedented roles, relationships, and classes have emerged.

Nevertheless, I would persist in arguing that the social drama is a well-nigh universal processual form and represents a perpetual challenge to all aspirations to perfection in social and political organization. In some cultures its profile is clear-cut and its style abrasive; in others, agonistic (contestative) action may be muted or deflected by elaborate codes of etiquette. In yet others conflict may be—to cite Richard Antoun on Arab village politics in Jordan—"low-key," eschewing direct confrontation and encounter in its style. Social dramas are in large measure political processes, that is, they involve competition for scarce ends—power, dignity, prestige, honor, purity—by particular means and by the utilization of resources that are also scarce—goods, territory, money, men and women. Ends, means, and resources are caught up in an interdependent feedback process. Some kinds of resources, for example, land and money, may be converted into other kinds, for instance, honor and prestige (which are simultaneously the needs sought). Or they may be employed to stigmatize rivals and deny them these ends. The political aspect of social dramas is dominated by star groupers; they are the main protagonists, the leaders of factions, the defenders of the faith, the revolutionary vanguard, the arch-reformers. They are the ones who develop to an art the rhetoric of persuasion and influence, who know how and when to apply pressure and force, and who are most sensitive to the factors of legitimacy. In phase three, redress, it is the star groupers who manipulate the machinery of redress, the law courts, the procedures of divination and ritual, and impose sanctions on those adjudged to have precipitated crisis, just as it may well be disgruntled or dissident star groupers who lead rebellions and provoke the initial breach.

The fact that a social drama, as I have analyzed its form, closely corresponds to Aristotle's description of tragedy in the *Poetics*—in that it is "the imitation of an action that is serious, complete, and of a certain magnitude . . . having a beginning, a middle, and an end"—is not, I repeat, because I have tried inappropriately to impose an etic Western model of stage action upon the conduct of an African village society but because there is an interdependent, perhaps dialectic, relationship between social dramas and genres of cultural performance in perhaps all societies. Life, after all, is as much an imitation of art as the reverse. Those who, as children in Ndembu society, have listened to innumerable stories about Yala Mwaku and Lweji Ankonde know all about inaugural motifs—"when the king was drunk and helpless, his sons beat and reviled him"—transitional motifs—"his daughter found him near death and comforted and tended him"—and terminal motifs—"the king gave his daughter the *lukanu* and excluded his sons from the royal succession." When these same Ndembu, now full-grown, wish to provoke a breach or to claim that some party has crucially disturbed the placid social order, they have a frame available to "inaugurate" a social drama, with a repertoire of "transitional" and "ending" motifs to continue the framing process and channel the subsequent agonistic developments. The story itself still makes important points about family relationships, and about the stresses between sex and age roles, and appears to be an emic generalization, clothed in metaphor and involving projection, of innumerable specific social dramas generated by these structural tensions; so does the story feed back into the social process, providing it with a rhetoric, a mode of emplotment, and a meaning. Some genres, particularly the epic, serve as paradigms which inform the action of important political leaders—star groupers of encompassing groups such as church or state—giving them style, direction, and sometimes compelling them subliminally to follow in major public crises a certain course of action, thus emplotting their lives.

I tried to show in chapter 2 of *Dramas, Fields, and Metaphors* how Thomas Becket, after his antagonistic confrontation with both Henry II and the bench of bishops at the council of Northampton, seemed to have been almost "taken over," "possessed" by the action-paradigm provided by the *via crucis* in Christian belief and ritual, sealing his love-hate relationship with Henry in the conjoined image of martyr and martyrizer—and giving rise to a subsequent host of narratives and aesthetic dramas. By paradigm I do not mean a system of univocal concepts, logically arrayed. I do not mean either a stereotyped set of guidelines for ethical, aesthetic, or conventional action. A paradigm of this sort goes beyond the cognitive and even the moral to the existential domain; and in so doing becomes clothed with allusiveness, implications, and metaphor—for in the stress of action firm definitional outlines become blurred by the encounter of emotionally charged wills. Paradigms

of this type, cultural root paradigms, so to speak, reach down to irreducible life stances of individuals, passing beneath conscious prehen-
sion to a fiduciary hold on what they sense to be axiomatic values, matters literally of life and death.

Richard Schechner has recently sought to express the relationship
between social drama and aesthetic or staged drama in the form of a
figure eight placed in a horizontal position and then bisected through
both loops:[10]

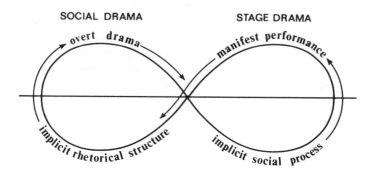

The left loop represents the social drama; above the line is the overt
drama, below it, the implicit rhetorical structure; the right loop represents stage drama; above the line is the manifest performance, below it,
the implicit social process, with its structural contradictions. Arrows
pointing from left to right represent the course of action. They follow
the phases of the social drama above the line in the left loop, descending
to cross into the lower half of the right loop where they represent the
hidden social infrastructures. The arrows then ascend and, moving now
from right to left, pass through the successive phases of a generalized
stage drama. At the point of intersection between the two loops, they
descend once more to form the hidden aesthetic model underpinning,
so to speak, of the overt social drama. This model, though effective, is
somewhat equilibrist in its implications, for my taste, and suggests cyclical
rather than linear movement. But it has the merit of pointing up the
dynamic relation between social drama and expressive cultural genres.

The social drama of Watergate is full of "stage business" during
every phase, from the Guy Fawkes-like conspiratorial atmosphere of the
breach episode, signaled by the finding of the incriminating tape on the
door, through the tough-minded fiction of the cover-up and all that
went into the crisis phase of investigation, with its Deep Throat revela-
tions and combinations of high-minded principle and low-minded political opportunism. The redressive phase was no less implicitly scripted by
theatrical and fictional models. I need not describe the hearings and the

10. Richard Schechner, personal communication.

Saturday Night Massacre. Now we have plays, films, and novels about Watergate and its natural *dramatis personae,* which are shaped—to use the aseptic language of social science—in accord with the structure and properties of the social field environing and penetrating their authors at the time of writing. At the deepest level we may anticipate an interpretive shift toward accommodation of the most acceptable texts to some deeply entrenched paradigm of Americanity. The American "myth," as Sacvan Bercovitch has recently argued in *The American Jeremiad,*[11] periodically produces "jeremiads" (polemical homilies in various cultural genres) against declension into ways of life which reek of the static, corrupt, hierarchical Old World and obviate movement toward an ever receding but ultimately reachable promised land to be carved from some unsullied wilderness, where an ideal, prosperous democracy can thrive "under God." Watergate is a superb target for the American jeremiad. Paradoxically, many of its personages have become celebrities, but this, after all, may not be so surprising. Pontius Pilate was canonized by the Ethiopean church, and if Dean and Ehrlichman will never perhaps be seen as saints, their mere participation in a drama which activated a major cultural paradigm has conferred on them an ambiguous eminence they might otherwise have never achieved. The winners of social dramas positively require cultural performances to continue to legitimate their success. And such dramas generate their "symbolic types": traitors, renegades, villains, martyrs, heroes, faithfuls, infidels, deceivers, scapegoats.[12] Just to be in the cast of a narrated drama which comes to be taken as exemplary or paradigmatic is some assurance of social immortality.

It is the third phase of a social drama, redress, that has most to do with the genesis and sustentation of cultural genres, both "high" and "folk," oral and literate. In *Schism and Continuity,* I argued that in Ndembu society when conflict emerges from the opposed interests and claims of protagonists acting under a single social principle, say, descent from a common ancestress, judicial institutions can be invoked to meet the crisis, for a rational attempt can be made to adjust claims that are similarly based. But when claims are advanced under different social principles, which are inconsistent with one another even to the point of mutual contradiction, there can be no rational settlement. Here Ndembu have recourse to divination of sorcery or ancestral wrath to account for misfortune, illness, or death occurring before or during the social drama. Ultimately, rituals of reconciliation may be performed, which, in their verbal and nonverbal symbolism, reassert and reanimate the over-

11. See Sacvan Bercovitch's *The American Jeremiad* (Madison, Wis., 1978).

12. See R. Grathoff's *The Structure of Social Inconsistencies: A Contribution to a Unified Theory of Play, Game and Social Action* (The Hague, 1970) and Don Handelman's "Is Naven Ludic?" *Social Analysis* 1 (1979).

arching values shared by all Ndembu, despite conflicts of norms and interests on the ground level.

Whether juridical or ritual processes of redress are invoked against mounting crises, the result is an increase in what one might call social or plural *reflexivity*, the ways in which a group tries to scrutinize, portray, understand, and then act on itself. Barbara Myerhoff has recently written of cultural performances in *Life History among the Elderly: Performance, Visibility, and Remembering* that they are "*reflective* in the sense of showing ourselves to ourselves. They are also capable of being *reflexive*, arousing consciousness of ourselves as we see ourselves. As heroes in our own dramas, we are made self aware, conscious of our consciousness. At once actor and audience, we may then come into the fullness of our human capability—and perhaps human desire to watch ourselves and enjoy knowing that we know."[13] I tend to regard the social drama in its full formal development, its full phase structure, as a process of converting particular values and ends, distributed over a range of actors, into a system (which is always temporary and provisional) of shared or consensual meaning. It has not yet reached the stage of Myerhoff's enjoying that we know that we know ourselves, but it is a step in that direction. I am inclined to agree with Dilthey that *meaning (Bedeutung)* arises in *memory*, in *cognition* of the *past*, and is concerned with negotiation about the "fit" between past and present; and *value (Wert)* inheres in the affective enjoyment of the *present*, while the category of *end (Zweck)* or *good (Gut)* arises from *volition*, the power or faculty of using the will, which refers to the *future*.[14] The redressive phase, in which feedback on crisis is provided by the scanning devices of law (secular ritual) and religious ritual, is a liminal time, set apart from the ongoing business of quotidian life, when an interpretation (*Bedeutung*) is constructed to give the appearance of sense and order to the events leading up to and constituting the crisis.

It is only the category of meaning, so Dilthey tells us, that enables us to conceive of an intrinsic affinity between the successive events of life or, one might add, of a social drama. In the redressive phase, the meaning of the social life informs the apprehension of itself, while the object to be apprehended enters into and reshapes the apprehending subject. Pure anthropological functionalism, whose aim is to state the conditions of social equilibrium among the components of a social system at a given time, cannot deal with meaning, for meaning always involves retrospection and reflexivity, a past, a history. Meaning is the only category which grasps the full relation of the part to the whole in life, for value, being dominantly affective, belongs essentially to an experience in a conscious present. Such conscious presents, regarded purely as present moments,

13. Barbara Myerhoff, *Life History among the Elderly: Performance, Visibility, and Remembering* (n.p., n.d.), p. 5.
14. See H. A. Hodges' *The Philosophy of Wilhelm Dilthey* (London, 1952), pp. 272–73.

totally involve the experiencer, even to the extent that these moments have no intrinsic connection with one another, at least of a systematic, cognitive kind. They stand behind one another in temporal sequence, and, while they may be compared as "values," that is, as having the same epistemological status, they do not form anything like a coherent whole, for they are essentially momentary, transient, insofar as they are values alone; if they are interconnected, the ligatures that bind them belong to another category—that of *meaning*, reflexivity arrived at. In stage drama, values would be the province of actors, meaning that of the producer. Reflexivity articulates experience. Dilthey eloquently hits off the unarticulated quality of value: "From the standpoint of value, life appears as an infinite assortment of positive and negative existence-values. It is like a chaos of harmonies and discords. Each of these is a tone-structure which fills a present; but they have *no musical relation* to one another" (my emphasis). To establish such a musical relation, the liminal reflexivity of the redressive phase is necessary if a crisis is to be rendered meaningful. Since crises *are* "like a chaos of harmonies and discords," some modern modalities of music try to replicate this chaos and let it stand as it is; for the meaning—ligatures inherited from the past—no longer bind. Here we must return to narrative.

For both legal and ritual procedures generate *narratives* from the brute facts, the mere empirical coexistence of experiences, and endeavor to lay hold of the factors making for integration in a given situation. Meaning is apprehended by *looking back* over a temporal process: it is generated in the narrative constructed by lawmen and judges in the process of cross-examination from witnesses' evidence or by diviners from their intuitions into the responses of their clients as framed by their specific hermeneutic techniques. The meaning of every part of the process is assessed by its contribution to the total result.

It will be noted that my basic social drama model is agonistic, rife with problem and conflict, and this is not merely because it assumes that sociocultural systems are never logical systems or harmonious *gestalten* but are fraught with structural contradictions and norm-conflicts. The true opposition should not be defined in these "objectivized" terms for it lies between indeterminacy and all modes of determination. Indeterminacy is, so to speak, in the subjunctive mood, since it is that which is not yet settled, concluded, and known. It is all that may be, might be, could be, perhaps even should be. It is that which terrifies in the breach and crisis phases of a social drama. Sally Falk Moore goes so far as to suggest that "the underlying quality of social life should be considered to be one of theoretical absolute indeterminacy."[15] Social reality is "fluid and indeterminate," though, for her, "regularizing processes" and "processes of situational adjustment" constantly represent human aspirations

15. Sally Falk Moore, *Law as Process* (London, 1978), p. 48.

to transform social reality into organized or systematic forms. But even where ordering rules and customs are strongly sanctioned, "indeterminacy may be produced and ambiguities within the universe of relatively determinate elements." Such manipulation is characteristic of breach and crisis. It may also help to resolve crisis.

The third phase, redress, reveals that "determining" and "fixing" are indeed processes, not permanent states or givens. These processes proceed by assigning meanings to events and relationships in reflexive narratives. Indeterminacy should not be regarded as the absence of social being; it is not negation, emptiness, privation. Rather, it is potentiality, the possibility of becoming. From this point of view social being is finitude, limitation, constraint. Actually it only exists as a set of cognitive models in actors' heads or as more or less coherent objectivized doctrines and protocols. Ritual and legal procedures mediate between the formed and the indeterminate. As Moore and Myerhoff argue, "ritual is a declaration of form *against* indeterminacy, therefore indeterminacy is always present in the background of any analysis of ritual."[16]

The social drama, then, I regard as the experiential matrix from which the many genres of cultural performance, beginning with redressive ritual and juridical procedures and eventually including oral and literary narrative, have been generated. Breach, crisis, and reintegrative or divisive outcomes provide the content of such later genres, redressive procedures their form. As society complexifies, as the division of labor produces more specialized and professionalized modalities of sociocultural action, so do the modes of assigning meaning to social dramas multiply—but the drama remains to the last simple and ineradicable, a fact of everyone's social experience and a significant node in the developmental cycle of all groups that aspire to continuance. The social drama remains humankind's thorny problem, its undying worm, its Achilles' heel—one can only use clichés for such an obvious and familiar pattern of sequentiality. At the same time it is our native way of manifesting ourselves to ourselves and of declaring where power and meaning lie and how they are distributed.

Rites of passage, like social dramas, involve temporal processes and agonistic relations—novices or initiands are separated (sometimes real or symbolic force is used) from a previous social state or status, compelled to remain in seclusion during the liminal phase, submitted to ordeal by initiated seniors or elders, and reaggregated to quotidian society in symbolic ways that often show that preritual ties have been irremediably broken and new relationships rendered compulsory. But, like other kinds of rituals, life-crisis rituals already exhibit a marked degree of generalization—they are the fairly late product of social reflexivity. They

---

16. Introduction to *Secular Ritual*, ed. Moore and Myerhoff (Amsterdam, 1977), p. 17; all further references to this work will be cited in the text.

confer on the actors, by nonverbal as well as verbal means, the experiential understanding that social life is a series of movements in space and time, a series of changes of activity, and a series of transitions in status for individuals. They also inscribe in the individuals the knowledge that such movements, changes, and transitions are not merely marked but also effected by ritual. Ritual and juridical procedures represent germinative components of social drama, from which, I suggest, many performative and narrative modes of complex culture derive. Cultural performances may be viewed as "dialectical dancing partners" (to use Ronald Grime's phrase) of the perennial social drama to which they give meaning appropriate to the specificities of time, place, and culture. However, they have their own autonomy and momentum: one genre may generate another; with sufficient evidence in certain cultural traditions one might be able to reconstruct a reasonably accurate genealogy of genres. (I use advisedly the terms genre, generate, genealogy, which are derived from the Indo-European root *gan* ["to beget or produce"] as metaphors for their ready cultural reproductiveness.) Or one genre might supplant or replace another as the historically or situationally dominant form of "social metacommentary" (to use Geertz's illuminating term). New communicative techniques and media may make possible wholly unprecedented genres of cultural performance and thus new modes of self-understanding. Once a genre has become prominent, however, it is likely to survive or be revived at some level of the sociocultural system, perhaps moving from the elite to the popular culture or vice versa, gaining and losing audiences and support in the process. Nevertheless, all the genres have to circle, as it were, around the earth of the social drama, and some, like satellites, may exert tidal effects on its inner structure. Since ritual in the so-called simpler societies is so complex and many-layered, it may not unfittingly be considered an important "source" of later (in cultural evolutionary terms), more specialized, performative genres. Often when ritual perishes as a dominant genre, it dies, a multipara, giving birth to ritualized progeny, including the many performative arts.

In earlier publications I defined "ritual" as "prescribed formal behavior for occasions not given over to technological routine, having reference to beliefs in invisible beings or powers regarded as the first and final causes of all effects"—a definition which owes much to those of Auguste Comte, Godfrey and Monica Wilson, and Ruth Benedict. I still find this formulation operationally useful despite Sir Edmund Leach, and other anthropologists of his ilk, who would eliminate the religious component and regard ritual as "stereotyped behavior which is potent in itself in terms of the cultural conventions of the actors, though not potent in a rational-technical sense," and which serves to communicate information about a culture's most cherished values. I find it useful because I like to think of ritual essentially as *performance*, as *enactment*, and not primarily as rules or rubrics. The rules frame the ritual process, but the ritual process transcends its frame. A river needs banks or it will be a dangerous flood, but banks without a river epitomize aridity. The term "performance" is, of course, derived from Old English *parfournir*, literally, "to furnish completely or thoroughly." To perform is thus to bring something about, to consummate something, or to "carry out" a play, order, or project. But in the carrying out, I hold, something new may be generated. The performance transforms itself. True, as I said, the rules may frame the performance, but the flow of action and inter-action within that frame may conduce to hitherto unprecedented in-sights and even generate new symbols and meanings, which may be incorporated into subsequent performances. Traditional framings may have to be reframed—new bottles made for new wine. It is here that I find the notion of orientation to preternatural and invisible beings and powers singularly apposite. For there is undoubtable transformative ca-pacity in a well-performed ritual, implying an ingress of power into the initial situation; and "performing well" implies the coinvolvement of the majority of its performers in a self-transcending flow of ritual events. The power may be drawn from the persons of the drama but drawn from their human depths, not entirely from their cognitive, "indicative" hold on cultural skills. Even if a rubrical book exists prescribing the order and character of the performance of the rites, this should be seen as a source of channelings rather than of dictates. The experience of subjective and intersubjective flow in ritual performance, whatever its sociobiological or personalogical concomitants may be, often convinces performers that the ritual situation *is* indeed informed with powers both transcendental and immanent.

Most anthropological definitions of ritual, moreover, including my own earlier attempts, have failed to take into account Arnold van Gen-nep's discovery that rituals nearly always "accompany transitions from one situation to another and from one cosmic or social world to another."[17]

As is well known, van Gennep divides these rituals into rites of separation, threshold rites, and rites of reaggregation, for which he also employs the terms "preliminal," "liminal," and "postliminal." The order in which the ritual events follow one another and must be performed, van Gennep points out, is a religious element of essential importance. To exist at all, writes Nicole Belmont about van Gennep's notion, "a ritual must first and foremost be inscribed in time and space or, rather, be reinscribed" if it follows "a prior model given in myth."[18] In other words, performative *sequencing* is intrinsic and should be taken into account in

---

17. Arnold van Gennep, *The Rites of Passage* (1908; London, 1960), p. 13.
18. Nicole Belmont, *Arnold van Gennep: The Creator of French Ethnography*, trans. Derek Coltman (Chicago, 1979), p. 64.

any definition of ritual. Here I would query the formal structuralist implication that sequence is an illusion and all is but a permutation and combination of rules and vocabularies already laid down in the deep structures of mind and brain. There *is* a qualitative distinction between successive stages in social dramas and rites of passage which renders them irreversible—their sequence is no illusion—the unidirectional movement is transformative. I have written at some length about the threshold or liminal phase of ritual and found it fruitful to extend the notion of liminality as metaphor beyond ritual to other domains of expressive cultural action. But liminality must be taken into account in any serious formulation of ritual as performance, for it is in connection with this phase that emic folk characterizations of ritual lay strongest stress on the transformative action of "invisible or supernatural beings or powers regarded as the first and final causes of all effects." Without taking liminality into account, ritual becomes indistinguishable from "ceremony," "formality," or what Myerhoff and Moore, in their introduction to *Secular Ritual,* indeed call *"secular* ritual." The liminal phase is the essential, *anti*secular component in true ritual, whether it be labeled "religious" or "magical." Ceremony *indicates,* ritual *transforms,* and transformation occurs most radically in the ritual "pupation" of liminal seclusion—at least in life-crisis rituals. The public liminality of great seasonal feasts exhibits its fantasies and "transforms"[19] to the eyes of all—and so does postmodern theater, but that is a matter for a different essay.

I have also argued that ritual in its performative plenitude in tribal and many post-tribal cultures is a matrix from which several other genres of cultural performance, including most of those we tend to think of as "aesthetic," have been derived. It is a late modern Western myth, encouraged perhaps by depth psychologists and, lately, by ethologists, that ritual has the rigid precision characteristics of the "ritualized" behavior of an obsessive neurotic or a territory-marking animal or bird, and it is also encouraged by an early modern Puritan myth that ritual is "mere empty form without true religious content." It is true that rituals may become mere shells or husks at certain historical junctures, but this state of affairs belongs to the senescence or pathology of the ritual process, not to its "normal working." Living ritual may be better likened to artwork than to neurosis. Ritual is, in its most typical cross-cultural expressions, a synchronization of many performative genres and is often ordered by a *dramatic* structure, a plot, frequently involving an act of sacrifice or self-sacrifice, which energizes and gives emotional coloring to the interdependent communicative codes which express in manifold

19. Akin here to the linguistic sense of "transform," that is, (*a*), any of a set of rules for producing grammatical transformations of a kernel sentence; (*b*), a sentence produced by using such a role.

ways the meanings inherent in the dramatic leitmotiv. Insofar as it is "dramatic," ritual contains a distanced and generalized reduplication of the agonistic process of the social drama. Ritual, therefore, is not "threadbare" but "richly textured" by virtue of its varied interweavings of the productions of mind and senses.

Participants in the major rituals of vital religions, whether tribal or post-tribal, may be passive and active in turn with regard to the ritual movement, which, as van Gennep and, more recently, Roland Delattre have shown, draws on biological, climatic, and ecological rhythms, as well as on social rhythms, as models for the processual forms it sequentially employs in its episodic structure. *All* the senses of participants and performers may be engaged; they *hear* music and prayers, *see* visual symbols, *taste* consecrated foods, *smell* incense, and *touch* sacred persons and objects. They also have available the kinesthetic forms of dance and gesture and perhaps cultural repertoires of facial expression to bring them into significant performative rapport. I should mention in this connection Judith Lynne Hanna's useful book *To Dance Is Human: A Theory of Nonverbal Communication* in which she attempts to construct a sociocultural theory of dance.[20] In song, participants merge (and diverge) in other ordered and symbolic ways. Moreover, few rituals are so completely stereotyped that every word, every gesture, every scene is authoritatively prescribed. Most often, invariant phases and episodes are interdigitated with variable passages in which, both at the verbal and nonverbal levels, improvisation may not be merely permitted but required. Like the black and white keys of a piano, like the yin and yang interplay in Chinese religious cosmology and Taoist ritual, constancy and mutability make up, in their contrariety, a total instrument for the expression of human meaning—joyous, sorrowful, and both at once, "woven fine," in William Blake's words. Ritual, in fact, far from being merely formal, or formulaic, is a symphony in more than music. It can be, and often is, a symphony or synesthestic ensemble of expressive cultural genres or a synergy of varied symbolic operations, an opus which unlike "opera" escapes opera's theatricality, though never life's inexpugnable social drama, by virtue of the seriousness of its ultimate concerns.

The "flat" view of ritual must go. So also must the notion, beloved until recently by functionalist anthropologists, that ritual could be best understood as a set of mechanisms for promoting a gross group solidarity, as a "sort of all-purpose social glue," as Robin Horton characterized this position; its symbols are *not* merely "reflections or expressions of components of social structure." Ritual, in its full performative flow, is not only many-leveled, "laminated," but also capable, under conditions

20. Judith Lynne Hanna, *To Dance Is Human: A Theory of Nonverbal Communication* (Austin, Tex., 1979).

of societal change, of creative modification on all or any of its levels. Since it is tacitly held to communicate the deepest values of the group regularly performing it, it has a "paradigmatic" function, in both of the senses argued for by Geertz. As a "model for," ritual can anticipate, even generate, change; as a "model of," it may inscribe order in the minds, hearts, and wills of participants.

Ritual, in other words, is not only complex and many-layered; it has an *abyss* in it and, indeed, it is an effort to make meaningful the dialectical relation of what the Silesian mystic Jakob Boehme, following Meister Eckhart, called "Ground and Unground," "Byss and Abyss" (= the Greek *a-bussos,* άβυσσος, from *a* ["without"] and the Ionic variant of the Attic *buthos,* βύθος, meaning "bottom" or, better, "depth" [finite], especially "of the sea." So "byss" is deep but "abyss" is beyond all depth). Many definitions of ritual contain the notion of "depth" but few of "infinite" depth. In other words, such definitions are concerned with finite structural depth but not with infinite "antistructural" depth. A homelier analogy, drawn from linguistics, would be to say that the passage form of ritual, as elicited by van Gennep, postulates a unidirectional move from the "indicative" mood of cultural process through culture's "subjunctive" mood back to the "indicative" mood, though this recovered mood has now been tempered, even transformed, by immersion in subjunctivity; this process roughly corresponds with van Gennep's preliminal, liminal, and postliminal phases.

In preliminal rites of separation the initiand is moved from the indicative quotidian social structure into the subjunctive antistructure of the liminal process and is then returned, transformed by liminal experiences, by the rites of reaggregation to social structural participation in the indicative mood. The subjunctive, according to *Webster's Dictionary,* is always concerned with "wish, desire, possibility, or hypothesis"; it is a world of "as if," ranging from scientific hypothesis to festive fantasy. It is "if it *were* so," not "it *is* so." The indicative prevails in the world of what in the West we call "actual fact," though this definition can range from a close scientific inquiry into how a situation, event, or agent produces an effect or result to a layperson's description of the characteristics of ordinary good sense or sound practical judgment.

Moore and Myerhoff, in *Secular Ritual,* did not use this pair of terms, "subjunctive" and "indicative," but, rather, saw social process as moving "between the formed and the indeterminate" (p. 17). They are, however, mostly discussing "ceremony" or "secular ritual," not pure ritual. I agree with them, as I said earlier, that "all collective ceremony can be interpreted as a cultural statement about cultural order as against a cultural void" (p. 16) and that "ceremony is a declaration against indeterminacy. Through form and formality it celebrates man-made meaning, the culturally determinate, the regulated, the named, and the explained. It banishes from consideration the basic questions raised by the made-upness of culture, its malleability and alterability. . . . [Every ceremony] seeks to state that the cosmos and social world, or some particular small part of them are orderly and explicable and for the moment fixed. A ceremony can allude to such propositions and demonstrate them at the same time. . . . Ritual [really "ceremony"] is a declaration of form *against* indeterminacy, therefore indeterminacy is always present in the background of any analysis of ritual" (pp. 16–17). Roy Rappaport in his recent book, *Ecology, Meaning, and Religion,* adopts a similar standpoint when he writes: "Liturgical orders [whose "sequential dimension," he says, is ritual] bind together disparate entities and processes, and it is this binding together, rather than what is bound together, that is peculiar to them. Liturgical orders are meta-orders, or orders of orders. . . . they mend ever again worlds forever breaking apart under the blows of usage and the slashing distinctions of language."[21]

While I consider these to be admirably lucid statements about ceremony, which for me constitutes an impressive institutionalized performance of indicative, normatively structured social reality and is also both a model *of* and a model *for* social states and statuses, I do not think such formulations can be applied with equal cogency to ritual. For ritual, as I have said, does not portray a dualistic, almost Manichaean, struggle between order and void, cosmos and chaos, form and indeterminacy, with the former always triumphing in the end. It is, rather, a transformative self-immolation of order as presently constituted, even sometimes a voluntary *sparagmos* or self-dismemberment of order, in the subjunctive depths of liminality. One thinks of Eliade's studies of the "shaman's journey" where the initiand is broken into pieces and then put together again as a being bridging visible and invisible worlds. Only in this way, through destruction and reconstruction, that is, transformation, may an authentic reordering come about. Actuality takes the sacrificial plunge into possibility and emerges as a different kind of actuality. We are not here in the presence of two like but opposed forces as in Manichaean myth; rather there is a qualitative incongruence between the contraries engaged, though Jung's daring metaphor of the incestuous marriage of the conscious ego with the unconscious seen as an archetypal mother poses that relationship in terms of paradoxical kinship and affinity. Subjunctivity is fittingly the mother of indicativity, since any actualization is only one among a myriad of possibilities of being, some of which may be actualized in space-time somewhere or somewhen else. The hard saying "except ye become as a little child" assumes new meaning. Unless the fixing and ordering processes of the adult, the *sociostructural* domain, are liminally abandoned and the initiand submits

---

21. Roy Rappaport, *Ecology, Meaning, and Religion* (Richmond, Cal., 1979), p. 206.

to being broken down to a generalized *prima materia,* a lump of human clay, he cannot be transformed or reshaped to encounter new experiences.

Ritual's liminal phase, then, approximates to the "subjunctive mood" of sociocultural action. It is, quintessentially, a time and place lodged between all times and spaces defined and governed in any specific biocultural ecosystem (Andrew Vayda, John Bennett, and the like) by the rules of law, politics, and religion and by economic necessity. Here the cognitive schemata that give sense and order to everyday life no longer apply but are, as it were, suspended—in ritual symbolism perhaps even shown as destroyed or dissolved. Gods and goddesses of destruction are adored primarily because they personify an essential phase in an irreversible transformative process. All further growth requires the immolation of that which was fundamental to an earlier stage—"lest one good custom should corrupt the world." Clearly, the liminal space-time "pod" created by ritual action, or today by certain kinds of reflexively ritualized theater, is potentially perilous. For it may be opened up to energies of the biopsychical human constitution normally channeled by socialization into status-role activities, to employ the unwieldy jargon of the social sciences. Nevertheless, the danger of the liminal phase conceded and respected by hedging it around by ritual interdictions and tabus, it is also held in most cultures to be regenerative, as I mentioned earlier. For in liminality what is mundanely bound in sociostructural form may be unbound and rebound. Of course, if a society is in hairline-precarious subsistence balance with its environment, we are unlikely to find in its liminal zones very much in the way of experimentation—here one does not fool around with the tried and tested. But when a "biocultural ecosystem," to use Vayda's term, produces significant surpluses, even if these are merely the seasonal boons of a naturally well-endowed environment, the liminality of its major rituals may well generate cultural surpluses too. One thinks of the Kwakiutl and other northwest Amerindian peoples with their complex iconographies and formerly rich hunting and gathering resources. New meanings and symbols may be introduced or new ways of portraying or embellishing old models for living, and so of renewing interest in them. Ritual liminality, therefore, contains the potentiality for cultural innovation as well as the means for effecting structural transformations within a relatively stable sociocultural system. For many transformations are, of course, within the limits of social structure and have to do with its internal adjustments and external adaptions to environmental changes. Cognitive structuralism can cope best with such relatively cyclical and repetitive societies.

In tribal and agrarian cultures, even relatively complex ones, the innovative potential of ritual liminality seems to have been circumscribed, even dormant, or pressed into the service of maintaining the existing social order. Even so, room for "play," Huizinga's *ludic*, abounds in many kinds of tribal rituals, even in funerary rituals. There is a play of *symbol*-vehicles, leading to the construction of bizarre masks and costumes from elements of mundane life now conjoined in fantastic ways. There is a play of *meanings*, involving the reversal of hierarchical orderings of values and social statuses. There is a play with *words*, resulting in the generation of secret initiatory languages as well as joyful or serious punning. Even the dramatic scenarios which give many rituals their processual armature may be presented as comedic rather than serious or tragic. Riddling and joking may take place, even in the liminal seclusion of initiatory lodges. Recent studies of Pueblo ritual clowns recall to us how widespread the clown role is in tribal and archaic religious culture. Liminality is peculiarly conducive to play, where it is not restricted to games and jokes, and extends to the introduction of new forms of symbolic action, such as word games or original masks.

But whatever happened to liminality as societies increased in scale and complexity, particularly Western industrial societies? With de-liminalization seems to have gone the powerful *play* component. Other religions of the Book, too, have tended regularly to stress the solemn at the expense of the festive. Religiously connected fairs, fiestas, and carnivals do continue to exist, of course, but not as intrinsic parts of liturgical systems. The great Oriental religions, Hinduism, Taoism, Tantric Buddhism, Shintoism, however, still recognize in many public performances that human ritual can be both earnest *and* playful. Eros may sport with Thanatos not as a grisly danse macabre but to symbolize a complete human reality and a nature full of oddities.

It would seem that with industrialization, urbanization, spreading literacy, labor migration, specialization, professionalization, bureaucracy, the division of the leisure sphere from the work sphere, the former integrity of the orchestrated religious gestalt that once constituted ritual has burst open and many specialized performative genres have been born from the death of that mighty *opus deorum hominumque*. These genres of industrial leisure would include theater, ballet, opera, film, the novel, printed poetry, the art exhibition, classical music, rock music, carnivals, processions, folk drama, major sports events, and dozens more. Disintegration has been accompanied by secularization. Traditional religions, their rituals denuded of much of their former symbolic wealth and meaning, hence their transformative capacity, persist in the leisure sphere but have not adapted well to modernity. Modernity means the exaltation of the indicative mood; but in what Ihab Hassan has called the "postmodern turn" we may be seeing a re-turn to subjunctivity and a rediscovery of cultural transformative modes, particularly in some forms of theater. Dismembering may be a prelude to remembering, which is not merely restoring some past intact but setting it in living relationship to the present.

There are signs, however, that those nations and cultures which came late to the industrial table, such as Japan, India, the Middle Eastern nations, and much of South and Central America, have succeeded, at least in part, in avoiding the dismemberment of important ritual types; they have incorporated into their ritual performances many of the issues and problems of modern urban living and succeeded in giving them religious meaning. When industrial development came to much of the Third World it had to confront powerfully consolidated structures of ritual performative genres. In the West similar institutions had been gradually eroded from within, from the revival of learning to the Industrial Revolution. Here the indicative mood triumphed, and subjunctivity was relegated to a reduced domain where admittedly it shone more brightly in the arts than in religion.

Religion, like art, *lives* insofar as it is performed, that is, insofar as its rituals are "going concerns." If you wish to spay or geld religion, first remove its rituals, its generative and regenerative processes. For religion is not a cognitive system, a set of dogmas, alone; it is meaningful experience and experienced meaning. In ritual one *lives through* events or through the alchemy of its framings and symbolings; one *re*lives semiogenetic events, the deeds and words of prophets and saints or, if these are absent, myths and sacred epics.

If, then, we regard narrative as an emic Western genre or metagenre of expressive culture, it has to be seen as one of the cultural grandchildren or great-grandchildren of "tribal" ritual or juridical process. But if we regard narrative etically, as the supreme instrument for binding the "values" and "goals," in Dilthey's sense of these terms, which motivate human conduct into situational structures of "meaning," then we must concede it to be a universal cultural activity, embedded in the very center of the social drama, itself another cross-cultural and transtemporal unit of social process.

"Narrate" is from the Latin *narrare* ("to tell") which is akin to the Latin *gnārus* ("knowing," "acquainted with," "expert in") both derivative from the Indo-European root *gnâ* ("to know") whence the vast family of words deriving from the Latin *cognoscere,* including "cognition" itself, and "noun" and "pronoun," the Greek *gignōskein,* whence *gnōsis,* and the Old English past participle *gecnawan,* whence the Modern English "know." Narrative is, it would seem, rather an appropriate term for a reflexive activity which seeks to "know" (even in its ritual aspect, to have *gnōsis* about) antecedent events and the meaning of those events. *Drama* itself is, of course, derived from the Greek *drân* ("to do or act"); hence narrative is knowledge (and/or *gnōsis*) emerging from action, that is, experiential knowledge. The redressive phase of social drama frames an endeavor to rearticulate a social group broken by sectional or self-serving interests; in like manner, the narrative component in ritual and legal action attempts to rearticulate opposing values and goals in a meaningful structure, the plot of which makes cultural sense. Where historical life itself fails to make cultural sense in terms that formerly held good, narrative and cultural drama may have the task of *poesis,* that is, of remaking cultural sense, even when they seem to be dismantling ancient edifices of meaning that can no longer redress our modern "dramas of living"—now evermore on a global and species-threatening scale.

Narrative Time

Paul Ricoeur

My aim in this paper is to investigate the topic of narrative time. My approach to the problem of the "illusion of sequence" is derived from two complementary claims. If by sequence we mean chronological time, and if by illusion of sequence we mean the illusion of chronology, we may be correct; but such a critique of chronology does not dispose of the question of time. On the contrary, such a critique opens the way for a more authentic reflection on narrative time. The complementary claim is that there is another response to the illusion of sequence than the recourse to a-chronological models, such as nomological laws in history or paradigmatic codes in literary criticism. This other response consists in elucidating a deeper experience of time, one that escapes the dichotomy between the chronology of sequence and the a-chronology of models.

1. Presuppositions

My first working hypothesis is that narrativity and temporality are closely related—as closely as, in Wittgenstein's terms, a language game and a form of life. Indeed, I take temporality to be that structure of existence that reaches language in narrativity and narrativity to be the language structure that has temporality as its ultimate referent. Their relationship is therefore reciprocal.

This structural reciprocity of temporality and narrativity is usually overlooked because, on the one hand, the epistemology of history and the literary criticism of fictional narratives take for granted that every narrative takes place within an uncriticized temporal framework, within a time that corresponds to the ordinary representation of time as a linear succession of instants. Philosophers writing on time, too, usually overlook the contribution of narrative to a critique of the concept of time. They either look to cosmology and physics to supply the meaning of time or they try to specify the inner experience of time without any reference to narrative activity. Narrative function and the human experience of time thus remain strangers. In order to show the reciprocity between narrativity and temporality, I shall conduct this study as an analysis with two foci: for each feature of narrative brought out by reflection on either history or fictional narrative, I shall attempt to find a corresponding feature of temporality brought out by an existential analysis of time.

A second working hypothesis intervenes here: starting from the pole of temporality, there are different degrees of temporal organization. While this idea stems from division II of Heidegger's *Being and Time,*[1] one will not find here a blind submission to Heidegger's analyses. Quite the contrary; on the essential points, important and even fundamental corrections in the Heideggerian conception of time will result from applying a Heideggerian framework to the question of narrativity, along with some recourse to other great philosophers of temporality and historicality, from Aristotle and Augustine to Gadamer. From the outset, however, I agree with Heidegger that the ordinary representation of time as a linear series of "nows" hides the true constitution of time, which, if we follow the inverse order of that presented in *Being and Time,* is divided into at least three levels.

At the level closest to that of the ordinary representation of time, the first temporal structure is that of time as that "in" which events take place. It is precisely this temporal structure that is leveled off by the ordinary representation of time. An analysis of narrative will help to show in what way this "within-time-ness" already differs from linear time, even though it tends toward linearity due to its datable, public, and measurable nature and as a result of its dependence on points of reference in the world.

1. Martin Heidegger, *Being and Time,* trans. John Macquarrie and Edward Robinson (New York, 1962); all further references to this work will be included in the text.

Paul Ricoeur is professor of philosophy at the Université de Paris (Nanterre) and John Nuveen Professor at the University of Chicago. His most recent works to appear in English are *Husserl: An Analysis of His Phenomenology, Main Trends in Philosophy,* and *The Conflict of Interpretations: Essays on Hermeneutics.* His previous contribution to *Critical Inquiry,* "The Metaphorical Process as Cognition, Imagination, and Feeling," appeared in the Autumn 1978 issue.

At a deeper level, time is more properly "historicality." This term does not coincide with the within-time-ness of which I have just spoken, nor with "temporality" as such, which refers to the deepest level. Let us restrict ourselves here to characterizing historicality in terms of the emphasis placed on the weight of the past and, even more, in terms of the power of recovering the "extension" between birth and death in the work of "repetition." This final trait is so decisive that, according to Heidegger, it alone permits objective history to be grounded in historicality. Finally, Heidegger invites us to move beyond historicality itself to the point at which temporality springs forth in the plural unity of future, past, and present. It is here that the analysis of time is rooted in that of "care," particularly as care reflecting on itself as mortal.

Joining this second working hypothesis to the first, I shall try to check the successive stages of the analysis of temporality itself against an analysis of narrativity, which is itself composed of several levels.

My third working hypothesis concerns the role of narrativity. The narrative structure that I have chosen as the most relevant for an investigation of the temporal implications of narrativity is that of the "plot." By plot I mean the intelligible whole that governs a succession of events in any story. This provisory definition immediately shows the plot's connecting function between an event or events and the story. A story is *made out of* events to the extent that plot *makes* events *into* a story. The plot, therefore, places us at the crossing point of temporality and narrativity: to be historical, an event must be more than a singular occurrence, a unique happening. It receives its definition from its contribution to the development of a plot. Still, the temporal implications of the plot, on which my whole paper focuses, are precisely those overlooked by anti-narrativist writers in the field of historiography and by structuralists in the field of literary criticism. In both fields, the emphasis on nomological models and paradigmatic codes results in a trend that reduces the narrative component to the anecdotic surface of the story. Thus both the theory of history and the theory of fictional narratives seem to take it for granted that whenever there is time, it is always a time laid out chronologically, a linear time, defined by a succession of instants.

My suspicion is that both anti-narrativist epistemologists and structuralist literary critics have overlooked the temporal complexity of the narrative matrix constituted by the plot. Because most historians have a poor concept of "event"—and even of "narrative"—they consider history to be an explanatory endeavor that has severed its ties with storytelling. And the emphasis on the surface grammar in literary narration leads literary critics to what seems to me to be a false dichotomy: either remaining caught in the labyrinthine chronology of the told story or moving radically to an a-chronological model. This dismissal of narrative as such implies a similar lack of concern in both camps for the properly *temporal* aspects of narrative and therefore for the contribution that the theory of narrative could offer to a phenomenology of time experience. To put it bluntly, this contribution has been almost null because *time* has disappeared from the horizon of the theories of history and of narrative. Theoreticians of these two broad fields seem even to be moved by a strange resentment toward time, the kind of resentment that Nietzsche expressed in his *Zarathustra*.

2. What Occurs Happens "in" Time

I will now fashion together a theory of narrative and a theory of time and, by moving back and forth between them, attempt to correlate the stages of the analysis of narrative with the different depths in the analysis of time. If, in this effort at comparison, the analysis of time most often performs the role of guide, the analysis of narrative, in its turn, serves as a critical and decisive corrective to it.

At the first level of our inquiry, the relation to time expressed by the preposition "in"—to happen "in" time—serves as our guide. What is at stake in an existential analysis—such as Heidegger's—is the possibility of discerning those characteristics by which within-time-ness differs from the ordinary representation of time, even though it is easily leveled off into this representation. I shall compare this existential analysis of time with the analysis of what may seem most superficial in narrativity, that is, the *development* of a plot and its correlate, the ability *to follow* a story.

First, a brief review of the main features of the Heideggerian analysis of within-time-ness: this level is defined by one of the basic characteristics of care—our thrownness among things—which makes the description of our temporality dependent on the description of the things of our concern. Heidegger calls these things of our concern *das Vorhandene* ("subsisting things which our concern counts on") and *das Zuhandene* ("utensils offered to our manipulation"). Heidegger calls this trait of concern "preoccupation" or "circumspection." As we shall see later, concern has other traits that are more deeply hidden, and because of these hidden, deep traits, it has fundamental temporal modes. But however inauthentic our relationship to things, to ourselves, and to time may be, preoccupation, the everyday mode of concern, nevertheless already includes characteristics that take it out of the external domain of the objects of our concern, referring it instead to our concern in its existential constitution. It is remarkable that in order to point out these properly existential characteristics, Heidegger readily turns to what we say and do with regard to time. This method is, not surprisingly, very close to that found in ordinary language philosophy: the plane on which we are placing ourselves in this initial phase of investigation is precisely the one on which ordinary language truly is what J. L. Austin and others have said it is, namely, a treasure-house of expressions appropriate to what is specifically human in experience. It is therefore language, with its storehouse of meanings, that keeps the description of concern, in the modality of preoccupation or circumspection, from slipping back into the description of the things of our concern and from remaining tied to the sphere of *vorhanden* and *zuhanden*.

Within-time-ness, then, possesses its own specific features which are not reducible to the representation of linear time, a neutral series of abstract instants. Being in time is already something quite different from measuring intervals between limiting instants; it is first of all *to reckon with* time and so to calculate. It is because we do reckon with time and make calculations that we have the need to measure, not the other way around. It should therefore be possible to give an existential description of this reckoning before the measuring it calls for. It is here that expressions such as "having time to," "taking time to," "wasting time," and so on, are most revealing. The same is true of the grammatical network of verbal tenses, and likewise of the far-ranging network of adverbs of time: then, after, later, earlier, since, till, while, until, whenever, now that, and so forth. All these extremely subtle and finely differentiated expressions point out the datable and public character of the time of preoccupation.

It is our preoccupation, not the things of our concern, that determines the sense of time. It is because there is a *time to do* this, a right time and a wrong time, that we can reckon *with* time. If within-time-ness is so easily interpreted in terms of the ordinary representation of time, this is because the first measurements of the time of our preoccupation are borrowed from the natural environment—first of all from the play of light and of the seasons. In this respect, a day is the most natural of measures. "Dasein," Heidegger says, "historizes *from day to day*" (p. 466). But a day is not an abstract measure; it is a magnitude which corresponds to our concern and to the world into which we are thrown. The time it measures is that in which it is *time to* do something *(Zeit zu)*, where "now" means "now that"; it is the time of labors and days. It is therefore important to see the shift in meaning that distinguishes the "now" belonging to this time of preoccupation from "now" in the sense of an abstract instant, which as part of a series defines the line of ordinary time. The existential now is determined by the present of preoccupation, which is a "making-present," inseparable from awaiting and retaining. It is because, in preoccupation, concern tends to contract itself into this making-present and to obliterate its dependency with regard to awaiting and retaining that the now isolated in this way can fall prey to the representation of the now as an isolated abstract instant. In order to preserve the meaning of now from this reduction to an abstraction, it is important to attend to the way in which we "say now" *(Jetzt-sagen)* in everyday acting and suffering. "Saying 'now,'" says Heidegger, "is the discursive Articulation of a *making-present* which temporalizes itself in a unity with a retentive awaiting" (p. 469). And again, "The making-present which interprets itself—in other words, that which has been interpreted and is addressed in the 'now'—is what we call 'time'" (p. 460). So we see how, as a result of certain practical circumstances, this interpretation is bent in the direction of the representation of linear time. Saying "now" becomes for us synonymous with reading the hour on the face of a clock. As long as the hour and the clock are still perceived as derivations of the day that links concern with the light of the world, saying "now" retains its existential significance; but when the machines used to measure time are cut off from this primary reference to natural measures, saying "now" is turned into a form of the abstract representation of time.

Turning to narrative activity, I shall now attempt to show that the time of the simplest story also escapes the ordinary notion of time conceived of as a series of instants succeeding one another along an abstract line oriented in a single direction. The phenomenology of the act of following a story may serve as our point of departure.[2] Let us say that a story describes a series of actions and experiences made by a number of characters, whether real or imaginary. These characters are represented either in situations that change or as they relate to changes to which they then react. These changes, in turn, reveal hidden aspects of the situation and of the characters and engender a new predicament that calls for thinking, action, or both. The answer to this predicament advances the story to its conclusion.

Following a story, correlatively, is understanding the successive actions, thoughts, and feelings in question insofar as they present a certain directedness. By this I mean that we are pushed ahead by this development and that we reply to its impetus with expectations concerning the outcome and the completion of the entire process. In this sense, the story's conclusion is the pole of attraction of the entire development. But a narrative conclusion can be neither deduced nor predicted. There is no story if our attention is not moved along by a thousand contingencies. This is why a story has to be followed to its conclusion. So rather than being predictable, a conclusion must be acceptable. Looking back from the conclusion to the episodes leading up to it, we have to be able to say that this ending required these sorts of events and this chain of actions. But this backward look is made possible by the teleological movement directed by our expectations when we follow the story. This is the paradox of contingency, judged "acceptable after all," that characterizes the comprehension of any story told.

2. Here I am borrowing from W. B. Gallie's *Philosophy and the Historical Understanding* (New York, 1964).

If we now compare this brief analysis of the development of a plot to the Heideggerian concept of within-time-ness, we can say that the narrative structure confirms the existential analysis. To begin, it is clear that the art of storytelling places the narrative "in" time. The art of storytelling is not so much a way of reflecting on time as a way of taking it for granted. We can apply to storytelling Heidegger's remark that "factical Dasein takes time into its reckoning, without any existential understanding of temporality" (p. 456). And it is indeed to factical *Dasein* that the art of storytelling belongs, even when the narrative is fictional. It is this art that makes all the adverbs enumerated above directly significant—then, next, now, and so on. When someone, whether storyteller or historian, starts recounting, everything is already spread out in time. In this sense, narrative activity, taken without further reflection, participates in the dissimulation both of historicality and, even more so, of the deeper levels of temporality. But at the same time, it implicitly states the truth of within-time-ness insofar as it possesses its own authenticity, the authenticity of its inauthenticity, if one may so put it, and it therefore presents an existential structure quite as original as the other two existential categories of time that frame it.

To take an example, the heroes of stories reckon *with* time. They have or do not have time *for* this or that. Their time can be gained or lost. It is true to say that we measure this time of the story because we count it and that we count it because we reckon with it. The time of the story retains this reckoning at the threshold of measurement, at the point where it reveals our thrownness, by which we are abandoned to the changing of day into night. This time already includes the sort of reckoning used in dating events, but it is not yet the time in which the natural measure of "days" is replaced by artificial measures, that is, measures taken from physics and based on an instrumentation that follows the progress of the investigation of nature. In a narrative, the measuring of time is not yet released from time reckoning because this reckoning is still visibly rooted in preoccupation. It is as true to say of narrative as of preoccupation that the "day" is the natural measure and that "Dasein historizes *from day to day*."

For these reasons, the time of a narrative is public time, but not in the sense of ordinary time, indifferent to human beings, to their acting and their suffering. Narrative time is public time in the same sense that within-time-ness is, before it is leveled off by ordinary time. Moreover, the art of storytelling retains this public character of time while keeping it from falling into anonymity. It does so, first, as time common to the actors, as time woven in common by their interaction. On the level of the narrative, of course, "others" exist: the hero has antagonists and helpers; the object of the quest is someone else or something else that another can give or withhold. The narrative confirms that "in the 'most intimate' Being-with-one-another of several people, they can say '*now*' and say it 'together.' . . . The 'now' which anyone expresses is always said in the publicness of Being-in-the-world with one another" (p. 463).

This first side of public time is, in some sense, internal to the interaction. But the narrative has a second relationship to public time: external public time or, we might say, the time of the public. Now a story's public is its audience. Through its recitation, a story is incorporated into a community which it gathers together. It is only through the written text that the story is open to a public that, to borrow Gadamer's expression, amounts to anyone who can read. The published work is the measure of this public. But even so, this public is not just anyone at all, it is not "they"; instead, it is they lifted out of anonymity in order to make up an invisible audience, those whom Nietzsche called "my own." This public does not fall back into they—in the sense in which a work is said to fall into the public domain—except through a leveling off similar to that by which within-time-ness is reduced to ordinary time, knowing neither day nor hour, recognizing no "right" time because no one feels concerned by it.

A final trait of within-time-ness is illustrated by the time of the narrative. It concerns the primacy of the present in preoccupation. We saw that for Heidegger, "saying now" is interpreting the making-present which is accorded a certain preference by preoccupation, at the expense of awaiting and retaining. But it is when within-time-ness is leveled off that saying "now" slips into the mathematical representation of the instant characteristic of ordinary time. "Saying now" must therefore continually be carried back to making-present if this abstract representation is to be avoided.

Now narratives invite a similar, yet quite original, reinterpretation of this "saying now." For a whole category of narratives, in fact (those which according to Robert Scholes and Robert Kellogg stem from the epic matrix[3] and those which Vladimir Propp and Algirdas Greimas place under the title of the quest), narrative activity is the privileged discursive expression of preoccupation and its making-present. It is privileged because these narratives exhibit a feature that the Heideggerian analysis of saying "present"—an analysis that is too brief and too centered around "reading the hour"—does not encounter, namely, the phenomenon of "intervention" (which, by way of contrast, is at the center of Henrik von Wright's analyses in action theory). These narratives, in fact, represent a person acting, who orients him- or herself in circumstances he or she has not created, and who produces consequences he or she has not intended. This is indeed the time of the "now that . . . ," wherein a person is both abandoned and responsible at the same time.

3. See Robert Scholes and Robert Kellogg's *The Nature of Narrative* (New York, 1966).

The dialectical character of this "now that . . ." appears, however, only as it is unfolded narratively in the interplay between being able to act and being bound to the world order. This interplay accentuates both what distinguishes within-time-ness from abstract time and what makes the interpretation of within-time-ness lean toward the representation of abstract time. On the one hand, the narrative's making-present is the instant of suffering and acting, the moment when the actor knowing, in a nonrepresentative way, what he or she can do, in fact does it. This is the moment when, according to Claude Bremond, possible action becomes actual, moving toward its completion.[4] This present of praxic intervention has, therefore, nothing in common with the mathematical instant; one could say of it, with Heidegger, that it "temporalizes itself in a unity with awaiting and retaining" (p. 459). Yet the fall into the representation of ordinary time is, in a sense, also lodged in this very structure of intervention. Days and hours are, of course, as much intimate measures of action caught up in circumstances as they are external measures punctuating the sovereign firmament. Nevertheless, in the instant of acting, when the agent seizes hold of such circumstances and inserts his or her action into the course of things, the temporal guides provided by the chain of meaning attached to manipulable objects tend to make world time prevail over the time of action. So it is in the phenomenon of intervention, in which our powers of action are linked to the world order, that what could be termed the structure of intersection characteristic of within-time-ness is constituted, in the nether zone between ordinary time and true historicality. Thus in this sense, narrative shows how concern "interprets itself" in the saying "now." The heroic quest is the privileged medium for this self-presentation. It, more than any other form, is the narrative of preoccupation.

The time of the plot, however, provides much more than an illustration of the existential analysis of within-time-ness. We have already seen that the actor's intervention in the course of the world affords a more refined and more dialectical analysis than Heidegger's analysis of making-present and saying "now." Turning our investigation now from narrative theory back to the theory of time, we must deal with a basic characteristic of plot that I have up to now neglected.

If so many authors have hastily identified narrative time and chronological time at the level of surface grammar—or, in Greimas' terms, at the level of manifestation—it is because they have neglected a fundamental feature of a narrative's temporal dialectic. This trait characterizes the plot as such, that is, as the objective correlate of the act of following a story. This fundamental trait, which was already implied in my definition of events made into story through the plot, may be

4. See Claude Bremond's "La Logique des possibles narratifs," *Communications* 8 (1966): 60–76.

described as follows: every narrative combines two dimensions in various proportions, one chronological and the other nonchronological. The first may be called the episodic dimension, which characterizes the story as made out of events. The second is the configurational dimension, according to which the plot construes significant wholes out of scattered events. Here I am borrowing from Louis O. Mink the notion of a configurational act, which he interprets as a "grasping together." [5] I understand this act to be the act of the plot, as eliciting a pattern from a succession. This act displays the character of a judgment or, more precisely, a reflective judgment in the Kantian sense of this term.[6] To tell and to follow a story is already to reflect upon events in order to encompass them in successive wholes. This dimension is completely overlooked in the theory of history proposed by anti-narrativist writers. They tend to deprive narrative activity of its complexity and, above all, of its twofold characteristic of confronting and combining both sequence and pattern in various ways. This antithetical dynamic is no less overlooked in the theory of fictional narratives proposed by structuralists, who take it for granted that the surface grammar of what they call the "plane of manifestation" is merely episodic and therefore purely chronological. They then conclude that the principle of order has to be found at the higher level of a-chronological models or codes. Anti-narrativist historians and structuralists thus share a common prejudice: they do not see that the humblest narrative is always more than a chronological series of events and that in turn the configurational dimension cannot overcome the episodic dimension without suppressing the narrative structure itself.[7]

The temporal implications of this twofold structure of the plot are so striking that we may already conjecture that narrative does more than just establish humanity, along with human actions and passions, "in" time; it also brings us back from within-time-ness to historicality, from "reckoning with" time to "recollecting" it. As such, the narrative function provides a transition from within-time-ness to historicality.

The temporal dialectic, then, is implied in the basic operation of eliciting a configuration from a succession. Thanks to its episodic dimension, narrative time tends toward the linear representation of time in

5. See Louis O. Mink's "Interpretation and Narrative Understanding," *The Journal of Philosophy* 69, no. 9 (1972): 735–37.
6. See also the work of William H. Dray on judgment.
7. In my "The Narrative Function" (*Semeia* 13 [1978]: 177–202), I contend that "if history may have been grafted, as inquiry, onto narrative activity, it is because the 'configurational' dimension of story-telling and story-following already paved the way for an activity that Mandelbaum rightly characterizes as subsuming parts to wholes. This activity is not a radical break with narrative activity to the extent that the latter already combines chronological and configurational order" (p. 184).

several ways: first, the "then" and "and then" structure that provides an answer to the question "What next?" suggests a relation of exteriority between the phases of the action; second, the episodes constitute an open-ended series of events that allows one to add to the "then" an "and then" and an "and so on"; and finally, the episodes follow one another in accordance with the irreversible order of time common to human and physical events.

The configurational dimension, in turn, displays temporal features that may be opposed to these "features" of episodic time. The configurational arrangement makes the succession of events into significant wholes that are the correlate of the act of grouping together. Thanks to this reflective act—in the sense of Kant's *Critique of Judgment*—the whole plot may be translated into one "thought." "Thought," in this narrative context, may assume various meanings. It may characterize, for instance, following Aristotle's *Poetics,* the "theme" *(dianoia)* that accompanies the "fable" or "plot" *(mythos)* of a tragedy.[8] "Thought" may also designate the "point" of the Hebraic *maschal* or of the biblical parable, concerning which Jeremias observes that the point of the parable is what allows us to translate it into a proverb or an aphorism. The term "thought" may also apply to the "colligatory terms" used in history writing, such terms as "the Renaissance," "the Industrial Revolution," and so on, which, according to Walsh and Dray, allow us to apprehend a set of historical events under a common denominator. (Here "colligatory terms" correspond to the kind of explanation that Dray puts under the heading of "explaining what.") In a word, the correlation between thought and plot supersedes the "then" and "and then" of mere succession. But it would be a complete mistake to consider "thought" as a-chronological. "Fable" and "theme" are as closely tied together as episode and configuration. The time of fable-and-theme, if we may make of this a hyphenated expression, is more deeply temporal than the time of merely episodic narratives.

The plot's configuration also superimposes "the sense of an ending"—to use Kermode's expression—on the open-endedness of mere succession. As soon as a story is well known—and such is the case with most traditional and popular narratives as well as with the national chronicles of the founding events of a given community—retelling takes the place of telling. Then following the story is less important than apprehending the well-known end as implied in the beginning and the well-known episodes as leading to this end. Here again, time is not abolished by the teleological structure of the judgment which grasps together the events under the heading of "the end." This strategy of

8. It may be noted in passing that this correlation between "theme" and "plot" is also the basis of Northrop Frye's "archetypal" criticism.

judgment is one of the means through which time experience is brought back from within-time-ness to repetition.

Finally, the recollection of the story governed as a whole by its way of ending constitutes an alternative to the representation of time as moving from the past forward into the future, according to the well-known metaphor of the arrow of time. It is as though recollection inverted the so-called natural order of time. By reading the end in the beginning and the beginning in the end, we learn also to read time itself backward, as the recapitulating of the initial conditions of a course of action in its terminal consequences. In this way, a plot establishes human action not only within time, as we said at the beginning of this section, but within memory. Memory, accordingly, *repeats* the course of events according to an order that is the counterpart of time as "stretching-along" between a beginning and an end.

This third temporal characteristic of plot has brought us as close as possible to Heidegger's notion of "repetition," which is the turning point for his whole analysis of historicality *(Geschichtlichkeit)*. Repetition, for Heidegger, means more than a mere reversal of the basic orientation of care toward the future; it means the retrieval of our most basic potentialities inherited from our past in the form of personal fate and collective destiny. The question, then, is whether we may go so far as to say that the function of narratives—or at least of some narratives—is to establish human action at the level of genuine historicality, that is, of repetition. If such were the case, the temporal structure of narrative would display the same hierarchy as the one established by the phenomenology of time experience.

3. Historicality and Repetition

I have shown how my analysis of narrative structure confirms the Heideggerian existential analysis of time. My purpose now is to show that the analysis of narrativity also affects and corrects Heidegger's corresponding analysis of historicality on one decisive topic.

Heidegger emphasizes three main traits as the criteria of historicality: first, time appears at this level as "extended" between birth and death. In a sense, we are already acquainted with this aspect of time thanks to the analysis of within-time-ness. This concept is one interpretation of the "extension" of time in terms of the "mundane" clues to which our preoccupation is submitted in the inauthentic realm of everyday life. The problem now is to disentangle the authentic meaning of this extension. Following an order of derivation that proceeds from the deep structure to our scattered interests, Heidegger must confront the concept of extension as a challenge, to the extent that temporality consists in the deep *unity* of future, past, and present—or, rather, of coming

forth, having been, and making present. Augustine had already faced
this paradox in the eleventh book of his *Confessions*. Starting from the
key experience of the unity of expectation, memory, and attention, he
had to ascribe to the soul a specific extension, which he called *distentio
animi,* as a sign of finitude and fallenness. Heidegger is confronted with a
similar enigma, that is, the transition from the deep unity of the three
dimensions of time to the dispersion of time in the realm of inauthenticity. Extension, at the intermediate level, is thus both cohesion
and change. This double meaning is preserved in the term *Geschehen,*
which usually means "becoming," but which Heidegger brings back to
some of its archaic implications, such as mobility, extending, and being
extended. Furthermore, he chooses this idiom by reason of its kinship
with *Geschichte* ("history").[9] What is ultimately at stake is the possibility of
grounding the idea of history as a science in the existential structure of time. *Geschehen* is the mediating structure between temporality (as
the unity of coming-forth, having-been, and making-present) and
within-time-ness.

This leads to a second trait of historicality: the priority given to the
past in the structure of care that underlies the unity of the three dimensions of time. This trait may no longer be taken for granted in an
analysis that proceeds from top to bottom; it must even appear as a
perplexing paradox. Indeed, according to Heidegger's analysis of the
unified experience of temporality, the past is not the primary direction
of care, nor is the present, as in Augustine, since the present is the
making-present of preoccupation which prevails only in the experience
of within-time-ness from which we started in our earlier move from
bottom to top. *The primary direction of care is toward the future.* Through
care, we are always already "ahead of" ourselves. Of course the shift
from future to past is understandable to the extent that any project
implies memory and that no authentic anticipation of what we may "have
to be" is possible without borrowing from the resources of what we
already "have been." Nevertheless, the exclusive concern for the past,
which generates history, must appear as an intriguing enigma when put
against the background of the existential analysis of care and its primary
orientation toward the future.

A third trait has still to be underlined: when we speak of becoming,
either in the field of nature or of history, we imply an indefinite extension of duration both backward and forward. The history of nature, like
that of mankind, knows no beginning and no end. But this vague notion
has no existential force. What first makes sense is the notion of an individual life extending *between* birth and death. This "in between" is the
appropriate temporal characteristic of the "extension" of life as

9. In order to preserve this kinship, the translators of *Being and Time* have translated
the German *Geschehen* as "historicizing."

stretching-along. Now the *finite* aspect of this stretching-along does not belong to the experience of extension as such. It comes from the more radical structure of temporality as governed by the structure of "being-toward-death." We hit here on an ontological presupposition which I will come to grips with later on when we confront temporality and narrativity. But the reader of *Being and Time* cannot escape the centrality of this notion. The impulse toward the future is, at the deep level of temporality, a finite movement to the extent that all genuine expectations are *limited from within* by being-toward-death. *This structure is the organizing pole of the Heideggerian analytic of time.* It is precisely what must appear scandalous to historians and narrators of all kinds for whom historicality opens an endless space for the course of events.

The gap between Heidegger's concept of historicality and our own concept of narrative time would be unbridgeable if Heidegger did not provide us with a mediating concept and if our analysis of narrative time could not be raised above the level of within-time-ness. As concerns Heidegger, the stroke of genius is to have ascribed to what he calls *Wiederholen* ("repetition" or "recollection") the fundamental structure thanks to which historicality is brought back to its origin in the originary structure of temporality. Through repetition, the character of time as stretching-along is rooted in the deep unity of time as future, past, and present, the backward move toward the past is retrieved in the anticipation of a project, and the endlessness of historical time is grafted on the finite structure of being-toward-death.

In *Being and Time* (par. 74, pp. 103–5), Heidegger broaches the topic of repetition in the following way: the analysis starts from the notion of a heritage as something transmitted and received. But because of the preceding analysis of temporality centered on the nontransferable experience of having to die, the perspective under which the notion of a heritage is introduced must remain radically monadic. Each person transmits from him- or herself to him- or herself the resources that he or she may "draw" from his or her past. (Notice that the German word for "drawing," as from a well, is *holen,* which is a basic component of *wiederholen* ["to re-peat" or "to re-collect"].) In this way, each of us receives him- or herself as "fate" *(Schicksal).* Repetition is "going back [*der Rückgang*] into the possibilities of the Dasein that has-been-there" (p. 437). And thanks to repetition as fate, retrospection is reconnected to anticipation, and anticipation is rooted in retrospection. Fate is the character of thrownness of all authentic projects. The German expressions here are very strong, since project and thrownness belong to the same semantic field: *Entwurf, Geworfenheit.* So Heidegger can even speak here of a "thrown project" *(ein geworfener Entwurf).*

But what makes this extraordinary analysis problematic is the monadic character of repetition as fate. It is only thanks to a transfer of the senses of fate, governed by the theme of being-toward-death, to the notion of a common "destiny" *(Geschick)* that we reach the communal dimension of historicality. Here Heidegger joins his previous analysis of *Mit-Sein* ("being-with") to his analysis of *Schicksal* to forge the composite expression *Mit-geschehen.* Destiny is the "cohistoricality" of a community, of a people.[10] This priority of fate over destiny in his analysis may explain the tragic or heroic account that pervades such declarations as the following:

> Only in communicating and in struggling does the power of destiny become free. Dasein's fateful destiny in and with its "generation" goes to make up the full authentic historizing of Dasein.
>   Fate is that powerless superior power which puts itself in readiness for adversities. [P. 436]

So there is a dark kernel of thought underlying the new equivalence between historicality and repetition.

It is at this point that the dialectic between historicality and narrativity may bring forth genuine insights, thanks to the reinterpretation of each term of the one by means of the other. What is needed is not just an "application" of the concept of historicality as repetition to the theory of narrative but a rereading of the latter capable, in turn, of rectifying the former.

Let us return to a suggestion made earlier, namely, that the art of narrating does not merely preserve within-time-ness from being leveled off by measured, anonymous, and reified time, it also generates the movement back from objective time to originary temporality. How does it do this?

The analysis of plot as configuration has already led us to the threshold of what could be called "narrative repetition." By reading the end into the beginning and the beginning into the end, we learn to read time backward, as the recapitulation of the initial conditions of a course of action in its terminal consequences. In this way, the plot does not merely establish human action "in" time, it also establishes it in memory. And memory in turn repeats—re-collects—the course of events according to an order that is the counterpart of the stretching-along of time between a beginning and an end.

Yet the concept of repetition implies still more: it means the "retrieval" of our most fundamental potentialities, as they are inherited from our own past, in terms of a personal fate and a common destiny. The question, therefore, is whether we may go so far as to say that the function of narrative—or at least of a selected group of narratives—is to

10. Heidegger never loses sight of the hidden semantic connections between *Geschehen, Geschick,* and *Schicksal.*

establish human action at the level of authentic historicality, that is, of repetition.

In order to acknowledge this new temporal structure of narrative or at least of some narratives, we have to question some of the initial presuppositions of the previous analysis as well as those that govern the selection of the paradigmatic case of narrative in modern literary criticism. Propp, in his *Morphology of the Folktale*,[11] opened the way by focusing on a category of tales—Russian folktales—which may be characterized as complying with the model of the heroic quest. In these tales, a hero meets a challenge—either mischief or some lack—which he is sent to overcome. Throughout the quest, he is confronted with a series of trials which require that he choose to fight rather than to yield or flee, and which finally end in victory. The paradigmatic story ignores the nonchosen alternatives, yielding and losing. It knows only the chain of episodes that leads the hero from challenge to victory. It was no accident that, after Propp, this schema offered so little resistance to the attempts made by structuralists to dechronologize this paradigmatic chain. After all, only the linear succession of episodes had been taken into account. Furthermore, the segmenting of the chain had led to the isolating of temporal segments taken as discrete entities that were externally connected. Finally, these segments were treated as contingent variations of a limited number of some abstract narrative components, the famous thirty-one "functions" of Propp's model. The chronological dimension was not abolished, but it was deprived of its temporal constitution as plot. The segmenting and the concatenating of functions thus paved the way for a reduction of the chronological to the logical. And in the subsequent phase of structural analysis, with Greimas and Roland Barthes, the search for the atemporal formula that generates the chronological display of functions transformed the structure of the tale into a machinery whose task it is to compensate for the initial mischief or lack by a final restoration of the disturbed order. Compared to this logical matrix, the quest itself appears as a mere diachronical residue, a retardation or suspension in the epiphany of order.

The question is whether the initial need to reduce the chronological to the logical—a need arising from the method employed—governs the strategy of structural analysis in Propp's successive phases: first, the selection of the quest as the paradigmatic case; then, the projection of its episodes on a linear time; then, the segmentation and the external connection of the basic "functions"; and finally, the dissolution of the chronological into the logical.

There is an alternative to such dechronologization. It is repetition. Dechronologization implies the logical abolition of time; repetition, its existential deepening. But to support this view, we have to question the

11. Vladimir Propp, *Morphology of the Folktale* (Austin, Tex., 1968).

implications and even the choice of the paradigmatic cases of narratives in current literary criticism.

Even with regard to the model of the quest, some temporal aspects have been overlooked. Before projecting the hero forward for the sake of the quest, many tales send the hero or heroine into some dark forest where he or she goes astray or meets some devouring beast (as in "Little Red Riding Hood") or where the younger brother or sister has been kidnapped by some threatening force (like the birds in "The Swan-Geese Tale"). These initial episodes do more than merely introduce the mischief that is to be suppressed; they bring the hero or heroine *back* into a primordial space and time that is more akin to the realm of dreams than to the sphere of action. Thanks to this preliminary disorientation, the linear chain of time is broken and the tale assumes an oneiric dimension that is more or less preserved alongside the heroic dimension of the quest. Two qualities of time are thus intertwined: the circularity of the imaginary travel and the linearity of the quest as such. I agree that the kind of repetition involved in this travel toward the origin is rather primitive, even regressive, in the psychoanalytic sense of the word. It has the character of an immersion and confinement in the midst of dark powers. This is why this repetition of the origin has to be superseded by an act of rupture (like, for example, the episode of the woodcutters breaking open the belly of the wolf with an ax in "Little Red Riding Hood"). Nevertheless, the imaginary travel suggests the idea of a metatemporal mode which is not the atemporal mode of narrative codes in structural analyses. This "timeless"—but not atemporal—dimension duplicates, so to speak, the episodic dimension of the quest and contributes to the fairylike atmosphere of the quest itself.

This first mode of repetition must, in turn, be superseded, to the extent that it constitutes only the reverse side of the time of the quest and conquest, brought forward by the call for victory. Finally, the time of the quest prevails over that of the imaginary travel through the break by which the world of action emerges from the land of dreams—as though the function of the tale is to elicit the progressive time of the quest out of the regressive time of imaginary travel.

Repetition thus tends to become the main issue in narratives in which the quest itself duplicates a travel in space that assumes the shape of a return to the origin. Odysseus' travels are the paradigm. As Mircea Eliade writes in *L'Epreuve du labyrinthe,*

> Ulysses is for me the prototype of man, not only modern man, but the man of the future as well, because he represents the type of the "trapped" voyager. His voyage was a voyage toward the center, toward Ithaca, which is to say, toward himself. He was a fine navigator, but destiny—spoken here in terms of trials of initiation which he had to overcome—forced him to postpone indefinitely his

return to hearth and home. I think that the myth of Ulysses is very important for us. We will all be a little like Ulysses, for in searching, in hoping to arrive, and finally, without a doubt, in finding once again the homeland, the hearth, we re-discover ourselves. But, as in the Labyrinth, in every questionable turn, one risks "losing oneself." If one succeeds in getting out of the Labyrinth, in finding one's home again, then one becomes a new being.[12]

The retardation that Eliade speaks of here is no longer a mere suspension in the epiphany of order; retardation now means growth.

The *Odyssey*, accordingly, could be seen as the form of transition from one level of repetition to another, from a mere fantasy repetition that is still the reverse side of the quest to a kind of repetition that would generate the quest itself. With the *Odyssey*, the character of repetition is still imprinted in time by the circular shape of the travel in space. The temporal return of Odysseus to himself is supported by the geographical return to his birthplace, Ithaca.

We come still closer to the kind of repetition suggested by Heidegger's analysis of historicality with stories in which the return to the origin is not just a preparatory phase of the tale and no longer mediated by the shape of the travel back to the birthplace. In these stories, repetition is constitutive of the temporal form itself. The paradigmatic case of such stories is Augustine's *Confessions*. Here the form of the travel is interiorized to such a degree that there is no longer any privileged place in space to which to return. It is a travel "from the exterior to the interior, and from the interior to the superior" *(Ab exterioribus ad interiora, ab interioribus ad superiora)*. The model created by Augustine is so powerful and enduring that it has generated a whole set of narrative forms down to Rousseau's *Confessions* and Proust's *Le Temps retrouvé*. If Augustine's *Confessions* tells "how I became a Christian," Proust's narrative tells "how Marcel became an artist." The quest has been absorbed into the movement by which the hero—if we may still call him by that name—becomes *who he is.* Memory, therefore, is no longer the narrative of external adventures stretching along episodic time. It is itself the spiral movement that, through anecdotes and episodes, brings us back to the almost motionless constellation of potentialities that the narrative retrieves. The end of the story is what equates the present with the past, the actual with the potential. The hero *is* who he *was.* This highest form of narrative repetition is the equivalent of what Heidegger calls fate (individual fate) or destiny (communal destiny), that is, the complete retrieval in resoluteness of the inherited potentialities that *Dasein* is thrown into by birth.

---

12. Mircea Eliade, *L'Epreuve du labryrinthe* (Paris, 1978), p. 109; my translation.

The objection could be made, at this point, that only fictional narra-tive, and not history, reaches this deep level of repetition. I do not think this is the case. It is not possible to ascribe only to inquiry—as opposed to traditional narrative—all the achievements of history in overcoming legendary accounts, that is, the release from mere apologetic tasks re-lated to the heroic figures of the past, the attempt to proceed from mere narrative to truly explanatory history, and, finally, the grasping of whole periods under a leading idea. We may thus wonder whether the shift from sequential history to explanatory history, described by Maurice Mandelbaum in his *Anatomy of Historical Knowledge,* does not find its complete meaning in the further shift from explanatory history to what he calls interpretive history.

> While an interpretive account is not usually confined to a single cross section of time but spans a period . . . the emphasis in such works is on the manner in which aspects of society or of the culture of the period, or both, fit together in a pattern, defining a form of life different from that which one finds at other times or in other places.[13]

Are we stretching the notion of interpretation too far if we put it in the Heideggerian terms of repetition? Mandelbaum may dislike this unexpected proximity to Heideggerian ideas. I find, neverthe-less, some confirmation and encouragement for taking this daring step in the profound analysis of action that Hannah Arendt gives in her brilliant work *The Human Condition.*[14] Arendt distinguishes among labor, work, and action. Labor, she says, aims merely at survival in the struggle between man and nature. Work aims at leaving a mark on the course of things. Action deserves its name when, beyond the concern for submit-ting nature to man or for leaving behind some monuments witnessing to our activity, it aims only at being recollected in stories whose function it is to provide an identity to the doer, an identity that is merely a narrative identity. In this sense, history repeats action in the figure of the memor-able.

Such is the way in which history itself—and not only fiction—provides an approximation of what a phenomenology of time experi-ence may call repetition.

To end this inquiry, I would like to indicate in what sense this mutual clarification of historicality and narrativity affects the

13. Maurice Mandelbaum, *The Anatomy of Historical Knowledge* (Baltimore, 1977), pp. 39 ff.

14. Hannah Arendt, *The Human Condition* (Chicago, 1958).

Heideggerian schema of our experience of time in order to rectify it, at least on one point, in a significant way.

First, we must say that the repetition that Heidegger calls fate is articulated in a narrative. Fate is recounted. This remark may not seem to separate us in any important way from Heidegger, inasmuch as it takes from him the idea that the most detailed chronicle, and eventually the most misleading one, remains bound to and guided in advance by the destiny of a people. This comment, however, leads us still further. In imposing the narrative form on repetition, the chronicle also imposes the priority of the communal form of destiny on the private form of fate. In other words, narrativity, from the outset, establishes repetition on the plane of being-with-others. My analysis of narrative on the level of within-time-ness anticipated this conclusion. The narrative of a quest, which is the paradigmatic example appropriate to this level, unfolds in a public time. This public time, as we saw, is not the anonymous time of ordinary representation but the time of interaction. In this sense, narrative time is, from the outset, time of being-with-others.

But if this is so, the whole structure of the Heideggerian analytic of time is called into question to the extent that it proceeds from being-toward-death. We know how much Heidegger emphasizes the non-transferable character of being-toward-death and that this un-communicable aspect of dying imposes the primacy of individual fate over common destiny in the subsequent analysis of historicality. Yet it is this primacy that the analysis of narrativity calls into question.

One might ask at this point whether the whole Heideggerian analysis is not then overturned. Is it not a certain fascination with death that gives the whole analysis its well-known heroic accents? We need only recall the dialectic of strength and weakness to which Heidegger submits the theme of fate. Does not narrativity, by breaking away from the obsession of a struggle in the face of death, open any meditation on time to another horizon than that of death, to the problem of communication not just between living beings but between contemporaries, pre-decessors, and successors?[15] After all, is not narrative time a time that continues beyond the death of each of its protagonists? Is it not part of the plot to include the death of each hero in a story that surpasses every individual fate?

Let us go even further. Must we not call into question the very first analysis on which the Heideggerian analysis of repetition is based, I mean the analysis of a heritage of potentialities understood as something that is transmitted from oneself to oneself? Is not a heritage always something that is transmitted from *another* to the *self*? If such is the case, the study of transmission between generations, to which I alluded

15. I here employ the terminology used by Alfred Schutz in his phenomenology of social existence.

earlier, may reveal a wider problematic, the one Gadamer calls the problem of "tradition."[16] It seems to me that this problem, even more than the Heideggerian analysis of a heritage and individual fate, is likely to build a bridge between the ontology of historicality and the epistemology of the philosophy of history. It is always a community, a people, or a group of protagonists which tries to take up the tradition—or traditions—of its origins.

It is this communal act of repetition, which is at the same time a new founding act and a recommencement of what has already been inaugurated, that "makes history" and that finally makes it possible to write history. Historiography, in this sense, is nothing more than the passage into writing and then to critical rewriting of this primordial constituting of tradition. The naive forms of narration are deployed between this constituting of tradition and the writing of history (for example, legends and chronicles). And it is at the level of this mediation, where the writing of history is preceded by something already recounted, that historicality and narrativity are confounded and confused. So it is in this sense that repetition may be spoken of as the foundation of historiography. But it is a repetition that is always articulated in a narrative mode. History only turns this first conjunction of temporality and narrative in what I am calling narrative repetition into inquiry: *Historia, Forschung, enquête*. In this sense, therefore, the theory of narrativity rectifies the theory of historicality to the extent that it receives its leaven for the theme of repetition from the theory of narrativity.

The unanswered question in this essay concerns the relationship between historicality and deep temporality. You will recall that for Heidegger, historicality, in the technical sense of this term, constitutes the first form derived from deep temporality. For us, who follow the inverse order, the question is whether the theory of narrative has anything to say concerning the return from historicality to this deep temporality. We have seen in what way narrativity leads from time conceived of as within-time-ness to historicality, that is, to extension and repetition. But perhaps the analysis of narrative can also accompany a still more radical movement that would go from historicality to deep temporality following the triple framework evoked at the beginning of the second part of this essay: the unity of the three "extases" of time (having-been, coming-forth, and making-present); the primacy of the future over the past and the present in the unitary constituting of time; and the closure of the future by being-toward-death in its untransferable individuality.

Three possibilities, I think, are open to us. First, we might conclude that due to the tight link between historicality and within-time-ness in narrative activity the art of storytelling is essentially incapable of this radical return toward the depth of temporality. This impotence would

16. See Hans-Georg Gadamer's *Truth and Method* (New York, 1975).

then express the internal limit of any meditation on time linked to a reflection on narrative. Such a conclusion would in no way signify the failure of such a meditation. On the contrary, a reflection on limits is always instructive. Without it, the critical investigation of any mode of discourse is incomplete.

As a second possibility, we might draw an argument from the phenomenology of the art of storytelling to contest the most important trait of the Heideggerian theory of temporality, namely, being-toward-death. My earlier comments on the place of the problematic of tradition and transmission, in a meditation on time directly inspired by the theory of narrative, uncontestably point in this direction.

However justified these comments may be at the level of an analysis of historicality, they in no way exclude another type of meditation, our third possibility, that would apply no longer to the theme of historicality as such but precisely to its radical genesis beginning from that unitary structure by virtue of which time temporalizes itself as future, past, and present. The concept of tradition, in the sense of a common destiny more fundamental than any individual and moral fate, does not exclude this other meditation; it calls for it. Some consideration of death is inherent in any meditation on the constitution of history. Must not something or someone die if we are to have a memory of it or him or her? Is not the otherness of the past fundamentally to be seen in death? And is not repetition itself a kind of resurrection of the dead, as any reader of Michelet will recognize?

It Was a Dark and Stormy Night; or,
Why Are We Huddling about the Campfire?

Ursula K. Le Guin

It was a dark and stormy night
and Brigham Young and Brigham Old
sat around the campfire.
Tell us a story, old man!
And this is the story he told:

It was a dark and stormy night
and Brigham Young and Brigham Old
sat around the campfire.
Tell us a story, old man!
And this is the story he told:

It was a dark and stormy night
and Brigham Young and Pierre Menard, author of the *Quixote,*
sat around the campfire,
which is not quite the way my Great-Aunt Betsy told it
when we said Tell us another story!
Tell us, *au juste,* what happened!
And this is the story she told:

> It was a dark and stormy night, in the otherwise unnoteworthy year
> 711 E.C. (Eskimo Calendar), and the great-aunt sat crouched at her
> typewriter, holding his hands out to it from time to time as if for
> warmth and swinging on a swing. He was a handsome boy of about
> eighteen, one of those men who suddenly excite your desire when
> you meet them in the street, and who leave you with a vague feeling
> of uneasiness and excited senses. On a plate beside the typewriter

lay a slice of tomato. It was a flawless slice. It was a perfect slice of a perfect tomato. It is perfectly boring. I hold out my hands to the typewriter again, while swinging and showing my delicate limbs, and observe that the rows of keys are marked with all the letters of the English alphabet, and all the letters of the French alphabet minus accent marks, and all the letters of the Polish alphabet except the dark *L*. By striking these keys with the ends of my fingers or, conceivably, a small blunt instrument, the aging woman can create a flaw in the tomato. She did so at once. It was then a seriously, indeed a disgustingly flawed tomato, but it continued to be perfectly boring until eaten. She expires instantly in awful agony, of snakebite, flinging the window wide to get air. It is a dark and stormy night and the rain falling in on the typewriter keys writes a story in German about a great-aunt who went to a symposium on narrative and got eaten in the forest by a metabear. She writes the story while reading it with close attention, not sure what to expect, but collaborating hard, as if that was anything new; and this is the story I wrote:

It was a dark and stormy night
and Brigham al-Rashid sat around the campfire with his wife
who was telling him a story in order to keep her head on
   her shoulders,
and this is the story she told:

The *histoire* is the what
and the *discours* is the how
but what I want to know, Brigham,
is *le pourquoi*.
Why are we sitting here around the campfire?

Tell me a story, great-aunt,
so that I can sleep.
Tell me a story, Scheherazade,
so that you can live.
Tell me a story, my soul, animula, vagula, blandula,
little Being-Towards-Death,
for the word's the beginning of being
if not the middle or the end.

    "A beginning is that which is not itself necessarily after any-thing else, and which has naturally something else after it; an end,

---

Ursula K. Le Guin, distinguished novelist, poet, and essayist, is the author of *The Left Hand of Darkness, Malafrena,* and *The Dispossessed,* for which she won both the Hugo and the Nebula Award. Her novel *The Lathe of Heaven* was recently made into a film by the Public Broadcasting System.

that which is naturally after something else, either as its necessary or usual consequent, and with nothing else after it; and a middle, that which is by nature after one thing and has also another after it."[1]

But sequence grows difficult in the ignorance of what comes after the necessary or at least the usual consequent of living, that is, dying,

and also when the soul is confused by not unreasonable doubts of what comes after the next thing that happens, whatever that may be.

It gets dark and stormy when you look away from the campfire.

Tell me what you see in the fire, Lizzie, Lizzie Hexam,
down in the hollow by the flare!
I see storm and darkness, brother.
I see death and running water, brother.
I see loving kindness, brother.
Is it all right to see that, teacher?
What would Alain Robbe-Grillet say?

Never mind what he says, Lizzie.
Frogs have a lot of trouble with the novel,
even though kissed right at the beginning by the
    Princesse de Clèves;
maybe they do not want to look down and see Victor Hugo
    glimmering *au fond du puits.*

Brigham, this is stupid stuff!
Tell us a story, old man,
or old woman as the case may be,
or old Tiresias, chirping like a cricket,
tell us a story with a proper end to it
instead of beginning again and again like this
and thereby achieving a muddle
which is not by nature after anything in particular
nor does it have anything consequent to it
but it just hangs there
placidly eating its tail.

In the Far West, where Brigham Young ended up and I started from, they tell stories about hoop snakes. When a hoop snake wants to get somewhere—whether because the hoop snake is after something, or because something is after the hoop snake—it takes its tail (which may or may not have rattles on it) into its mouth, thus forming itself into a hoop, and rolls. Jehovah enjoined snakes to crawl on their belly in the dust, but Jehovah was an Easterner. Rolling along, bowling along, is a lot quicker

1. Aristotle, *On the Art of Poetry,* trans. Ingram Bywater (Oxford, 1920), p. 40.

and more satisfying than crawling. But, for the hoop snakes with rattles, there is a drawback. They are venomous snakes, and when they bite their own tail they die, in awful agony, of snakebite. All progress has these hitches. I don't know what the moral is. It may be in the end safest to lie perfectly still without even crawling. Indeed it's certain that we shall all do so in the end, which has nothing else after it. But then no tracks are left in the dust, no lines drawn; the dark and stormy nights are all one with the sweet bright days, this moment of June—and you might as well never have lived at all. And the moral of *that* is, you have to form a circle to escape from the circle. Draw in a little closer around the campfire. If we could truly form a circle, joining the beginning and the end, we would, as another Greek remarked, not die. But never fear. We can't manage it no matter how we try. But still, very few things come nearer the real Hoop Trick than a good story.

There was a man who practiced at the Hoop Trick named Aneirin. But let us have the footnotes first.

"We have to bear in mind that the *Gododdin* [and its associated lays] are not narrative poems. . . . Nowhere is there any attempt to give an account of what it was really all about."[2] I disagree with this comment and agree with the next one, which points out that the work goes rolling and bowling all about what it is all about. "While some of these [early Welsh poems] will 'progress' in expected fashion from a beginning through a middle to an end, the normal structure is 'radial,' circling about, repeating and elaborating the central theme. It is all 'middle.' "[3]

This is the Gododdin; Aneirin sang it.   [I]

Men went to Catraeth, keen their war-band.   [VIII]
Pale mead their portion, it was poison.
Three hundred under orders to fight.
And after celebration, silence.

Men went to Catraeth at dawn: [X]
All their fears had been put to flight.
Three hundred clashed with ten thousand.

Men went to Catraeth at dawn: [XI]
Their high spirits lessened their lifespans.
They drank mead, gold and sweet, ensnaring;
For a year the minstrels were merry.

Three spears stain with blood   [XVIII]
Fifty, five hundred.
Three hounds, three hundred:

2. K. H. Jackson, *The Gododdin: The Oldest Scottish Poem* (Edinburgh, 1969), pp. 3–4.
3. Joseph P. Clancy, *The Earliest Welsh Poetry* (London and New York, 1970), quotation from introduction.

Three stallions of war
From golden Eidin,
Three mailclad war-bands,
Three gold-collared kings.

In the great hall I drank wine and mead.   [XIX]
Many were his spears;
In the clash of men
He fashioned a feast for eagles.

Men went to Catraeth, they were renowned,   [XXI]
Wine and mead from gold cups was their drink,
A year in noble ceremonial,
Three hundred and sixty-three gold-torqued men.
Of all those who charged, after too much drink,
But three won free through courage in strife:
Aeron's two warhounds and tough Cynon,
And myself, soaked in blood, for my song's sake.

My legs at full length   [XLVIII]
In a house of earth,
A chain of iron
About both ankles,
Caused by mead, by horn,
By Catraeth's raiders.
I, not I, Aneirin,
Taliesin knows it,
Master of wordcraft,
Sang to Gododdin
Before the day dawned.

None walk the earth, no mother has borne   [XLIX]
One so fair and strong, dark as iron.
From a war-band his bright blade saved me,
From a fell cell of earth he bore me,
From a place of death, from a harsh land,
Cenan fab Llywarch, bold, undaunted.

Many I lost of my true comrades.   [LXI]
Of three hundred champions who charged to Catraeth,
It is tragic, but one man came back.

On Tuesday they donned their dark armour,   [LXIX]
On Wednesday, bitter their meeting,
On Thursday, terms were agreed on,
On Friday, dead men without number,
On Saturday, fearless, they worked as one,
On Sunday, crimson blades were their lot,
On Monday, men were seen waist-deep in blood.
After defeat, the Gododdin say,

Before Madawg's tent on his return
There came but one man in a hundred.

Three hundred, gold-torqued,   [XCI]
Warlike, well-trained,
Three hundred, haughty,
In harmony, armed.
Three hundred fierce steeds
Bore them to battle.
Three hounds, three hundred:
Tragic, no return.[4]

"I, not I, Aneirin"—"won free"—"for my song's sake." What is Aneirin telling us? Whether or not we allow that a story so muddled or all middle can be a narrative, or must be lyric or elegiac, but do classic Greek definitions fit Welsh Dark Ages traditions?—so, as Barbara Myerhoff pleaded, in all courtesy let us not argue about it at this point, only perhaps admitting that the spiral is probably the shortest way of getting through spacetime and is certainly an effective way to recount the *loss* of a battle—in any case, what is Aneirin trying to tell us? For all we know or shall ever know of the Battle of Catraeth is what he tells us; and there is no doubt that he very much wanted us to know about it, to remember it. He says that he won free for his song's sake. He says that he survived, alone, or with Cynan and two others, or with Cenan—he seems to have survived in several different ways, also, which is very Welsh of him—he says that he survived in order to tell us about his friends who did not survive. But I am not sure whether he means by this that he must tell the story because he alone survived; or that he survived because he had the story to tell.

And now for quite another war. I am going to speak in many voices now for a while. Novelists have this habit of ventriloquy.[5]

"The SS guards took pleasure in telling us that we had no chance of coming out alive, a point they emphasized with particular relish by insisting that after the war the rest of the world would not believe what had happened; there would be no evidence" (a survivor of Dachau).

"Those caught were shot, but that did not keep Ringelblum and his friends from organizing a clandestine group whose job was to gather information for deposit in a secret archive, much of which survived. Here survival and bearing witness became reciprocal acts" (Des Pres).

"In Treblinka the dead were being unearthed and burned, by work

---

4. Ibid., Clancy's translation of the text of the *Gododdin*.

5. The following citations appear in Terence Des Pres' *The Survivor: An Anatomy of Life in the Death Camps* (Oxford, 1976; New York, 1977). Some of the citations from Des Pres' own text are rephrased.

squads; after that the work squads were to be shot and burned. If that had come to pass Treblinka would never have existed. The aim of the revolt was to ensure the memory of that place. We know the story of Treblinka because forty survived" (Des Pres).

"I found it most difficult to stay alive, but I had to live, to give the world this story" (Glatstein, from Treblinka).

"Even in this place one can survive, and therefore one must want to survive, to tell the story, to bear witness" (Primo Levi, from Auschwitz).

"It is a man's way of leaving a trace, of telling people how he lived and died. If nothing else is left, one must scream. Silence is the real crime against humanity" (Nadyezhda Mandelshtam).

"Conscience is a social achievement; on its historical level it is the collective effort to come to terms with evil, to distill a moral knowledge equal to the problems at hand. . . . Existence at its boundary is intrinsically significant. The struggle to live, to survive, is rooted in, and a manifestation of, the form-conferring potency of life itself " (Des Pres).

"We may speculate that survival depends upon life considered . . . as a set of activities evolved through time in successful response to crises, the sole purpose of which is to keep going. . . . Living things act as they do because they are so organized as to take actions that prevent their dissolution into their surroundings" (J. Z. Young).

"It seems as if Western culture were making a prodigious effort of historiographic *anamnesis*. . . . We may say . . . this *anamnesis* continues the religious evaluation of memory and forgetfulness. To be sure, neither myths nor religious practices are any longer involved. But there is this common element: the importance of precise and total recollection. . . . The prose narrative, especially the novel, has taken the place of the recitation of myths. . . . The tale takes up and continues 'initiation' on the level of the imaginary. . . . Believing that he is merely amusing himself or escaping, the man of the modern societies still benefits from the imaginary initiation supplied by tales. . . . Today we are beginning to realize that what is called 'initiation' coexists with the human condition, that every existence is made up of an unbroken series of 'ordeals,' 'deaths,' and 'resurrections.' . . . Whatever the gravity of the present crisis of the novel, it is nonetheless true that the need to find one's way into 'foreign' universes and to follow the complications of a 'story' seems to be consubstantial with the human condition."[6]

"For Heaven only knows why one loves it so, how one sees it so, making it up, building it round one, tumbling it, creating it every moment afresh. . . . In people's eyes, in the swing, tramp, and trudge; in the bellow and the uproar; the carriages, motor cars, omnibuses, vans, sandwich men shuffling and swinging; brass bands; barrel organs; in the

6. Mircea Eliade, *Myth and Reality,* trans. Willard R. Trask (New York, 1963), pp. 136, 138, and 202.

triumph and the jingle and the strange high singing of some aeroplane overhead was what she loved; life; London; this moment of June."[7]

Why are we huddling about the campfire? Why do we tell tales, or tales about tales—why do we bear witness, true or false? We may ask Aneirin, or Primo Levi, we may ask Scheherazade, or Virginia Woolf. Is it because we are so organized as to take actions that prevent our dissolution into the surroundings? I know a very short story which might illustrate this hypothesis. You will find it carved into a stone about three feet up from the floor of the north transept of Carlisle Cathedral in the north of England, not all that far from Catterick which may have been Catraeth. It was carved in runes, one line of runes, laboriously carved into the stone. A translation into English is posted up nearby in typescript under glass. Here is the whole story:

Tolfink carved these runes in this stone.

Well, this is pretty close to Barbara Herrnstein Smith's earliest form of historiography—notch-cutting. As a story, it does not really meet the requirement of Minimal Connexity. It doesn't have much beginning or end. The material was obdurate, and life is short. Yet I would say Tolfink was a reliable narrator. Tolfink bore witness at least to the existence of Tolfink, a human being unwilling to dissolve entirely into his surroundings.

It is time to end, an appropriate time for a ghost story. It was a dark and stormy night, and the man and the woman sat around the campfire in their tent out on the plains. They had killed the woman's husband and run away together. They had been going north across the plains for three days now. The man said, "We must be safe. There is no way the people of the tribe can track us." The woman said, "What's that noise?" They listened, and they both heard a scratching noise on the outside of the tent, low down, near the ground. "It's the wind blowing," the man said. The woman said, "It doesn't sound like the wind." They listened and heard the sound again, a scraping, louder, and higher up on the wall of the tent. The woman said, "Go and see what it is. It must be some animal." The man didn't want to go out. She said, "Are you afraid?" Now the scraping sound had got very loud, up almost over their heads. The man jumped up and went outside to look. There was enough light from the fire inside the tent that he could see what it was. It was a skull. It was rolling up the outside of the tent, so that it could get in at the smokehole at the top. It was the skull of the man they had killed, the husband, but it had grown very big. It had been rolling after them over the plains all along and growing bigger as it rolled. The man shouted to the woman, and she came out of the tent, and they caught each other by the hand and ran. They ran into the darkness, and the skull rolled down the tent

7. Virginia Woolf, *Mrs. Dalloway* (New York, 1925), p. 5.

and rolled after them. It came faster and faster. They ran until they fell down in the darkness, and the skull caught up with them there. That was the end of them.

There may be some truth in that story, that tale, that discourse, that narrative, but there is no reliability in the telling of it. It was told you forty years later by the ten-year-old who heard it, along with her great-aunt, by the campfire, on a dark and starry night in California; and though it is, I believe, a Plains Indian story, she heard it told in English by an anthropologist of German antecedents. But by remembering it he had made the story his; and insofar as I have remembered it, it is mine; and now, if you like it, it's yours. In the tale, in the telling, we are all one blood. Take the tale in your teeth, then, and bite till the blood runs, hoping it's not poison; and we will all come to the end together, and even to the beginning: living, as we do, in the middle.

Afterthoughts on Narrative

I

On the How, What, and Why of Narrative

Paul Hernadi

I am impressed with Ursula Le Guin's way of correlating three questions that have been repeatedly asked at this conference:

> The *histoire* is the what
> and the *discours* is the how
> but what I want to know, Brigham,
> is *le pourquoi.*
> *Why* are we sitting here around the campfire?

After some remarks on the "how" and "what" of narratives, I will sketch an answer to the third and probably most troublesome question.

I fail to discern a genuine temporal quality in what Seymour Chatman calls "discourse-time"—the sequential order of narrative presentation. It seems to me that a narrative sequence requires the lived time of its perceiver's imagination if it is to evoke the narrated events with a temporal dimension of their own (Chatman's "story-time"). This applies even to cinematographic narratives. The celluloid discourse subdivides into frames rather than moments. Its spatial footage turns into temporal brainage only if someone is watching.

To be sure, movies are meant to run at a speed foreseen by the filmmakers. Yet Chatman himself did not hesitate to alter Jean Renoir's intended "discourse-time"—I would prefer to say "performance-time"—when he showed us some shots repeatedly, others in slow motion. Such techniques of film analysis can be very instructive if we keep a crucial difference in mind: the difference between how the film is experienced by a person viewing it continuously at the intended speed and how it is experienced by a person viewing certain parts of it repeatedly and in the temporal blowup of slow motion. The two kinds of experience may shed light on each other. But selectively repeated scenes and slow-motion viewings force us to infuse privileged amounts of time (both physical *temps* and lived *durée*) into certain units of the film's "discourse." The "how" of the *discours* having thus been altered, can the "what" of the perceived *histoire* remain the same?

Such a question should not take thoughtful students of the cinema by surprise. Most literary critics, however, seem to ignore the effect of their carefully slow and selectively repetitive reading on both the *discours* and the *histoire* of, say, a particular novel. Unlike filmmakers or even composers, writers have no overt means of prescribing the speed at which the sequence of their work should be given temporal reality. This is why Frank Kermode can say that a "collusion between novelist and public" ensures the success of certain types of narratives through "underreading." In contrast, professors of literature with sufficient leisure on their hands may well be suspected to "overread" by looking out for suppressed secrets in the purposefully unlit background of a novel's plot and characters.

But aren't at least some of the "secrets" Kermode has extracted from Joseph Conrad's *Under Western Eyes* the writer's signals as much as they are symptoms of the writing? To answer this question we would need to know whether we are meant to read a given passage or the entire novel presto, largo, or perhaps allegretto. Yet there is no literary convention for indicating the proper tempo of a text. To make matters worse (or better?) for the literary critic, even stage directions seldom parallel the composer's forte or pianissimo or crescendo, and comparable instructions for the dynamics of reading are almost totally absent from nondramatic works. It seems, therefore, both unavoidable and justifiable to countenance very different tempi and dynamics in the readings of a text. At the same time, we should not assume that the circumspectly erudite professor's analysis of his or her reading experience is automatically relevant to the story that a faster, nonprofessional reading might elicit from the "same" discourse. The "how" of different readings and their "what" cannot fail to differ for they reflect different responses to the more basic question "why."

Paul Hernadi teaches English and comparative literature at the University of Iowa. He is the author of *Beyond Genre: New Directions in Literary Classification* and the editor of *What Is Literature?* and *What Is Criticism?*

Why, then, do we huddle in the dark around the campfires of our flickering narratives? There are obviously many different reasons for doing so. Yet, having heard various *récits*—whether "stories" or "accounts"—during the narrative conference, I am more inclined than ever to see self-assertive entertainment and self-transcending commitment as two kinds of ultimate motivation for our countless narratives. Stories and histories and other narrative or descriptive accounts help us to *escape boredom and indifference*—ours as well as that of other people. Those nearly vacant states of mind at the zero degree of entertainment and commitment bring us frightfully close to the experience of nonexistence. Hence our desire to replace boredom by thrilling or gratifying entertainment (remember Edmund Burke's contrast between the Sublime and the Beautiful?) and to replace indifference by the social or cosmic commitment either to change the world or to change ourselves. In a world of unmixed colors and pure literary genres, tragedy, comedy, satire, and romance might answer distinct needs for thrill, gratification, indignation, and admiration. But, as Roy Schafer and Victor Turner have reminded us, the private and social dramas underlying psychoanalytical and anthropological accounts are even less pure than most works of literature. Couldn't we conclude that life's internal and external dramas stem from a compound desire for self-assertion and self-transcendence—a desire which, in the realm of literary entertainment and commitment, motivates the emergence and appreciation of tragicomedy?

Afterthoughts on Narrative

II

Language, Narrative, and Anti-Narrative

Robert Scholes

Narrative is a place where sequence and language, among other things, intersect to form a discursive code. I shall attempt to sketch out a few of the salient features of this code as it has operated in the narrative tradition of Western culture, but first it is necessary to consider the nature of language itself.

We *must* consider the nature of language because many of the problems and confusions in our thought about narrative stem from what seem to me to be a set of misconceptions about language itself. Saussure demonstrated that the link between "sound-image" and concept in language, that is, between the signifier and the signified, was arbitrary in most cases, which is unexceptionable; but he went on to assume that he had demonstrated the arbitrariness of all concepts themselves, which he had not. Charles S. Peirce argued most persuasively that every sign (Saussure's "signifier") must be interpreted by another sign (Peirce's "interpretant"), so that meaning is an endless network linking sign to sign to sign. Some of the most formidable later investigators into these matters, Umberto Eco and Jacques Derrida, for example, have followed Peirce in this, but I would argue that they have not always kept Peirce's notion of sign clearly enough in mind. For Saussure himself the word "sign" meant "verbal sign" most of the time, and this is what it means for nearly all of those who have followed him.

In this manner, taking from Peirce the notion that every sign must be interpreted by another sign and translating this into Saussurian terms, it is fatally easy to conclude that every verbal sign is connected to another verbal sign: crudely, every word is defined by another word, in an endless chain which is hopelessly cut off from nonverbal affairs. This is the situation Fredric Jameson so aptly called the "prison house of language," and it is the basic misconception which underlies much of our present confusion. One way out of this situation is to attend more closely to Peirce's notion of semiosis:

> (It is important to understand what I mean by *semiosis*. All dynamical action, or action of brute force, physical or psychical, either takes place between two subjects [whether they react equally upon each other, or one is agent and the other patient, entirely or partially] or at any rate is a resultant of such actions between pairs. But by "semiosis" I mean, on the contrary, an action, or influence, which is, or involves, a coöperation of *three* subjects, such as a sign, its object, and its interpretant, this tri-relative influence not being in any way resolvable into actions between pairs. . . .)[1]

Peirce's "tri-relative" notion of semiosis places him close to Frege, to Carnap, and to Ogden and Richards and far from Saussure and his followers. We can display their terminologies in the following way, placing the comparable (but by no means identical) terms of each formulation in the same column:

Frege	Expression (*Ausdruck*)	Sense (*Sinn*)	Reference (*Bedeutung*)
Carnap	Expression	Intension	Extension
Ogden/Richards	Symbol	Thought	Referent
Peirce	Sign	Interpretant	Object
Saussure	Signifier	Signified	—————

The Saussurian formulation, like most "linguistic" views of language, eliminates the third column and with this gesture erases the world. There are two possible justifications for this. One is that questions of reference are outside linguistic discourse. A discipline may set its own boundaries, and in the case linguistic scholars have chosen to eliminate

1. Charles Sanders Peirce, "Pragmatism in Retrospect: A Last Formulation," *Philosophical Writings of Peirce*, ed. Justus Buchler (New York, 1955), p. 282.

Robert Scholes is professor of English and comparative literature and director of the semiotics program at Brown University. He is the author of *Structuralism in Literature: An Introduction* and *Fabulation and Metafiction*.

a potentially awkward portion of their possible field. The second justification is more ambitious, more philosophical. It argues that reference is a mirage of language, that there is no simple reference or unmediated perception, that the world is always already textualized by an arche-writing or system of differentiation which effectively brackets or sets aside questions of reference, eliminating the terms in the third column not by choice but by necessity. This is (very roughly) the position articulated by Derrida in *Of Grammatology*.

In this view, the medium of language—the material out of which linguistic signs are constructed, whether conceived as "writing" (Derrida's *"écriture"*) or as "speaking" (Saussure's "sound-image")—is based on "difference." Whether one conceives of language grammatologically or phonologically, the linguistic medium is generated by a series of differentiations or displacements. For spoken language to exist, human sounds must be organized into a system of phonemic differences. If we assume that these differences have priority over perception, then we must accept that we are indeed in a prison house of language. This is why Derrida says, "I don't know what perception is and I don't believe that anything like perception exists."[2]

One great question, it seems to me, is whether we have to accept the *priority* of difference over perception. But I must confess myself unequal to the task of debating that question. Therefore, I suggest that we grant that major premise—at least provisionally—in order to raise some lesser but still crucial issues. Assuming the priority of difference over perception, does it make sense to equate all sign processes with difference? Do we, by our processes of signification, give a spurious order to chaos, creating selves and worlds both bounded by language? Or is there an order always already in place before we seek to shape it? Does the differentiating process meet no resistance in the phenomena it orders? Or is the play of difference itself shaped and systematized by a necessity outside itself we call "the world"?

To allow difference priority does not mean that we must allow it a solipsistic authority over the world. The arbitrariness of the sound-image does not guarantee the nonreferentiality of the concept. Perceptions are not pure, granted; they are affected by the very languaging process that enables them. But language is not pure either; to the extent that it deals with sensory data, it is contaminated by the resistances it encounters. In language, a play of difference and a necessary order of phenomena are engaged with one another, and what is produced by their interaction cannot properly be reduced to a neat Saussurian formula.

2. Jacques Derrida, "Structure, Sign, and Play in the Discourse of the Human Sciences," in *The Structuralist Controversy: The Languages of Criticism and the Sciences of Man,* ed. Richard Macksey and Eugenio Donato (Baltimore and London, 1970), p. 272.

A verbal sign is never simply a matter of a signifying sound-image tied to a single signified concept. A word in any language carries with it a semantic field of potential meanings which is partly governed by a social code and partly individualized by the unique features of whoever utters or interprets the word. When a word is incorporated in an utterance, the semantic field is narrowed by its situation in a syntactic structure, in a discursive pattern, in a social situation, and in a referential context. Thus each interpreter generates a distinct interpretant for each textual sign, and, to the extent that communication is achieved, the interpretants of all interpreters of the same utterance will correspond with one another and with that of the person who employed the sign in the original act of communication. This correspondence will never be perfect, of course.

Let me elaborate on this a bit. In terms of Saussure's indispensable distinction between language (*langue*) and utterance (*parole*), a verbal sign in language should be conceived of not in terms of a signifier/signified relationship (as Saussure himself formulated it) but in terms of a sign/semantic field relationship: one sign with many potential meanings, some determinate, some indeterminate. But when such a sign is employed in a speech act (or utterance), each interpreter (including the speaker) narrows the field down and so isolates an interpretant for that sign in this particular utterance, discourse, context, and situation. The interpretant is generated by the interpreter through a process of selection from and perhaps modification of the semantic field which the interpreter has developed for that particular sign in terms of its previous appearances in other utterances. A dictionary or lexicon of any language is simply an attempt to codify the results of this process.

Now comes the crucial question: Of what does the semantic field for any given verbal sign consist? The oversimple view which I am trying to correct suggests that one verbal sign is defined by another, and so on ad infinitum. The view I am offering here suggests, on the contrary, that each verbal sign is potentially defined by a semantic field and then acquires a more precise definition in any given utterance or speech act. But beyond that—and I believe this is the most important and controversial part of what I am suggesting—it seems to me self-evident that *the semantic field for many verbal signs is not exclusively verbal.* That is, we carry with us as part of our interpretive equipment—indeed, as a part of language itself—an enormous amount of information that is not normally considered linguistic. This information, which we need in order to interpret utterances of all sorts, is derived from our interactions with things and states of affairs other than words. If I say, "Beck's beer has a pleasantly skunky smell," those interpreters whose semantic field for the word **"skunky" includes olfactory experiences with skunks will construct a dif**ferent interpretant for my statement than those who have not had any sensory experience of skunkiness. Furthermore, our experience with the odor of skunk is not in itself a linguistically determined experience. The smell of a skunk will wake most human beings from a sound sleep—whether or not they have a word for the sensation they encounter. My point is simply that sensations and perceptions of all sorts are a part of our languaging equipment. Beyond this, I would argue that traces of sensory data are a regular feature of our interpretants and that the vividness of this data contributes to the superiority of certain individuals' interpretations of certain signs.

Peirce, of course, has suggested that there are three distinct modes of signification and that any given sign situation may partake of one, two, or all three modes. In Peirce's terminology, a *symbol* refers to something by virtue of an arbitrary agreement (this is Saussure's "sign"); an *icon* represents something by virtue of qualities in the iconic sign itself—qualities that resemble aspects of the object that it represents, as in a portrait or a diagram; and an *index* indicates neither arbitrarily nor by resemblance but by carrying traces of the thing that caused its own existence or by pointing to this object in some other existential way. A portrait of Gertrude Stein by Picasso will be an icon of Stein but an index of Picasso. A photograph, on the other hand, will be both an icon and an index of its subject since the light rays bouncing from the subject to the film have "caused" this visible sign to appear. Peirce also argues that any successful act of designation must be indexical: when the symbol "this" is used to refer to a particular object, it functions as an index; proper names are also indexical.

I go over this familiar ground from Peirce primarily to direct attention to a less familiar aspect of his theory. He points out that the interpretant of a symbol will often include both indexical and iconic qualities. Put simply, for the phrase "Ezekiel loveth Huldah" to be meaningful, the interpreter must be able to identify Ezekiel and Huldah (an indexical process) and must also be able to generate an iconic interpretant for the verb "loveth." Peirce is quite specific on this matter: "Now the effect of the word 'loveth' is that the pair of objects denoted by the pair of indices Ezekiel and Huldah is represented by the icon, or the image we have in our minds of a lover and his beloved."[3]

In the development of any language, metaphors are made through the activation of this conceptual iconicity. Language—that system of phonemic and grammatical differentiation—grows and changes partly through semantic shifts that depend upon what Aristotle called "an eye for resemblances." The most able makers of metaphors—call them poets—are undoubtedly those whose semantic fields have the highest degree of iconicity. Metonymy, it is worth pointing out, is a highly indexical process of signification since it is based upon an existential contiguity, whether spatial, temporal, or causal. Both metaphor and metonymy function as linguistic processes in the perpetual motion of

3. Peirce, "Logic as Semiotic: The Theory of Signs," *Philosophical Writings,* p. 113.

any given language. In this function, they keep language open to life, preventing closure of the arbitrary system of symbols by continually altering the symbolic fields that surround each symbol with potential meanings.

This long digression into language was necessary because we cannot understand verbal narrative unless we are aware of the iconic and indexical dimensions of language. Narrative is not just a sequencing, or the illusion of sequence, as the title of our conference would have it; narrative is a sequencing of something for somebody. To put anything into words is to sequence it, but to enumerate the parts of an automobile is not to narrate them, even though the enumeration must mention each part in the enumeration's own discursive order. One cannot narrate a picture, or a person, or a building, or a tree, or a philosophy. Narration is a word that implicates its object in its meaning. Only one kind of thing can be narrated: a time-thing, or to use our normal word for it, an "event." And strictly speaking, we require more than one event before we recognize that we are in the presence of a narrative. And what is an event? A real event is something that happens: a happening, an occurrence, an event. A narrated event is the symbolization of a real event: a temporal icon. A narration is the symbolic presentation of a sequence of events connected by subject matter and related by time. Without temporal relation we have only a list. Without continuity of subject matter we have another kind of list. A telephone directory is a list, but we can give it a strong push in the direction of narrative by adding the word "begat" between the first and second entries and the words "who begat" after each successive entry until the end. This will resemble certain minimal religious narratives, even down to the exclusion of female names from most of the list (the appearance of nonpersonal listings in the phone book complicates things, of course).

Any set of events that can be sequenced and related can also be narrated: stages in the growth of a plant, the progress of a disease, the painting of a picture, the building of an automobile, the wrecking of an automobile, or the erosion of a stone. A narration, then, is a text which refers, or seems to refer, to some set of events outside of itself. Such a text always involves its interpreter in the construction of a very specific kind of iconic interpretant which we have learned to call "diegesis."

A narrative is a specific sort of collective sign or text which has for its object (in Peirce's sense) a sequence of events and for its interpretant a diegesis (the icon of a series of events). It is a formal feature of narrative texts—a part of their grammar—that the events are always presented in the past tense, as having already happened. Even if the grammatical tense of the discourse shifts to the present, as in certain epistolary novels, the fact of textualization ensures that interpretation follows the event.

The difference between drama and narrative is not that characters speak in drama but that we hear them; not that they have bodies but that we see them. Drama is presence in time and space; narrative is past, always past. In viewing film, of course, we are not in the presence of actors but of their traces on a screen. To speak of events in the future tense is not to narrate them either. Science fiction novels are always told in the past tense. To speak of the future is to prophesy or predict or speculate— never to narrate.

A narration involves a selection of events for the telling. They must offer sufficient continuity of subject matter to make their chronological sequence significant, and they must be presented as having happened already. When the telling provides this sequence with a certain kind of shape and a certain level of human interest, we are in the presence not merely of narrative but of story. A story is a narrative with a certain very specific syntactic shape (beginning-middle-end or situation-transformation-situation) and with a subject matter which allows for or encourages the projection of human values upon this material. Virtually all stories are about human beings or humanoid creatures. Those that are not invariably humanize their material through metaphor and metonymy.

When we speak of narrative, we are usually speaking of story, though story is clearly a higher (because more rule-governed) category. And it is story of which I wish to speak in the remainder of this essay. My intention is to try to clarify certain aspects of "story" by examining the whole process of encoding and decoding stories in the light of the Peircean triad of semiosis: sign, object, and interpretant. The object of a story is the sequence of events to which it refers; the sign of a story is the text in which it is told (print, film, etc.); and the interpretant is the diegesis or constructed sequence of events generated by a reading of the text. Let us call these three aspects of a story simply the *events,* the *text,* and the *interpretation.*

Now, each of these three aspects of "story" has its own temporal structure. Events flow in "natural" time and receive there both an order and a duration that are fixed. A text is a set of signs that refer to a selection of events. These signs have their own order and duration which will not necessarily correspond to that of the events in their natural state. An *interpretation* of a textual story always includes an attempt to recapitulate the natural order and duration of events. It is this structure that enables all of the intricate analytical treatment of narrative order, duration, and frequency developed by Gérard Genette in *Narrative Discourse.*[4] We must also observe that there is a necessary sequence among the three elements of story that we have been discussing. Narrative is

4. See Gérard Genette's *Narrative Discourse: An Essay in Method,* trans. Jane E. Lewin (Ithaca, N.Y., 1980).

always presented *as if* the events came first, the text second, and the interpretation third, so that the interpretation, by striving toward a re-creation of the events, in effect completes a semiotic circle. And in this process, the events themselves have become humanized—saturated with meaning and value—at the stage of entextualization and again at the stage of interpretation.

Our customary distinction between historical and fictional narrative can be clarified in terms of this structure. History is a narrative discourse with different rules than those that govern fiction. The producer of a historical text affirms that the events entextualized did indeed occur prior to the entextualization. Thus it is quite proper to bring extra-textual information to bear on those events when interpreting and evaluating a historical narrative. Any important event which is ignored or slighted by a historical narrative may properly be offered as a weak-ness in that narrative. It is certainly otherwise with fiction, for in fiction the events may be said to be created by and with the text. They have no prior temporal existence, even though they are presented *as if* they did. As Sidney rightly pointed out four centuries ago, the writer of fiction does not *affirm* the prior existence of his events, he only pretends to through a convention understood by all who share his culture.

Once this major distinction between fictional and historical dis-courses is accepted, we must acknowledge that they still have much in common. Both history and fiction assume the normal flow of events, and the interpretation of both kinds of texts involves the construction of a diegesis in which this flow is re-created by the interpreter with every event in order and all relationships as clear as possible. The reader's desire to order and to know are the sources of what Roland Barthes has called (in *S/Z*) the proairetic and hermeneutic codes in narrative. These codes, like all codes, are cultural; that is, they are the common property of all members of a cultural group. Or to invert the metaphor, all mem-bers of such a group are possessed by those codes. Our need for chronological and causal connection defines and limits all of us—helps to make us what we are.

Post-modernist anti-narratives, such as the one discussed at this con-ference by Jacques Derrida, can quite properly be seen as attempts to frustrate our automatic application of these codes to all our event-texts. Such anti-narratives are in this sense metafictional because they ulti-mately force us to draw our attention away from the construction of a diegesis according to our habitual interpretive processes. By frustrating this sort of closure, they bring the codes themselves to the foreground of our critical attention, requiring us to see them *as* codes rather than as aspects of human nature or the world. The function of anti-narrative is to problematize the entire process of narration and interpretation for us.

To what end? One may well ask. These metafictional gestures must be seen, I believe, as part of a larger critical or deconstructive enterprise which is revolutionary in the deepest sense. From this standpoint, traditional narrative structures are perceived as part of a system of psychosocial dependencies that inhibit both individual human growth and significant social change. To challenge and lay bare these structures is thus a necessary prelude to any improvement in the human situation. In this view, narrativity itself, as we have known it, must be seen as an opiate to be renounced in the name of the improvements to come. I understand this project somewhat and even sympathize with it to some extent, but I must confess that I am not sanguine about its success. Even with respect to the narrative processes we are considering here, it seems to me likely that they are too deeply rooted in human physical and mental processes to be dispensed with by members of this species. We can and should be critical of narrative structuration, but I doubt if even the most devoted practitioner of anti-narrativity can do without it.

Afterthoughts on Narrative

III

Narrative Versions, Narrative Theories

Barbara Herrnstein Smith

Contemporary narrative theory is, in many respects, a quite sophisticated area of study: it is international and interdisciplinary in its origins, scope, and pursuits and, in many of its achievements, both subtle and rigorous. It also appears to be afflicted, however, with a number of dualistic concepts and models, the continuous generation of which betrays a lingering strain of naive Platonism and the continued appeal to which is both logically dubious and methodologically distracting.

The sort of dualism to which I refer is discernible in several of the present essays and is conspicuous in the title of Seymour Chatman's recently published study, *Story and Discourse*. That doubling (that is, story *and* discourse) alludes specifically to a two-leveled model of narrative that seems to be both the central hypothesis and the central assumption of a number of narratological theories which Chatman offers to set forth and synthesize. The dualism recurs throughout his study in several other sets of doublet terms: "deep structure" and "surface manifestation," "content plane" and "expression plane," *"histoire"* and *"récit," "fabula"* and *"sjužet,"* and "signified" and "signifier"—all of which, according to Chatman, may be regarded as more or less equivalent distinctions: "Structuralist theory argues that each narrative has two parts: a story *(histoire)* [that is,] the content . . . and a discourse *(discours),* that is, the expression, the means by which the content is communicated."[1]

---

1. Seymour Chatman, *Story and Discourse: Narrative Structure in Fiction and Film* (Ithaca, N.Y. and London, 1978), p. 19; all further references to this work will be included in the text.

Chatman outlines various arguments that have been presented by various narrative theorists to support this model, one of which originates in the observation that the same story may exist in many different versions and, indeed, in many different modes and media. Thus, in his essay, he notes that *Cinderella* may be manifested "as verbal tale, as ballet, as opera, as film, as comic strip, as pantomime, and so on"[2] and, in *Story and Discourse,* elaborates Claude Bremond's claim that every narrative contains

> a layer of autonomous significance, endowed with a structure that can be isolated from the whole of the message. . . . [This basic and autonomous structure] may be transposed from one to another medium without losing its essential properties. . . . [Thus,] the subject of a story may serve as argument for a ballet, that of a novel can be transposed to stage or screen, one can recount in words a film to someone who has not seen it.[3]

"This transposability of the story," remarks Chatman, "is the strongest reason for arguing that narratives are indeed structures independent of any medium" (p. 20). Among the other related reasons are (1) that there is a difference between "discourse-time" and "story-time," that is, between the length of time it takes to read (or hear) a narrative and the length of time occupied by the events referred to in it, and (2) that a set of events that occurred in one order can be narrated in another order or in what is called "nonlinear sequence." These facts and phenomena, it is claimed, require us to posit the existence of two independent levels of narrative structure: the first or basement level, underlying every narrative, is its "deep structure" or "basic story"; the second or upper level is the *narrative discourse* itself, where the basic story is "actualized," "realized," "expressed," or "manifested" in some form—or in many different forms, modes, media, and, thus, *versions* (pp. 22–28).

There are many grounds, logical and empirical, on which one could take issue with this set of claims and arguments, and I shall not attempt

2. Chatman, "What Novels Can Do That Films Can't (and Vice Versa)," p. 118.
3. Claude Bremond, "Le Message narratif," *Communications* 4 (1964): 4; translated by Chatman and cited in *Story and Discourse,* p. 20.

Barbara Herrnstein Smith is professor of English and communications and the director of the Center for the Study of Art and Symbolic Behavior at the University of Pennsylvania. She is the author of *Poetic Closure* and *On the Margins of Discourse.*

to stake them all out here.[4] I shall attempt to demonstrate, however, that the set of narrative "properties" or "phenomena" frequently invoked by Chatman and other narratologists in connection with the two-leveled model of narrative structure neither requires nor supports that model but, on the contrary, reveals its major logical flaws and methodological limitations. In the first section I shall examine the related concepts of narrative versions and basic stories and, in the second, what narratologists refer to as "anachrony" or the various disparities between "the dual time orders" of narrative structure. I shall be concerned, in both sections, not merely to indicate certain weaknesses of the structuralist model but to suggest alternate ways of formulating the problems and explaining the phenomena in question. And, in the concluding section, I shall outline an alternative conception of narrative discourse which, when developed further, would, I believe, permit us to construct richer and more coherent accounts of the nature of narratives generally.

1. Versions and Variants

There are a number of senses in which narratives are commonly said to *be* versions and, conversely, to *have* versions. To recall some of the most familiar: we speak of the King James version of Genesis, Shakespeare's version of Plutarch's *Life of Antony,* an abridged version of *Clarissa,* an expurgated version of *Lady Chatterley's Lover,* a movie version of *Barry Lyndon,* the star witness' version of the shooting, and my teenaged daughter's version of what happened in the girls' bathroom at school on Monday. Most of these versions seem to involve some sort of translated, transformed, or otherwise modified retelling of a particular prior narrative text; the last two seem to involve a narrative account from a particular perspective or from a perspective that is rather pointedly understood to be but one among many (actual or possible). These two major senses of narrative "versions"—that is, as *retellings* of other narratives and as accounts told from a particular or partial *perspective—* will concern us throughout this discussion. I should like to turn now, however, to a specific example to which Chatman alludes, namely, *Cinderella,* and ask to what extent the existence of its many versions, in many modes and media, either supports or illustrates the two-leveled model of narrative.

We may consider, first, the claim that in any narrative the two levels are "autonomous": that is, the repeated reference to a basic story that is

4. I have taken issue with a number of them elsewhere; see "Surfacing from the Deep," *PTL: A Journal for Descriptive Poetics and Theory* 2 (1977): 151–82 (rpt. in *On the Margins of Discourse: The Relation of Literature to Language* [Chicago, 1978], pp. 157–201), for a general critique of the use of models and concepts drawn from transformational-generative linguistics in literary criticism and theory.

independent of any of its versions, independent of any surface manifestation or expression in any material form, mode, or medium—and thus presumably also independent of any teller or occasion of telling and therefore of any human purposes, perceptions, actions, or interactions. As this description suggests, the narratologist's own versionless version of *Cinderella*—that is, its hypothetical basic story—bears an unmistakable resemblance to a Platonic ideal form: unembodied and unexpressed, unpictured, unwritten and untold, this altogether unsullied *Cinderella* appears to be a story that occupies a highly privileged ontological realm of pure Being within which it unfolds immutably and eternally. If this is what is meant by the basic story of *Cinderella,* it is clearly unknowable—and, indeed, literally unimaginable—by any mortal being.

The narratologist might observe, at this point, that although the basic story of *Cinderella* is indeed "an abstraction," its features are not at all difficult to imagine, for it is simply the underlying plot of the fairy tale or what all the versions have in common. This basic story or deep-plot structure is revealed, he might say, whenever we construct a plot summary of any—or all—of the versions. Indeed, he might add, it is the fact that each of us would construct the *same* plot summary of *Cinderella* that demonstrates our intuitive apprehension of its basic story.

It will be instructive, however, to take note of the five hundred-page volume, published in 1893 by the British Folk-lore Society, entitled *Cinderella; three hundred and forty-five variants . . . abstracted and tabulated; with a discussion of mediaeval analogues and notes,* by Marian Roalfe Cox.[5] This volume does not include the cartoon version or the musical version, but it does include the familiar Grimm brothers' version, the earlier version by Charles Perrault, and abstracts of hundreds of other versions from all over Europe, North Africa, India, and the Middle East. In most of them, we find an initially ill-treated or otherwise unfortunate heroine, though sometimes her name is not Cinderella but Cencienta or Aschenputtel, Echenfettle, Fette-Mette or Tan Chan; and sometimes she isn't the youngest stepchild but the oldest daughter; and sometimes she is not a heroine but a hero; and usually the fairy godmother is a cat, a cow, or a tree; and the glass slipper is often a gold ring. Moreover, the turns of plot in many of these tales are likely to be disturbing or intriguing to someone who knows only one set of versions of the Grimm brothers' version. There is, for example, an Icelandic tale, collected in 1866, in which after Cinderella (who is named Mjadveig) marries the prince (who is the captain of a ship), the married couple invite the wicked stepmother to a feast on board the ship at which they serve her salted meat from twelve barrels which contain the remains of the ugly stepsisters, whom Mjadveig and her husband have previously murdered.[6]

5. Cox, *Cinderella* (London, 1893).
6. Abstracted by Cox, pp. 144–45.

I shall return to Cox and some other folklorists but, for the moment, I should like to draw a few morals from the 345 versions of *Cinderella.* The first, which I shall not belabor, is simply that all of us—critics, teachers and students of literature, and narratologists—tend to forget how relatively homogeneous a group we are, how relatively limited and similar are our experiences of verbal art, and how relatively confined and similar are the conditions under which we pursue the study of literature. It is likely that if each reader of this article were asked to give a plot summary of *Cinderella,* the individual summaries would indeed resemble each other fairly closely. The shape of the data is not in dispute; the question is how best to explain it, and I do not believe that we need invoke a two-leveled model to do it. For what the similarities would reveal, I think, is not the uniformity of the intuitively apprehended deep-plot structure of all the versions of *Cinderella* but rather (1) the similarity of our individual prior experiences of particular individual tellings designated *Cinderella;* (2) the similarity of the particular ways in which almost all of us have learned to talk about stories generally; and (3) the fact that all of us, in attempting to construct a plot summary in this particular context and in connection with these particular issues, would be responding to similar conditions and constraints. Because we are so accustomed to performing certain kinds of abstraction, abbreviation, and simplification in the name of "giving plot summaries," those operations come to seem natural, obvious, and nonarbitrary to us. The inclination and ability to perform precisely those operations are, however, by no means innate; they must be learned, and they may be learned differently—or not at all—and therefore performed differently, or not at all.

There is a second point here with even broader implications for narrative theory. Not only will different summaries of the same narrative be produced by people with different conventions, habits, and models of summarizing, but even given the *same* conventions, their summaries will be different if the motives and purposes of their summarizing are different. Thus, one would present a different plot summary of a given novel if one's motive were to advertise it to potential buyers or to deplore its sexism to a friend and still different if one were summarizing the novel in the course of presenting a new interpretation of it or of writing a critical biography of its author. Each of these summaries would simplify the narrative at a different level of abstraction, and each of them would preserve, omit, link, isolate, and foreground different features or sets of features in accord with the particular occasion and purposes of the summarizing. It is evident, moreover, that each of these summaries would, in effect, be another *version* of the novel: an abridged and simplified version, to be sure, but, in that respect, like the one-volume version of *Clarissa* constructed for busy or impatient readers or like the abridged and simplified *Gulliver's Travels* constructed for the amusement of children. My point here is that what narratologists refer to as the basic stories or deep-plot structures of narratives are often not abstract, disembodied, or subsumed entities but quite manifest, material, and particular retellings—and thus versions—of those narratives, constructed, as *all* versions are, by someone in particular, on some occasion, for some purpose, and in accord with some relevant set of principles.

This point will be given further concreteness if we return to Cox's study of *Cinderella* and to its rather touching preface. Clearly the task of collecting, transcribing, classifying, and abstracting those 345 variants was an arduous one. Nevertheless, she wrote, she would "in no wise begrudge the time which that labor has absorbed" if it helped to settle certain difficult questions, "especially [the question] of the origins, independent or otherwise, of stories similar in their incident and widespread in their distribution"[7]: that is, whether all the French, Spanish, German, and Italian Cinderellas, Aschenputtels, and Fette-Mettes were translations or transmissions, migrations or distortions, elaborations or degenerations of some single original story and, if so, whether that archetype or ur-story originated in Europe, or came from India by way of North Africa, or from Iceland by way of Norway, and so forth. Those questions were not, of course, settled by Cox's labors. Nor were they settled by the labors of her successor, Anna Birgitta Rooth, although the latter's study (*The Cinderella Cycle,* published in Lund in 1951) took into account several hundred additional variants and was conducted in accord with a considerably more sophisticated folkloristic methodology. Nor were the questions quite settled in 1974 by the Chinese folklorist Nai Tung-Ting who, after concluding from his examination of eighteen newly discovered Far Eastern variants that "the earliest complete version of Cinderella on record seems to have arisen in North Vietnam," nevertheless ends his book as follows:

> Finally, this writer is not maintaining that Cinderella *certainly* originated in this region. He is merely pointing out that, with our limited knowledge, such a possibility cannot be ruled out. . . . This writer hopes that his humble study has added a little to our knowledge; he hopes as earnestly that he has also shown how much there is still to learn. [Italics mine][8]

In short, the origin of "*the* story of Cinderella" has not yet been determined. Moreover, in the view of most modern folklorists, it cannot be determined: not because the evidence is so meager—or so overwhelming—but rather because it becomes increasingly clear that to ask the question in that form is already to beg it.

By now, folklorists around the world have collected about a

---

7. Cox, pp. lxxi–lxxii.
8. Nai Tung-Ting, *The Cinderella Cycle in China and Indo-China* (Helsinki, 1974), p. 40.

thousand variants of *Cinderella*. All of these stories are in some respects similar and in some respects dissimilar. The incidence, nature, and degrees of resemblance and disparity are so diverse, however, that they allow of just about every conceivable type of causal relation among the stories, including none at all. Cox left no record of her own more desperate speculations, but I think she began to suspect not only that the original version of the Cinderella story could not in the nature of things be tracked down but that the very concept of "the story of Cinderella" might be an artifact of folkloristic assumptions and methodology. In any case, we might now say that the basic Cinderella who was sought by the early folklorists was neither before, behind, nor beneath the 345 variants but was, rather, *comprised* of them—and, more generally, that what *anyone* could mean by "the story of Cinderella" would have to be some set of particular tellings that he or she determined (or agreed) were covariants of each other in accord with some particular, but arbitrary, set of relational criteria.

I emphasized a bit earlier that no narrative version can be independent of a particular teller and occasion of telling and, therefore, that we may assume that every narrative version has been constructed in accord with some set of purposes or interests. The significance of this point for the concept of basic stories will be clearer if we recognize the potential range and variability of such purposes and interests. It will be useful, then, to take brief note of certain types of narratives which Cox did not include in her catalog of variants but which we would nevertheless have good reason to speak of as "versions" of *Cinderella*.

There are, to begin with, such narratives as one might read in popular magazines about the careers of those movie stars and rock musicians who seem to rise recurrently from poverty and obscurity to exalted status in the glittering world of Hollywood or New York. One such magazine advertises on its cover: "Read the Real-Life Cinderella-Story of Sylvester Stallone"; and it is clear that the story within *is* a version of *Cinderella* and that both are "basically the same story"—rags-to-riches, as we sometimes put it, in a neat three-word plot summary (and version) of *Cinderella*.

There are also such retellings of the tale as the one that appears in Julius E. Heuscher's volume, *A Psychiatric Study of Myths and Fairy Tales: Their Origin, Meaning and Usefulness*. Heuscher offers a reading of *Cinderella* as basically a story of psycho-sexual development. The three visits to the prince's ball, he suggests, are occasions for erotic arousal from which the young girl flees, trying to evade sexual maturity. "Eventually," however, Heuscher tells us, "Cinderella is able to confront her lover, and painlessly she lets the foot slip into the slipper."[9] This reading is, of

9. Julius E. Heuscher, *A Psychiatric Study of Myths and Fairy Tales* (Springfield, Ill., 1974), p. 225.

course, an "interpretation" of *Cinderella*. It is also a retelling and thus a version of the tale; indeed, it also represents an attempt to identify the basic story of *Cinderella*, though it is certainly not the *same* basic story that might be identified by a folklorist or narratologist.

A supplementary catalog of *Cinderella*-variants might include other readings produced by other types of literary scholars—such as critics, biographers, and historians—who have had occasion to discover and/or construct versions of *Cinderella*. I recall, for example, a colleague who was able to demonstrate that all of Charles Dickens' novels are basically versions of *Cinderella*. Since this scholar did not claim that Dickens intended his novels as adaptations of or allusions to the fairy tale, it would be hard to say whether his own readings of *David Copperfield, Oliver Twist,* and *Great Expectations* as Cinderella-stories actually made those novels into versions of *Cinderella* or only discovered that they were versions. When we reconsider the work of Cox, Heuscher, and the magazine writer, we see that a troubling question arises here, namely, who is responsible for a version *being* a version? Can it be only someone who, like Rossini and Walt Disney, *designs and intends* a narrative as such? Or can it also be someone who, like Cox and the other folklorists, *identifies and classifies* it as such? And, in that case, can it not also, apparently, be someone who, like the Dickens scholar, *perceives and interprets* it as such?

Before attempting to solve that puzzle, I should mention a theological-minded friend who, when I revealed my interest in *Cinderella,* revealed to me in turn that the story is, basically, an allegory of Christian redemption: Cinderella is the soul, he said; her initial consignment to a place in the ashes represents the soul's initial confinement to the flesh; the fairy godmother is Grace, the transformation of the pumpkin is transubstantiation, and the prince. . . . I stopped him at that point, just as he was warming to the subject and beginning to explain how *Cinderella* is thus basically the same story as *The Divine Comedy, Pilgrim's Progress, King Lear,* and the *Aeneid.* I thought once more of Cox and the 345 variants, one of which is, in fact, what she called "the King Lear branch" of the story.[10] I thought especially of her uneasy feeling, as she intimated it in the preface, that if she had continued her labors long enough, all stories would have turned out to be versions of *Cinderella*—and of my own increasing suspicion, as my friend spoke, that *Cinderella* would turn out to be basically all stories.

It has not been my intention here to display a chaos of paradoxes and infinite regresses. It has been, rather, to suggest how a consideration of the phenomenon of narrative versions leads repeatedly to certain conclusions that challenge either the validity or the necessity of the two-leveled model of narrative structure. I alluded earlier, in connection with the Platonic version of *Cinderella* projected by that model (dis-

10. Cox, pp. lxvii *et passim.*

embodied, untold, unheard, and so forth), to the evident absence from that version of any tellers or occasions of telling and thus the absence of any human purposes, perceptions, actions, or interactions. I was not indulging there in the familiar humanistic pieties commonly directed against structuralist theories. My point was, rather, that *to the extent that contemporary narrative theory omits consideration of such variables, it drastically constricts its own explanatory resources.* I shall return to those variables in the second and third sections. Here, however, I should like to review and summarize the preceding general points:

1. For any particular narrative, there is no single *basically* basic story subsisting beneath it but, rather, an unlimited number of other narratives that can be *constructed in response* to it or *perceived as related* to it.

2. Among the narratives that can be constructed in response to a given narrative are not only those that we commonly refer to as "versions" of it (for example, translations, adaptations, abridgements, and paraphrases) but also those retellings that we call "plot summaries," "interpretations," and, sometimes, "basic stories." None of these retellings, however, is more absolutely basic than any of the others.

3. For any given narrative, there are always *multiple* basic stories that can be constructed in response to it because basic-ness is always arrived at by the exercise of some set of operations, in accord with some set of principles, that reflect some set of interests, all of which are, by nature, variable and thus multiple. Whenever we start to cut back, peel off, strip away, lay bare, and so forth, we always do so in accord with certain assumptions and purposes which, in turn, create hierarchies of relevance and centrality; and it is in terms of these hierarchies that we will distinguish certain elements and relations as being central or peripheral, more important or less important, and more basic or less basic.

4. The form and features of any "version" of a narrative will be a function of, among other things, the particular motives that elicited it and the particular interests and functions it was designed to serve. Some versions, such as translations and transcriptions, may be constructed in order to preserve and transmit a culturally valued verbal structure. Others, such as adaptations and abridgements, may be constructed in order to amuse or instruct a specific audience. And *some* versions, such as "interpretations," "plot summaries," and "basic stories," may be constructed in order to advance the objectives of a particular discipline, such as literary history, folklore, psychiatry—or, of course, narratology. None of these latter versions, however, is any less motivated or, accordingly, formally contingent than any of the other versions constructed to serve other interests or functions.

5. Among any array of narratives—tales or tellings—in the universe, there is an unlimited number of potentially perceptible *relations*. These relations may be of many different kinds and orders, including formal and thematic, synchronic and diachronic, and causal and non-

causal. Whenever these potentially perceptible relations become actually perceived, it is by virtue of some set of interests on the part of the perceiver: thus different relations among narratives will be perceived by anthropologists and anthologists, theologians and folklorists, literary historians and narratologists. Since new sets of interests can emerge at any time and do emerge continuously, there can be no ultimately basic sets of relations among narratives, and thus also no "natural" genres or "essential" types, and thus also no limit to the number or nature of narratives that may sometime be seen as versions or variants of each other.

* * *

Some of the methodological confusions that are encouraged by the conception of narrative versions as sets of differing surface realizations of a single basic story are illustrated in Chatman's essay. He offers to demonstrate how, by closely studying "film and novel versions of the 'same' narrative," the narratologist can "reveal...the peculiar powers of the two media. Once we grasp those peculiarities," he observes, "the reasons for the differences in form, content, and impact of the two versions strikingly emerge."[11] His analysis of Maupassant's story and Renoir's film is certainly painstaking in its comparison of various features and effects of the two works. Nevertheless, it is questionable whether any sturdy generalizations regarding the peculiar powers of the two media could be derived from the analysis, and it is also questionable to what extent Chatman did establish the reasons for the differences between the two works.

First, it should be noted that in comparing the film and the story Chatman confuses several *different kinds of differences,* among them the following:

1. the different technical properties of distinct media: thus, "film" as images photographed on celluloid and projected at a certain speed onto a screen versus "novels" as the orthographic characters of a particular linguistic notational system printed on the pages of a book;

2. the different conventions of distinct semiotic systems: thus, "film" as the conventions of cinematic representation versus "novels" as the conventions of verbal discourse;

3. the different traditions and conventions of distinct narrative modes, genres, and styles: thus "film" as French feature movies of the mid-thirties versus "novels" as late nineteenth-century realistic prose fiction;

4. the different skills and more or less idiosyncratic techniques and

11. Chatman, "What Novels Can Do," p. 119. I quote here from the text of the essay circulated among participants in the narrative conference. In the version of this passage reprinted in this volume, the quotation marks around "same" disappear but the equivocation (discussed below) does not.

personal styles of individual artists: thus "film" as the work of Renoir versus "novels" as the work of Maupassant; and, to add a somewhat different but equally significant order of confusion:

5. the particular responses of an individual reader or viewer to two distinct works as a function of his particular expectations, assumptions, interests, and dispositions, the latter being themselves a function of, among other things, his innate temperament and the extent and nature of his prior personal and cultural experiences with all of the above (that is, 1 through 5): thus "film" as Chatman's particular responses to and interpretation of Renoir's *Une Partie de campagne* versus "novel" as his particular responses to and interpretation of Maupassant's story.

Not all of these confusions can be attributed to a dualistic conception of narrative structure, and many of them recur in other compare-and-contrast discussions of different "media." Nevertheless, it was evidently that conception that was reponsible for Chatman's equivocal allusion to the works by Renoir and Maupassant as "two versions of the 'same' narrative," simultaneously suggesting that each of the two works had an independent but parallel relation to some *other* narrative, while also acknowledging (by the bracketing of "same" in inverted commas in the passage cited and more explicitly elsewhere in his essay) that there was, in fact, a specific asymmetrical relation between the two "versions," the Renoir film being an adaptation of that particular Maupassant story. The equivocation was required because the only way that Chatman could, in this case, retain the concept of narrative versions as multiple realizations of a single basic story was for him to *construct* such a story himself on the basis of both works and to treat it as if it had an existence independent of either of them.

The *explanatory* limits and liabilities of the dualistic model are also illustrated in Chatman's presentation; for the manufacture and invocation of this altogether too handy "hypothetical construct" (that is, the basic story) has effectively obscured the existence, operation, and significance of numerous "reasons for the differences in form, content, and impact" of the two works *other than* those lumped together here as differences in their respective "media." I refer, of course, to all those social, cultural, and other contextual conditions that might otherwise have been examined for their relevance to the differences between a particular narrative and the *retelling* of it a half-century later—after a great deal of water had passed under the bridges of the French countryside.

2. Narrative Anachronies and the Legacy of Linguistic Dualism

As indicated earlier, there are certain phenomena relating to *temporality* that are frequently invoked by theorists as evidence for the validity or necessity of the double-leveled model of narrative structure. I should like to turn now to a consideration of two of the most prominent of these:

(1) what Chatman, in *Story and Discourse,* refers to as the distinction between "discourse-time" and "story-time" and explains as the fact that there is commonly a disparity between "the time it takes to peruse [or to "present"] the discourse" and "the duration of the purported [or "actual"] events of the narrative" (pp. 62–63) and (2) what Nelson Goodman, in his analysis of time-twisted tales, refers to as the possible "disparity between the order of telling [the incidents in a narrative] and the order of occurrence."[12]

One would not deny, of course, that the time it takes someone to read *War and Peace* may differ from the time it took the Russians to defeat Napoleon—or Pierre and Natasha to live out their lives. It is certainly also the case that a narrator may relate events in a non-chronological order, telling us, for example, about someone's funeral before telling us about his childhood, as Tolstoy does in "The Death of Ivan Ilych." The question at issue, however, is neither the existence of these possibilities nor their interest and significance in the experience of narrative. Rather, it is whether either of these temporal disparities—or both of them taken together—requires us to posit the existence of two distinct, independent time orders for every narrative or, conversely, whether they can be understood in terms that do not already *assume* a dual-leveled model of narrative structure.

With respect to the first of the temporal disparities mentioned above—that is, the possibility of a difference between the *durations* of discourse-time and story-time—we may begin by observing that it is not clear what makes this disparity especially remarkable, or especially relevant to narrative, or especially relevant to narrative time. After all, there is also a difference between the length of time occupied by the siege of Moscow and the length of time it takes me to *say* "the siege of Moscow," as well as a difference between the area of space covered by Moscow, the city, and the area covered by the inscribed *word,* "Moscow."[13] All of these disparities—along with those cited as "phenomena," "features," and "salient properties" of narrative time—are what we learn to take for granted as the consequences of the conventional nature of language: that is, the fact that there may be and usually are *differences* between the formal properties of a linguistic event and the set of conditions conventionally implied by the occurrence of an event of that form.

12. Nelson Goodman, "Twisted Tales; or, Story, Study, and Symphony," p. 100.
13. Indeed, see *Story and Discourse,* pp. 96–106, for a corresponding and equally problematic discussion of "story-space" and "discourse-space." (The disparity of *area* mentioned above does not, it should be noted, receive any attention from Chatman or, to my knowledge, from any other narratologist.)

The question then becomes why, in view of their considerable sophistication concerning literary, linguistic, and semiotic conventions, narrative theorists appear to regard these temporal disparities as so phenomenal in connection with *narratives* and in need of special explanations and explanatory models. Part of the answer, I suspect, is the prominence given to such disparities in early Formalist theory—often as illustrations of, precisely, the taken-for-granted conventions of language and fiction and their possible "defamiliarization" in such novels or anti-novels as *Tristram Shandy*.[14]

There may be another part to the answer, however, and it brings us closer to the issue at hand, that is, to the relation between the various phenomena of narrative time and the dualistic model of narrative structure. Specifically, I would suggest that temporal disparities or anachronies will appear especially noteworthy only to the extent that one expects them to be otherwise: only, in other words, if one expects these two time orders to be conformant, equivalent, synchronic, or otherwise *correspondent*. As Gérard Genette remarks, the narratologist, in "pinpointing and measuring these narrative *anachronies* . . . implicitly assume[s] the existence of a kind of zero degree that would be a condition of perfect temporal correspondence between narrative and story."[15] Such an expectation of conformity is encouraged and supported by a conception of discourse as consisting of sets of discrete signs which, in some way, *correspond to* (depict, encode, denote, refer to, and so forth) sets of discrete and specific ideas, objects, or events. It is precisely such a conception of discourse that dominates contemporary narrative theory, and it is the dualism at the heart of that model of *language* that provides the scaffolding for the two-leveled model of narrative. (This model of language has, of course, been the major one in Western intellectual history and, in spite of some epistemological doubts and technical modifications introduced recently by various linguists and philosophers of language, it continues to be the model that dominates not only narratology but literary studies generally.)

An alternative conception of language views utterances not as strings of discrete signifiers that represent corresponding sets of discrete signifieds but as *verbal responses*—that is, as *acts* which, like any acts, are *performed in response to various sets of conditions*. These conditions consist of all those circumstantial and psychological variables of which every utter-

14. See esp. Viktor Shklovsky's classic essay, "Sterne's *Tristram Shandy:* Stylistic Commentary" (originally published in 1925), in *Russian Formalist Criticism: Four Essays*, trans. and ed. Lee T. Lemon and Marion J. Ries (Lincoln, Neb., 1965).

15. Gérard Genette, *Narrative Discourse: An Essay in Method,* trans. Jane E. Lewin (Ithaca, N.Y., 1980), pp. 35–36. Genette's immediately subsequent observation, that "this point of reference is more hypothetical than real," is discussed below in connection with nonlinear sequence.

ance is a function. Although *some* of these conditions are conventionally implied by and are, accordingly, inferable from the linguistic form of an utterance, they are not confined to and cannot be reduced to specific "referents" or "signifieds." In accord with this alternative view of language, individual narratives would be described not as sets of surface-discourse-signifiers that represent (actualize, manifest, map, or express) sets of underlying-story-signifieds but as the verbal acts of particular narrators performed in response to—and thus shaped and constrained by—sets of multiple interacting conditions. For any narrative, these conditions would consist of (1) such circumstantial variables as the particular context and material setting (cultural and social, as well as strictly "physical") in which the tale is told, the particular listeners or readers addressed, and the nature of the narrator's relationship to them, and (2) such psychological variables as the narrator's motives for telling the tale and all the particular interests, desires, expectations, memories, knowledge, and prior experiences (including his knowledge of various events, of course, but also of other narratives and of various conventions and traditions of storytelling) that elicited his telling it on that occasion, to that audience, and that shaped the particular way he told it.[16] Since all the formal properties of an individual narrative would be regarded as *functions of all these multiple interacting conditions* rather than as *representations of* specific, discrete objects, events, or ideas, the expectation of a conformity or formal correspondence between any of the properties of a narrative and anything else in particular simply would not arise. I would suggest, moreover, that the development of this sort of alternative conception of discourse and symbolic behavior generally may help clarify why traditional assumptions and latter-day affirmations of a correspondence between "language" and "the world" are untenable and thus move us beyond the mere *denial* of such a correspondence (as in the Heideggerian and post-structuralist insistence on "discrepancies," "failures," "ruptures," and "absences")—in short, beyond the whole "problematic of language."[17]

16. As I have stressed elsewhere, we cannot and need not draw a strict line between the "internal" and "external" or "physical" and "psychological" variables to which any act is a response; see *On the Margins of Discourse,* p. 17. On the narrator's prior "knowledge of events," see the discussion below.

17. The conception of language and symbolic behavior to which I allude here is developed further in *On the Margins of Discourse;* see esp. pp. 15–24 and 85–104. For related discussions representing a number of disciplines and intellectual traditions, see Kenneth Burke, *The Philosophy of Literary Form: Studies in Symbolic Action* (Baton Rouge, La., 1941; New York, 1957); B. F. Skinner, *Verbal Behavior* (New York, 1957); V. N. Vološinov, *Marxism and the Philosophy of Language,* trans. Ladislav Matejka and I. R. Titunik (Leningrad, 1930; New York, 1973); Dell Hymes, *Foundations in Sociolinguistics* (Philadelphia, 1974); Erving Goffman, *Frame Analysis: An Essay in the Organization of Experience* (New York, 1974); and Morse Peckham, *Explanation and Power: The Control of Human Behavior* (New York, 1979).

Given this alternative view of language, much of the scaffolding of the double-leveled model disappears; but so does the need for that model, for an alternative conception of narrative accordingly becomes available.

* * *

Most of the foregoing remarks concerning narrative anachrony in the sense of the disparities between the duration of discourse-time and story-time may be extended directly to the phenomenon of nonlinear sequence, that is, to the fact that, as narrative theorists sometimes put it, the sequence of events "in a given story" can be rearranged "at the discourse-level." I shall consider nonlinear sequence separately, however, because it constitutes one of the major arguments for the two-leveled model of narrative structure and because that argument in turn raises questions of more general interest for narrative theory.

We may first note that most descriptions of nonlinear sequence imply the possibility of *linear* sequence: the possibility, once again, of there being an exact match or correspondence, here between the chronological order of some set of events and the temporal deployment of the elements of some narrative utterance. The question that is raised or begged, then, is whether—or to what extent—such a correspondence ever can or does occur. Genette, who has extensively explored the various aspects of narrative anachrony, remarks that the possibility of such a correspondence is "more hypothetical than real" but continues: "Folklore narrative habitually conforms, at least in its major articulations, to chronological order, but our (Western) literary tradition, in contrast, was inaugurated by a characteristic effect of anachrony."[18] He then goes on to describe in some detail the "beginning *in medias res*" of the *Iliad*. There is reason, however, to question the propriety of that contrast between folklore and literary tradition, especially the implication of a literary-historical progression from some presumably prehistoric naive narrative synchrony to a subsequent more sophisticated narrative anachrony. For it can be demonstrated not only that absolute chronological order is as *rare* in folkloric narratives as it is in any literary tradition but that it is virtually *impossible* for any narrator to sustain it in an utterance of more than minimal length. In other words, by virtue of the very nature of discourse, nonlinearity is the rule rather than the exception in narrative accounts. Indeed, for that reason, the literary-historical "progression" is probably closer to being the reverse of what Genette implies: that is, to the extent that *perfect* chronological order may be said to occur at all, it is likely to be found only in acutely self-conscious, "artful," or "literary" texts.

18. Genette, *Narrative Discourse*, p. 36.

There is, however, a second and even more significant question raised by narrative theorists' allusions to the fact that the chronological order of "a given set of events" (or the sequence of events "in a given story" or "the succession of episodes" in the "underlying plot") can be *re*-arranged (or "reordered," "distorted," "deformed," "twisted," or "zig-zagged") in or by "the narrative."[19] For they all imply that prior to and independent of the narrative in question there existed some particular determinate set of events in some particular determinate (untwisted) order or sequence. And the question here is whether, for every time-twisted narrative (which is to say, for virtually every narrative), there always is such a prior and independent set and sequence of events—and also in what sense any of those stories or sets of events are "given."

The answer to the first part of this question is, I think, *no*. There are, of course, narratives (such as chronicles, news reports, gospels, and personal anecdotes) that are the accounts of events that have presumably already occurred in some determinate chronological sequence. There are also narratives (such as latter-day versions of *Cinderella* or *The Life of Jesus*) that relate events (whether presumed to be historical or fictional) which are already known to their narrators (and probably to their audiences) from prior tellings or other sources. And, in these cases, it makes some sense to speak of the narrative in question as having rearranged the sequence of some given set of events or the events of some given story. Indeed, one suspects that these two types of narrative (that is, historical reports and twice-told tales) serve as unconscious paradigms for the narratologist, which may, in turn, help explain his need to posit underlying plot structures or basic stories to account for the sequential features of those rather different narratives that he *does* study most closely, namely, works of literary fiction. For in addition to the two types of narrative just mentioned, there are all those fictive narratives which consist neither of the reports of particular historically determinate events nor the retellings of more or less familiar tales. And, in these instances, which would include such works as "The Death of Ivan Ilych," *The Good Soldier,* and *Absalom, Absalom!,* there evidently are *no* sets and sequences of events that, already arranged in some particular way, could be spoken of as *re*arranged—unless one *posits* them in the form of subterranean plots or immaterial Platonic stories in which all the events that are "twisted," "zig-zagged," or "deformed" up above in the narrative level are, by definition, always "given" in proper chronological sequence.

It may be objected here by those who are not especially committed to the two-leveled model that novels and other works of fiction nevertheless *do* have certain prior and independent sets and sequences of events, these being the particular plots or sets of events that their

19. I quote here from Genette and from the papers delivered at the narrative conference by Chatman, Goodman, and Ricoeur.

authors *thought of* or *imagined* prior to composing those narratives. But this objection simply begs the original question in another way. To be sure, a novelist is likely to have had images of particular incidents which, together with various more or less articulated ideas and more or less vivid recollections of actual incidents, persons, and places, formed the creative materials from which a novel was ultimately fashioned. There is, however, no reason to suppose that these images, ideas, recollections, and so forth were themselves narrative in structure—that is, no reason to suppose that they comprised plots or storylike sets of events arranged in some determinate sequence—prior to and independent of the very narrative by which their author made them manifest.

We may, in fact, extend this point back to those paradigm narratives, mentioned above, that report not imaginary events but events which presumably occurred at some particular prior time. For like our imaginings of events that never occurred, our knowledge of *past* events is usually *not* narrative in structure or given in storylike sequences: on the contrary, that knowledge is most likely to be in the form of general and imprecise recollections, scattered and possibly inconsistent pieces of verbal information, and various visual, auditory, and kinesthetic images—some of which, at any given time, will be more or less in or out of focus and all of which will be organized, integrated, and apprehended as a specific "set" of events only in and through the very act by which we narrate them as such.[20]

It appears, then, that there are very few instances in which we can sustain the notion of a set and sequence of events altogether prior to and independent of the discourse through which they are narrated. Indeed, it appears that the best way to conceive of the sets of events that narratives seem to relate is not as specific, historically determinate, or otherwise stable and given phenomena but, rather, as the variable inferences and constructs that narratives characteristically elicit from their audiences or, indeed, as the various processes and activities of inferring, construing, projecting, hypothesizing, imagining, anticipating, and so forth that constitute our characteristic cognitive *responses to* narratives.

Two points should be emphasized here. One is that the audience of a narrative may not ever have any reason or occasion to arrest, stabilize, or verbally articulate this set of responses, in which case his inferences

20. At the narrative conference, comparable observations were made by Roy Schafer in connection with the "life-histories" achieved through psychoanalysis. See also Hayden White, "The Historical Text as Literary Artifact," *Clio* 3, no. 3 (1974), rpt. in his *Tropics of Discourse* (Baltimore, 1978), pp. 81–100, and Jonathan Culler's discussion of the recurrent opposition between "the priority and determining power of events and the determination of events by structures of signification" in "Fabula and Sjuzhet in the Analysis of Narrative," *Poetics Today* 1, no. 3 (1980): 27–37. The general intellectual movement from assumptions of "a world fixed and found" to the recognition of "a diversity of . . . versions or worlds in the making" is one in which Goodman himself has vigorously participated: see his *Ways of Worldmaking* (Indianapolis, 1978), p. x.

and constructs will *remain* in a fluid and mutable state. In other words, if no one ever asks us to *tell* "what happened" in *King Lear* or in *Madame Bovary,* our sense of what happened in the play or novel will remain indeterminate and unfixed, moving from an active process of imagining and inferring to a subsequent condition of variable recollection or potential retrieval. The second point is that the degree of specificity and richness of our inferences will, in any case, always depend upon, among other things, the nature of our *interest* in that narrative. Thus, if one is a jury member attending to a witness' account of a shooting or a professor of literature preparing a lecture on *King Lear* or *Madame Bovary,* one is likely to attempt to draw maximally specific and detailed inferences, perhaps rehearsing the narrative many times over, covertly or overtly, in an effort to visualize details with maximum vividness and to arrange the sequence of events with maximum coherence. If, on the other hand, a colleague rambles on about some car accident he passed driving to work that morning, one's inferences and constructions in response to *that* narrative are likely to be relatively vague and thin, and the entire cognitive engagement that it elicits is likely to be exhausted fairly rapidly.

It is clear from the foregoing discussion that an adequate account of the phenomenon of nonlinear sequence must turn that phenomenon around: that is, what must be described and explained is not how (or within what limits)[21] a narrator can *re*arrange the chronology of a given set of events but rather how, on what bases, and, sometimes, whether his audience will infer from his narrative the chronology of some set of events that is *not given.* I suggested above that, as part of the total process of a listener's (reader's or viewer's) engagement with any narrative, he will usually attempt to construe some chronology of events, more or less stable or unstable, rough or precise, depending on the nature of his interest in the narrative. It may be further observed that he will always tend to do so on the basis of some combination of the following: (1) his prior knowledge or beliefs concerning the chronology of those implied events as derived from other sources, including other narratives; (2) his familiarity with the relevant conventions of the language in which that narrative is presented (verb tenses, adverbs, and adverbial clauses, and so forth, and comparable time markers in other modes and media); (3) his familiarity with the relevant conventions and traditions of the style and genre of that narrative; (4) his knowledge and beliefs, including cultural assumptions, with respect to how things in general, and the particular kinds of things with which that narrative is concerned, happen and "follow from" each other—that is, his sense of the "logic" of temporal and causal sequence; and (5) certain more or less universal perceptual and cognitive tendencies involved in his processing—apprehending and organizing—information in any form.

21. See Goodman's "Twisted Tales."

Narrators, literary and other, characteristically assume the potency and operation of all these tendencies in their audiences and design their tales to exploit them accordingly. Commonly, a narrator will design his tale so as to lead his audience to make certain more or less specific and stable inferences appropriate to the nature of his *own* interests in the narrative transaction. The success of his design cannot, of course, ever be insured, and it is most unlikely to be total for all present, presumed, or potential audiences. It might be noted here, moreover, that (as the Formalists delighted in demonstrating and as the works of Sterne, Borges, Robbe-Grillet, and Barth, among others, exemplify—and as Derrida's contribution to the narrative conference was perhaps meant to remind us) the narrator always has the option of subverting the conventions and thwarting the operation of any or all of the cognitive tendencies listed above. The result may be a tale that provides for its audience an increased measure of cognitive interest at the expense of a smooth and efficient access to information. And, at the extremes noted above, it may offer, if that much less of the profit and pleasure provided by *un récit bien fait,* then that much more of the gratification one derives from observing (and perhaps having the occasion to exhibit) the twist and play of one's own mind in its engagement with a well-made narrative toy.[22] Contemporary narrative theorists have certainly recognized the existence of conventional linguistic and generic time markers and of the various cognitive tendencies outlined above. Indeed, a number of narratologists, including Genette and Chatman, have made them the focus of very substantial attention. What they apparently fail to appreciate, however, is the extent to which a consistent recognition of the operation of these conventions and tendencies would eliminate the need for such concepts and entities as dual time orders and underlying plot structures in describing and explaining the phenomena of narrative temporality.

3. *Narrative Acts and Transactions*

In the preceding two sections, I have suggested that descriptions and accounts based on a dualistic model of narrative discourse are not only empirically questionable and logically frail but also methodologically distracting, preventing us from formulating the problems of narrative theory in ways that would permit us to explore them more fruitfully in connection with whatever else we know about language, behavior, and culture. As already indicated, an alternative to the current narratological model would be one in which narratives were regarded not only as *structures* but also as *acts,* the features of which—like the features of all

22. On the relation between art and "cognitive play," see *On the Margins of Discourse,* pp. 116–24.

other acts—are functions of the variable sets of conditions in response to which they are performed. Accordingly, we might conceive of narrative discourse most minimally and most generally as verbal acts consisting of *someone telling someone else that something happened.* Among the advantages of such a conception is that it makes explicit the relation of narrative discourse to other forms of discourse and, thereby, to verbal, symbolic, and social behavior generally.

It is certainly the case that a narrative action may be accomplished, as Chatman and Bremond observe, through gestures, the display of pictures, and various other nonlinguistic modes and media. It is important to recognize, however, that, even in the narrow linguistic sense, narrative discourse may be composed of quite brief, bare, and banal utterances as well as such extensive and extraordinary tellings as might occupy 1,001 nights or pages. It is also important to recognize that narrative discourse is not necessarily—or even usually—marked off or segregated from other discourse. Almost any verbal utterance will be laced with more or less minimal narratives, ranging from fragmentary reports and abortive anecdotes to those more distinctly framed and conventionally marked tellings that we are inclined to call "tales" or "stories." Indeed, narrative discourse is, at one extreme, hardly distinguishable from description or simply assertion. That is, "telling someone that something happened" can, under certain circumstances, be so close to "saying that something is (or was) the case" that it is questionable if we can draw any logically rigorous distinction between them or, more generally, if any absolute distinction can be drawn between narrative discourse and any other form of verbal behavior.

To be sure, the common opposition of such terms as "report" versus "describe" and our ability to teach children to discriminate between such phrases as "telling a story" and "having a conversation" attest to the *functional* integrity and clarity of such categories and distinctions. Also, narratologists themselves may, in accord with their particular interests and purposes, always establish technically useful distinctions and demarcation points: stipulating, for example (as they sometimes do), that a telling counts as a hardcore narrative only if it describes a transition from one state to an antithetical state or only if the something-that-happened comprises at least two temporally sequential and causally related events. Nevertheless, it is also useful to be mindful of the continuities of narrative with all other discourse and of the extent to which these definitions and distinctions are drawn, not discovered, by narratologists.

A second, related advantage of conceiving of narrative this way— which is to say, as part of a *social transaction*—is that it encourages us to notice and explore certain aspects of narrative that tend to remain obscure or elusive when we conceive of it primarily as a kind of text or structure or any other form of detached and decontextualized entity.[23] For it suggests not only that every telling is produced and experienced under certain social conditions and constraints and that it always involves two parties, an audience as well as a narrator, but also that, as in any social transaction, each party must be individually motivated to participate in it: in other words, that each party must have some *interest* in telling or listening to that narrative.

In view of the fact that things are always happening, it may be reasonably asked why, in any given instance of narrative discourse, someone has chosen (or agreed) to tell someone else that something happened and why the latter has chosen (or agreed) to listen. The general answer to this question is that participation in the narrative transaction is sufficiently in the interest of each party to win out over all currently competing activities for both of them.[24] To make this answer useful, however, we must emphasize that the *nature* of the interests involved on both sides may vary greatly from one transaction to another as may the total *structure of motivation,* that is, the dynamics of the interaction between the narrator's interests and those of his audience. The significance of this emphasis for narrative theory is that it suggests why, in seeking to account for either the forms and features of individual narratives or the similarities and differences among sets of narratives, we might profitably direct our attention to the major variables involved in those transactions: that is, to the *particular* motives and interests of narrators and audiences and to the *particular* social and circumstantial conditions that elicit and constrain the behavior of each of them.

It is clear, for example, that quite *different* sets of interests, motives, and constraints would be involved in each of the following situations: (1) two junior executives in the club car of a commuter train pass the time by exchanging office anecdotes and off-color stories; (2) a radio broadcaster, during the evening news, reports to an audience of several thousand Americans the events surrounding a military coup in central Asia; (3) a political prisoner, under torture, recounts to his interrogators the events leading to the formation of an underground organization; (4) an eminent scholar, whose previously published works have come under attack by revisionist historians, is typing out the final draft of his monumental new history of the antebellum South. It is also clear, I think, that the nature of the particular tale that got told in each of these situations

23. For comparable reasons, a comparable conception of narrative is urged upon folklorists by Robert A. Georges in "Toward an Understanding of Story-Telling Events," *Journal of American Folklore* 82 (1969): 313–29.

24. This is an application to narrative discourse of a law that holds for all discourse, namely: *The fact that something is true is never a sufficient reason for saying it.* The law, some of its implications, and some other related aspects of the economics of verbal transactions are discussed in *On the Margins of Discourse,* pp. 16–17 and 85–106.

would be a function of the sorts of conditions I have been emphasizing: the social and circumstantial context of the narrative and the structure of motivation that sustained the narrative transaction between the teller and his audience.

This last point can be elaborated just a bit. Any narrator's behavior will be constrained in part by various assumptions he will have made concerning his present or presumed audience's motives for listening to him. Although these assumptions will usually be formed on the basis of the narrator's prior knowledge of that audience, they may also be *re*-formed on the basis of feedback from the listener during the transaction itself. The efforts and ability of listeners to shape the tales they hear are evident from the sort of proddings and promptings that are familiar in face-to-face narrative transactions: "And then what happened? But what did he look like? Weren't you frightened? Why don't you just summarize that part? Yes, but what's the point?" I would emphasize, however, that face-to-face transactions are not exceptional in this respect. For we all inevitably learn to anticipate and re-create such reactions: that is, we learn in effect to impersonate our own audiences in advance, and, therefore, this sort of feedback controls the structure of our tales even when our audience is silent or absent—as when we compose narrative texts.

Of course, human motives and interests are always to some extent unpredictable or unknowable, even in face-to-face transactions. Moreover, individual narrators may vary greatly in their ability to gauge accurately their audience's interests and in their sensitivity and responsiveness to feedback. In any case, we know that not every story is "a good story." What may be added is that the conception of narrative discourse outlined here would permit us to describe the necessarily contingent *value* of a narrative in terms of how successfully it accommodates the interests of the parties involved in any of the particular transactions in which, at any time, it figures.

Pursuing this point, we might observe that under certain sets of constraints—for example, during a "prime-time" newscast—the interests of all the parties involved in the transaction will be served best by a narrative of utmost concision, while in other kinds of situations—for example, while attempting to "kill" or "pass" time on the commuter train—the total structure of motivation will accommodate and elicit the most highly elaborated development and extensive digression in the stories that are narrated. The general point suggested here is that the features of *individual* narratives, including literary and fictional works, can be described and accounted for as functions of certain variables that control the features of *all* narratives, including nonliterary and nonfictional ones, and, as a corollary, that similarities and differences among *sets* of narratives can be explored and explained on the basis of similarities and differences in the specific conditions that elicit and constrain them.

Two further methodological implications of the view of narrative outlined here may be briefly noted. One is that, in seeking to account for the distinctive nature, value, and effects of *fictional* narratives, we may take a less travelled road by observing that *the extent to which* a narrator takes or claims responsibility for the veridicality of his tale will serve different interests and, accordingly, have a different sort of value for himself and his audience depending on the nature and constraints of the transaction between them and, conversely, that different situations and structures of motivation will elicit and reward different *kinds and degrees* of truth claims. It is evident, for example, that claims and assumptions of veridicality will have a different significance for each of the parties in the transactions between the prisoner and his interrogators and between the historian and his readers. It is also evident that, under *some* conditions, as when we exchange narrative jokes or present certain other kinds of fictive tellings, such as fables and folktales, the interest and value of an account-of-something-that-happened may be altogether independent of the extent to which veridicality might be claimed for or attributed to it.[25] What these observations suggest is that a number of key problems of narrative theory that are commonly posed and analyzed in philosophic terms—for example, as questions of the "truth value" of fictional "propositions"—could be profitably reformulated in terms of the variable constraints, conventions, and dynamics of verbal transactions and explored accordingly. There is, in fact, no good reason to give logical priority or methodological sovereignty to the traditional preoccupations and procedures of philosophy when, as narrative theorists, we undertake to explore such problems.

Similarly, in seeking to identify the *functions* of storytelling for the individual narrator or his community, a recognition of the variety of possible narrative transactions and the range of interests that they may thereby serve should encourage us to acknowledge and explore the *multiplicity* of functions that may be performed by narratives generally and by any narrative in particular. We would, accordingly, be less likely to expect to find (or to claim to have identified) any single fundamental political purpose or psychological (or transcendental) effect of narratives, whether it be to reflect reality or to supplement it, to reinforce ruling ideologies or to subvert them, to console us for our mortality or to give us intimations of our immortality.

I have offered here only a partial survey of how narratives might be explored from the alternative perspective outlined above, and that perspective is itself only a partial one. My general purpose here, however, has not been to launch an altogether new or preemptive theory of narrative but to suggest that to the extent that our current theories remain

25. For a further discussion of the relation of fictive narratives to narrative discourse generally, see *On the Margins of Discourse,* pp. 127–31 and 194–97.

tied to dualistic models of language and confined to the examination of decontextualized structures, they are deficient in descriptive subtlety and explanatory force—and, conversely, that our accounts of narrative, literary and other, will be richer, sturdier, and more coherent when they are developed as part of a *comprehensive* theory of narrative which reflects a better appreciation of the nature of verbal transactions and the dynamics of social behavior generally. In short, our current versions of narrative are not the whole story or the only story.

Critical Response

I

Everyman His or Her Own Annalist

Louis O. Mink

Historians tell a story of their own profession, and the sequence annals-chronicle-history proper is so firmly ensconced in their history of progress (a historian who will reject every other example of "progress" will not question this one) that it takes a supreme effort of will to entertain Hayden White's hypothesis that annals and chronicles are not naive or degenerate forms of proper history but representations (possibly) of different conceptions of historical reality itself. There are other such conceptions—myth, for example—but annals and chronicles have a primary claim to attention since they are commonly seen as the main stages by which the modern conception of history came into being.

It may not be entirely clear what White's conclusion is about his own hypothesis. In one way it is less a hypothesis than a device which enables him to reconstruct the beliefs and attitudes of the annalist and chronicler. What isn't there in their accounts becomes important for our self-understanding just because it so obviously wasn't important for theirs. The annalist lacked, for example, a principle for assigning importance or significance to events; and he lacked such a principle because he lacked a notion of a social system for whose survival or change some events had more significance than others. This illuminates *our* propensity for narrative by revealing some of its presuppositions. But at the same time it suggests that these presuppositions are themselves not human universals. The annalist did not *fail* to achieve narrative understanding because he didn't have the presuppositions which give meaning to any attempt to achieve it. We in turn lack his presuppositions, one of which was that the chronology of years is not an artificial device but the sequence of

The present essay is a reply to Hayden White, "The Value of Narrativity in the Representation of Reality."

the years of Our Lord and therefore has in its form the fullness and continuity which for us the calendar can have only by virtue of its content of events. For us dates signify events (and we can never fill in all the blanks); for the annalist, on the contrary, events signify dates, unfolding in their own continuity. Thus what for us are discontinuities of events, demanding inquiry, for the annalist are not. Which, White asks, is the more "realistic" expectation?

His answer, as I understand it, is that neither is more realistic. Our demand for narrative intelligibility is no doubt more complex (and in any event it is ours) but not because it brings us closer to the reality of events in their interconnections and relative importance. Rather, the value of narrativity derives from the force of an impulse to moralize events by investing them with a "coherence, integrity, fullness, and closure" that is imaginary—a fiction, though a necessary one which inherits its necessity not from the determinateness of the world but from our inability (however one explains that inability) to contemplate events without redescribing them as connected within a moral order.

All this is as challenging to a nonhistorian as it must be distasteful to a historian (or, shall we say, to a typical historian). I find my thoughts revolving around two centers, one critical and one not, though the latter inevitably leads to the former. The critical center is a doubt whether narrativizing and moralizing are necessarily or universally linked. My counterclaim is that while every story permits a moral interpretation, at least some stories do not demand or presuppose it. The uncritical point extends White's argument and assumes the correctness of everything he says about the annals and the chronicle (though not of everything he says about narrative history proper). Let's begin with the latter.

Historians have never much liked the analogy between history and memory—largely, I believe, because they know history to be hard work while recollection seems passive, noninferential, and unverified. But White's description of annals suggests a renewed consideration of the analogy. It seems to me that the annals form, in all of its characteristics, is exactly modeled on at least one of the ways by which we experience memory. For example, if I were to write down an autobiographical chronology of my primary memories (that is, those summoned up directly and not by their connection with other memories), it would look something like this:

Louis O. Mink, Kenan Professor of Humanities at Wesleyan University, is the author of *Mind, History, and Dialectic: The Philosophy of R. G. Collingwood* and *A "Finnegans Wake" Gazetteer.* He is currently at work on a commentary of Kant's *Critique of Judgment.*

1960.   Kennedy elected President. First year of College of Social Studies.
1961.
1962.
1963.   Carleton College, second semester. Family camping trip through West, Canada, Mexico. Kennedy shot.
1964.
1965.   Family camping trip through Greece, Yugoslavia. For the first time came to see Vietnam as a national disaster.

1966.⎫
1967.⎭ Semester sabbatical somewhere along here.

1968.   Collingwood book finished.
etc.

Now of course the blank years are not unrecallable. Still, this personal annals faithfully records those memories that thrust themselves forward unbidden, at the suggestion of the sequence of years. Other memories may occur more frequently and be felt with greater depth and poignancy, but they appear as it were undated, though not without a general sense of temporal distance. Many recollections I can date only inferentially, by linking them with others until a datable one is reached. Others, like the memory of a particular conversation with someone frequently seen, may be undatable absolutely unless one goes beyond memory to records. The primary chronology, however, remains as the model of historical annals, blank years and all. Both lack a central subject (in the annals of memory, even the self is not necessarily the central subject; I remember the event of Kennedy's assassination, not, in the first instance, my reaction to it or the circumstances of learning of it); both lack organization and anything like narrative coherence; both lack the closure of a story reaching its end or point and having a "meaning." Moreover, and perhaps most importantly, there is (for me) in the annals of primary memory no discomfort about the gaps and discontinuities of the record, just as White suggests was the case for the annalist of events. I don't expect primary memory to be a representation of reality any more than I expect my occasional glances at my wristwatch to be a representation of the continuity and directionality of time. It seems to me that I simply note two things: what memory announces without solicitation and which memories bear—or seem to bear, which amounts to the same thing—chronological markers.

Of course we are seldom content with the deliverances of primary memory, and with any encouragement at all we begin to solicit recollections by questioning, inferring, and imagining. (Proust's memory was a little *madeleine* and a lot of imagination.) Thus from the protocols of annalistic memory we become recollective chroniclers. Now I think that, even uninstructed by White about the differences between chronicle and history, one would quite independently arrive at similar differences between types of recollection. The pursuit of recollection corresponding to chronicle is first of all the attempt to fill in the gaps of unbidden memory; but that requires the institution of a "central subject" because otherwise there is no way of identifying what is a gap in the sequence and what isn't. Moreover, chronicle recollection summons up the past with a faithfulness to detail no conclusion could justify. As White says, a chronicle ends, but the ending does not reveal a structure that retrospectively can be seen to have been immanent in the events all along; historical narrative proper does that.

This is why chronicle recollections are fascinating to the teller, whose recollections they are, and boring to the listener, who has only the pointless story without the vividness of recollected content. When our recollections are truly narrativized—when, that is, they achieve a coherence and point which are the same for the hearer as for the teller—I think we must admit that the witness of recollection no longer attests to their truth in any but a negative sense. That is, we may falsely claim to remember what in fact we don't remember, and then our claim to narrative recollection is false; but even though every memory claim is veridical, the truth of the narrative is not thereby guaranteed since the narrative itself is precisely what is not remembered but constructed. What White says of history proper is exactly true of narrative recollection: to qualify, an event must be susceptible to at least two narrations of its occurrence. If someone tells us a chronicle story of events we both experienced, we may say, "I don't remember that" or, "you forgot to mention such-and-such"; but when someone tells us a fully narrativized story about events we both experienced, we may very well say, "I don't remember it *that way.*" ("Yes, I remember that he didn't respond to the question; but he wasn't deliberately evading it, he just didn't understand it." Intentions and states of mind are not events, but their ascription may be a necessary part of any narration of these events.)

If the differences among types of recollection (or, more precisely, among different ways of employing recollection) correspond to differences among annals, chronicles, and histories as types, White's argument, or part of it, seems additionally confirmed. For the latter differences are thereby grounded in general human capacities and exemplified in common experience. To each of us, at times, the personal past of memory appears in the same discontinuous form as that by which the anonymous annalist of Saint Gall represented the collective record. But at the same time the analogy dehistoricizes the differences among types of historical representation. One may ask, at least, whether these types represent different conceptions of historical reality (which is White's hypothesis) or simply the relations between different interests and what could be essentially identical conceptions of historical reality.

That my chronology of primary recollections contains blanks, like the annalist's record, doesn't at all imply that I believe that events are discontinuous and lack meaning; it is simply a fact about the phenomenology of memory. And while no doubt a good deal could be inferred about me from the annalistic memories I recorded above, what could not be inferred is my conception of historical reality. I simply recorded the deliverances of recollection without reflection; and one might suppose that the annalist simply recorded what was accessible to him without inquiry. The annals form, that is, reveals not the informing principles of a different world view but the absence of a conception of research. Of course this doesn't imply that the annalist didn't have a different conception of historical reality but only that it can't be inferred from the form of his record. Perhaps the annalist was just not a very good diarist; but perhaps he was just not a diarist at all, in the same way that my gap-filled primary memories do not constitute the story of my life and do not even purport to do anything of the sort.

Still, we ordinarily move on from primary memories to recollective chronicle and then to the narrativization of recollection. However even if one agrees that types of recollection correspond to types of historiography, the analogy of memory and history clearly breaks down if one considers not the stages in themselves but the process of moving from one stage to the next. For White the process of narrativization, which is absent from annals, introduced in chronicle, and perfected in history proper, depends on the growing self-consciousness of the centrality of a social system—how it is sustained by notions of law and authority, and how these notions in turn require at least implicit moral justification, not just description. Nothing so elaborate is involved in the series of memory analogues. Of course narrative recollections *might* be presented as moral tales, but they don't have to be, and most are not. (Imagine a Mark Twain-like story of "My First Haircut.") But perhaps the analogy between memory and history doesn't break down, and in histories too the connection between narrative and moral presumption is contingent rather than necessary.

There is of course one sense of "moral" for which White's thesis would certainly be true, and that is when moral simply means "human," as contrasted with "natural." Human beings have intentions and make choices (including choices not to choose); *any* situation in which choice is possible, or by circumstance is rendered impossible, is a moral situation in this broadest sense. Thus the most casual conversation about the weather would in the chronicling of it be a moral account, since every response involves a choice between speech and silence and between saying this and saying something else. But in this sense of moral, White's thesis would be true but vacuous. It would amount merely to observing that accounts of human actions and responses are necessarily in narrative form (which is not vacuous) and necessarily about human actions and

responses (which is). But this isn't White's argument, although the ambiguity of moral may lurk in the background of its apparent persuasive-
ness. Instead White ostensibly argues that narrative proper requires
closure, an ending of the story, and that nothing in the representation
of real events can *count* as an ending except "the passage from one moral
order to another." This seems a lot to ask; are there really as many
passages from one moral order to another as there are narrative histories?

White gives (I think) two reasons for this bold conclusion. The first
is that a narrative must show *a* sequence of real events as coming to an
end while recognizing that *the* sequence of real events goes on: that's
what it is to be "real." In White's words, there is "another story 'waiting
to be told' just beyond the confines of 'the end' " (p. 22). But since no
ending can be found in the endless sequence of real events, it must be
attributed by a moral interpretation which endows a particular sequence
with moral closure. (Failure and success are equally kinds of closure.)
But it can't be a closure unless the succeeding story "waiting to be told"
is in, so to speak, a different key. Otherwise the succeeding story would
merely reveal that the closure of the preceding story was specious. Now
while this argument is cogent, I think it depends on a vacuous interpretation of moral. As W. D. Gallie pointed out, narratives are, in general,
teleological: a narrative moves across a series of contingencies toward
a promised but open conclusion. But every story includes its own past
as both determinate and consequential, and the conclusion toward which
it moves becomes less and less open; when the conclusion is reached, it's
no longer open at all. Stories end, I think, when, from the standpoint
of the story itself (and its protagonists), it's *too late to change.*

That's one answer to White's question, "But on what other grounds
[than moralism] could a narrative of real events *possibly* conclude?" (p.
22). In every story of human affairs, intentions, choices, and actions
move toward the fulfillment or frustration of partially envisioned and
often changing ends. The end reflects meaning back on the events leading up to it, but what in turn *counts* as the end is constituted by the
intentions, choices, and actions referred to in the descriptions of the
events themselves. It may well be, as White says, that in such descriptions
we endow reality with meaning. My point is that it is not only and not
necessarily in representing closure as the passage from one moral order
to another that our activity of narrativizing takes effect. Of course if
"moral order" means just the coherent sequence of a specific story, then
the difference of two narratives entails a difference of moral orders; but
this is clearly the vacuous sense of the thesis in which it becomes necessarily but trivially true.

White's second argument (presented in the last paragraph of his
essay, modestly enough in the form of rhetorical questions) is (1) that
the world is not given to us in the form of well-made stories; (2) that we

make such stories; (3) that we give them referentiality by imagining that in them the world speaks itself; and (4) that the motive for doing so is not the cognitive but the moral need for establishing a moral authority, which historical narratives express as immanent in (the meaning of) events but which, in fact, derives only from our narrativizing. Now I agree entirely with the first three propositions. And I don't doubt that some, perhaps many, historical narratives express a moral (or political or ideological) impulse to render thinkable the notion of a specific social reality with its forms of authority and legitimacy. Nietzsche taught us how fundamental that need is by confronting, on our behalf, the nausea that results when the *terra firma* of a conception of social reality is revealed as itself afloat on the sea of imagination. But White's thesis is not just that narratives *may* express the need to moralize but that narrativizing is uniquely and necessarily the instrument of that need. And this means that narrativizing is never in the first instance cognitive and never a primary and irreducible human capacity but a creature of something more primary—the "moral impulse," which sounds strangely to me like Nietzsche's "will." Even granting that there is such a moral need and that it is expressed in the structure of many narratives, I don't see that White has shown the relation to be necessary. Narrative form is not the unique expression of the legitimation of actual or ideal social reality: myth and its associated rituals are other types of expression and may exist side by side with historical narrative or be conflated with it. And, on the other hand, narrative structure is discernible in a wide range of human activities, from dreams (or at least the recounting of dreams) through play to the stories of cultures which lack even a concept of history. So narrativization seems to me primary, not, as White would have it, derivative—so primary, in fact, that the real wonder is that the historians were so late in discovering it.

Critical Response

II

"The Otherwise Unnoteworthy Year 711": A Reply to Hayden White

Marilyn Robinson Waldman

Hayden White has done more than anyone to bring *historical* narrative to the attention of narratologists. As demonstrated in "The Value of Narrativity in the Representation of Reality," his particular strength is to be able to uncover the world view and assumptions behind a given strategy for presenting history.[1] Yet curiously, White presents a seeming anomaly: historical texts (annals and chronicles) that apparently cannot be read for his purposes as historical narratives; texts that are too rudimentary because the societies that produced them did not have the necessary degree of social "centeredness" to make their "completion" possible, to give them the necessary moral voice and authority to make them readable as complete historical narratives with "full narrativity."

If one reflects on the title of White's paper, one realizes that White presents the not fully narrative forms not so much to comment on them as to use them to explore the significance of "full" narrativity, which involves, among other things, the formal elements of stories, explicit comments on the connections between events, and some kind of "moralizing" closure, when full narrativity does in fact make its appearance in European historiography. However, what White says about "rudi-

---

My title is taken from Ursula K. Le Guin, "It Was a Dark and Stormy Night; or, Why Are We Huddling about the Campfire?." When, in my response to Hayden White's presentation at the symposium, I called attention to the significance of the year 711, I never expected it to become so apt a metaphor.

1. All references to White's article will be included in the text. For another discussion of White's approach, see his *Metahistory: The Historical Imagination in Nineteenth Century Europe* (Baltimore, 1973).

mentary" forms raises serious questions about his evaluation of fully narrative forms and the significance of full narrativity as well.

It is useful to begin a critique of White's approach by formulating five basic questions he seems to raise:

1. Is narrative a manner of speaking or a form?
2. Are real events spoken about or narrated differently from imaginary ones?
3. Are "nonnarrative" histories alternatives to narrative ones or stages on the way to them?[2]
4. Does the possibility of narrativity rely on the availability of a social center to which it is somehow tied, and, as an extension of this question, can nonnarrativity still predominate where a social center does exist?
5. Is the distinction between narrative and discourse relevant to historiography?

Because of his orientation, White finds the answers to these questions problematic. First, there is his fundamental and unavoidable Europocentrism. White allows that annals and chronicles could be seen as different rather than as lower or earlier forms but tends to read them for what they lack that "full" narratives have. This approach assumes that these earlier texts are in fact *part* of the later tradition with which they are identified and in terms of which they are evaluated. White is relatively unfamiliar with cultures in which the listing strategy that is used in his annals and chronicles continues to be present (in more or less elaborate guises). As a matter of fact, it continues in our own culture as an alternative to fully narrative histories, even when the latter appear or become dominant. A Europocentric reading may be inappropriate or misleading, especially in connection with very early medieval "European" narrative, and particularly for areas like Gaul in close proximity to, if not contact with, the Muslim-dominated territory of Andalusia. Even later European historiography needs to be read in conjunction

---

2. White presents both possibilities (see, e.g., pp. 11 and 20); but cf. Barbara Herrnstein Smith, "Narrative Versions, Narrative Theories," for an understanding of the "alternatives" approach.

Marilyn Robinson Waldman is an associate professor of history and chairs the division of comparative studies in the humanities at the Ohio State University. She is the author of *Toward a Theory of Historical Narrative: A Case Study in Perso-Islamicate Historiography* and is currently working on a critical study of another Perso-Islamicate historical text.

with the better-developed, more extensive historiographical traditions of Islam. Second, White fails to make use of the growing literature on the implicit "stories" told through key elements of the listing strategy, such as ordering, juxtaposition, selection, association, and omission. Much of what we are now learning about listing is particularly relevant to medieval Europe and premodern non-Western societies, which tended to rely on indirection and esotericism for certain types of listing techniques.[3]

Let me now offer an alternate reading of the section of the *Annals of Saint Gall* on which White concentrates his analysis. While my hypothetical reading makes certain assumptions about the context in which the text was produced, White's reading begins with a considerably more assertive inference:

> This list immediately locates us in a culture hovering on the brink of dissolution, a society of radical scarcity, a world of human groups threatened by death, devastation, flood, and famine. All of the events are extreme, and the implicit criterion for their selection is their liminal nature. Basic needs—food, security from external enemies, political and military leadership—and the threat of their failing to be provided are the subjects of concern; but the connection between basic needs and the conditions for their possible satisfaction is not explicitly commented on. [Pp. 7–8]

My basic assumption is a negative one: we cannot assume that a text like this one tells no story because it does not make its story explicit, formally organized, and finished (that is, fully narrative); we cannot even assume that explicitness is universally a sign of "full" narrativity. In fact, my studies of Islamic historiography have shown that even explicit commentary on events presented cannot be universally considered as a sign of social and conceptual development. If the *Annals of Saint Gall* cannot be taken beyond White's reading, then there are many other, *too* many other, historical texts in "nonnarrative" historiographical genres that are equally unreadable. In other cultures there is so much not fully narrative material (and this in stable, "centered" societies where historians worked for the rulers) that we must find a way to read it without reference to a relatively late Europocentric norm.

Let me make some observations about the text that strike someone used to working primarily with annalistic texts. First, its chronology is measured in clear-cut annual intervals—by no means a universal form of organization; the dominance of the annual calendar needs further

---

3. See, e.g., Jack Goody, *The Domestication of the Savage Mind* (Cambridge, 1977), and Marshall G. S. Hodgson, "Two Pre-Modern Muslim Historians: Pitfalls and Opportunities in Presenting Them to Moderns," in *Towards World Community*, ed. John U. Nef (The Hague, 1965), pp. 53–68.

explanation as a conceptual mode. What should strike the reader of this text is the power of the annual-chronological classification system to set a rigid framework. Second, social and material disorder (and order) are closely, if not causally, related, and that relationship is at the center of the story being told. Highs and lows in one sphere are associated with highs and lows in the other. Again, this association is not inherent in the world: it has to be made (it is, by the way, made frequently in Islamic historiography, not always with explicit comment). Third, regularity, order, and perhaps even reassurance are tied to official personages, in life or death. One recalls how the famous ninth-century historian Tabari annually interrupts the account of the most threatening disorder of early Islamic history—the rise of the Abbasid Revolution—to give the name of the leader of that year's pilgrimage. No matter how varied the verse, as it were, the refrain, in this case annual, is reassuringly the same. In fact, in the *Annals of Saint Gall,* the disorder implied by some of the events is also stabilized by the regular, unbroken procession of years. Fourth, the battle of Poitiers (neither Poitiers nor Tours is significant in Arab-Islamic historiography, which views them as nonterminal border skirmishes since neither put an end to Arab raids across the Pyrenees) was fought between Muslims and Christians on Saturday, the day between their respective sabbaths. And finally, the most disastrous event, the Arab conquest of Andalusia in 711, is avoided and excluded as an explanation for Gaul's bad fortune. Admittedly, this is a tendentious reading, since I cannot know that the author (or authors) was aware of it. However, internal evidence shows that the author was aware of the presence of the "Saracens" by 725, when they are said to have arrived for the first time, and it is at least reasonable to assume that such an author would not have been unaware of the event which made the Arabs' presence possible, an event of lasting significance for medieval Europeans. One thing is clear: a reading of whatever "story" such a list may be telling would be greatly aided by its comparison with contemporary Hispano-Arabic accounts and by techniques developed to ascertain implicit meanings. We need to know much more about historiographical conventions of the time before we can conclude, with White, that "there are too many loose ends—no plot in the offing" (p. 8).

Three interrelated issues deserve much more attention: how this text's empty entries are to be explained; how listing strategies are to be understood in general; and how lists figure in other historiographical traditions. First, we cannot assume simply from the presence of empty years, as White does, that the writer of the *Annals of Saint Gall* had nothing more to say or that he thought nothing happened in them, just as we cannot assume, as White himself acknowledges, that any account is *complete* because it has no obvious empty spaces (pp. 10–11).

The presence of chronological charts in the backs of contemporary American textbooks is instructive, existing side by side as they do with accounts which have by White's standards attained full narrativity. In such charts, considering any thematic or topical unities, one can easily imagine that some years are less full than others or some even empty. Such charts are in widespread use for certain purposes and obviously do not imply the lack of social authority or the absence of narrative conceptualization in the society that produced them. To expand this point, one could note that classification systems that persist in the absence of entries are not at all uncommon, for example, menus on a day when a category is unavailable, or state-by-state listings of repair shops for a particular item, or lists of annual prize winners including a year in which no award is made. In fact, two stories could be said to be told in such cases: the story of what should or could be and the story of what could be (as opposed to what is) significant. What matters in each case is whether the framework is expressed by the former or the latter; the ability to read such stories cannot be assumed to rely solely on their formal characteristics. In fact, the story such lists might be telling may be less like White's full narrative than like Nelson Goodman's visual constellations, to be apprehended rather than followed.[4] That is, even though the lists appear in a fixed order, they may be read by a complex reordering and rearranging process.

The presence of so many empty years suggests, then, the possibility that the author is establishing a level of significance for included events, a level we do not yet comprehend and which is underscored by the emptinesses.[5] However, it may be that this list *is* rudimentary, not with regard to social authority but with regard to literacy. Jack Goody argues that techniques for storing, managing, and disseminating information, especially the list in its various forms and degrees of elaboration, must be viewed in terms of the level and professionalization of literacy in any given society.[6] He suggests that such lists (read techniques) may generate the conceptual apparatus they seem to imply rather than reflect it. That is, Goody raises the possibility that the development of the annalistic list in historiography may have *preceded* the ability of the user to conceptualize a full narrative sequence and ultimately encouraged its development. In this sense, Goody's analysis seems to approach White's, except for the important fact that Goody's context is literacy and its professionalization, presumably an equally significant one for White's annalist, rather than White's social-center and authority context. The appeal of Goody's context is that it can explain the presence of different

4. See Nelson Goodman, "Twisted Tales; or, Story, Study, and Symphony."

5. It is interesting to note, by the way, how Seymour Chatman's distinction between story-time (e.g., our annual entries) and discourse-time (e.g., our filled-in annual entries) might apply, even in light of Smith's critique of the distinction. See Chatman, "What Novels Can Do That Films Can't (and Vice Versa)," p. 118, and Smith, "Narrative Versions," pp. 209–10.

6. See Goody, *The Savage Mind.*

types of lists and narratives in stable, fully elaborated societies (a full narrative, for example, may itself ultimately be seen as a type of expanded list).

This comparison of contexts forms a natural transition to the final issue: how lists in the form of annalistic presentation figure in non-Western historiography. The evidence from Islamic historiography is extensive and suggests that we need some kind of definition of narrative that will allow us to view "rudimentary" narratives as potentially alternative strategies, not as stages in the evolution of a genre. Chart-form tabular history was composed by well-educated individuals in Islamic societies long after full-blown narrative appeared.[7] Annalistic accounts are even more widespread, alongside what White would call narrative histories, and both are supported by court patronage. The skills needed to read the less continuous annals, often presented in the form of lists of *hadith* reports (individual, discrete accounts of the same event, often not commented on by the author), are just beginning to be developed. The best attempt has been made by Marshall Hodgson, who analyzes the selection, ordering, omissions, and juxtapositions in Tabari's annalistic account of a critical event in the history of the early Islamic community, the assassination of the third caliph Uthman.[8] Hodgson's analysis reinforces a point made above, that the selection and ordering process itself tells a metastory that enriches the accounts of specific events.

My investigations of Islamic historiography raise a rather different issue concerning social authority and its potentially subversive effect. White argues that the ranking of events, which he sees as essential to full narrativity and absent in nonnarrative, is made possible by the author's "consciousness of a *social* center" and that the authority to write such a narrative is associated with authority more generally.[9] But as I have demonstrated elsewhere, in cultures where all the narrative weight is borne by *historical* narrative, it can undermine and question the authority by which it is supposedly fostered and buttressed.[10] What remains unclear in much of the present volume on narrative, and in most of the literature on historical narrative, is what makes White's distinction between "discourse of the real" and "discourse of the imaginary" mean-

7. For example, in the Ghaznavid-period (eleventh-century Iran) historical text, *Ta'rikh-i Jadval* (of whose existence I was orally informed by Abbas Zaryab Khu'i at Princeton in the spring of 1977). The manuscript of this chart-form history is held in the Majlis Library in Tehran. See also the discussion of Smith's minimal definition below.

8. See Hodgson, "Two Pre-Modern Muslim Historians."

9. Mary Louise Pratt makes a similar argument, pushing beyond and, in effect, back to White's "beginning," to the deterioration of narrative in the twentieth century due to the loss of authority and a social center. See Pratt, *Toward a Speech Act Theory of Literary Discourse* (Bloomington, Ind., 1977).

10. See my *Toward a Theory of Historical Narrative: A Case Study in Perso-Islamicate Historiography* (Columbus, Ohio, 1980), esp. chaps. 1, 3, and 4.

ingful, especially in light of his remarks elsewhere.[11] Robert Scholes, for example, distinguishes history from fiction but in terms of the difference in the various authors' truth claims and the relevance of extratextual information, not in terms of any effect these elements have on the way the subject matter is actually presented.[12] Perhaps White meant his passing reference to the distinction between narrative (told by the narrator) and discourse (which tells itself) to be useful in this regard. But again, there are serious transtemporal and transcultural obstacles to our knowing what tells itself in a given time and place. If White's example of annals tells a story of some sort, no matter how simple, it will *tell itself*, since it clearly is not told by the narrator, at least not explicitly. But then how could such rudimentary historical presentation be considered discourse as White means it? In a culture where indirection and esotericism are the rule, where the narrator constantly withdraws and tries to get his "real" story to tell itself, would not historical accounts be more discourse than narrative? But as White asserts, "*real* events should not speak, should not tell themselves" (p. 4). The utility of the distinction for world historiography is, then, still not at all clear.

The best way out of many of the problems in White's formulation is offered by Barbara Herrnstein Smith, who refuses to separate narrative from other discourse and whose alternative position has important implications for historical texts:[13]

> An alternative conception of language views utterances not as strings of discrete signifiers that represent corresponding sets of discrete signifieds but as *verbal responses*—that is, as *acts* which, like any acts, are *performed in response to various sets of conditions*. These conditions consist of all those circumstantial and psychological variables of which every utterance is a function. Although *some* of these conditions are conventionally implied by and are, accordingly, inferable from the linguistic form of an utterance, they are not confined to and cannot be reduced to specific "referents" or "signifieds." In accord with this alternative view of language, individual narratives would be described not as sets of surface-discourse-signifiers that represent (actualize, manifest, map, or express) sets of underlying-story-signifieds but as the verbal acts of particular narrators performed in response to—and thus shaped and constrained by—sets of multiple interacting conditions. [Pp. 221–22]

11. See White, "The Fictions of Factual Representation," in *The Literature of Fact*, ed. Angus Fletcher (New York, 1976), pp. 22–44, where White seems to argue that representations are not all that different. For a similar argument, see Jeffrey Mehlmann, *Revolution and Repetition: Marx/Hugo/Balzac* (Berkeley and Los Angeles, 1977).

12. See Robert Scholes, "Language, Narrative, and Anti-Narrative," p. 207.

13. All references to Smith's article will be included in the text. Cf. Pratt, *Toward a Speech Act Theory*, chap. 1.

Smith's position allows historical narrative, usually distinguished from fiction by the nature of its referents and signifieds, to be reincorporated into its proper universe. Her position also helps overcome the tendency to evaluate historical representation in terms of its accuracy of correspondence to what we assume, or decide, to be given or preexisting sequences. What Smith goes on to say applies as much to history as to fiction, although she does not immediately develop the applicability. The relevant point results from her discussion of the problem of anachrony in narrative, just after she has argued that nonlinearity is the rule rather than the exception: "And the question here is whether, for every time-twisted narrative (which is to say, for virtually every narrative), there always is such a prior and independent set and sequence of events—and also in what sense any of those stories or sets of events are 'given' " (p. 224).

At first Smith seems to overlook the fact that her positions reincorporate history into narrative; but as she finds her way back to what I view as the correct relationship among the various types of narrative, she rejects a reconciliation that is based on the fact that fiction could also be said to rely on a prior set of facts and argues instead that even for narratives overtly based on events that their authors view as given, the givenness does not control the narration:

> We may, in fact, extend this point back to those paradigm narratives, mentioned above, that report not imaginary events but events which presumably occurred at some particular prior time. For like our imaginings of events that never occurred, our knowledge of *past* events is usually *not* narrative in structure or given in storylike sequences: on the contrary, that knowledge is most likely to be in the form of general and imprecise recollections, scattered and possibly inconsistent pieces of verbal information, and various visual, auditory, and kinesthetic images—some of which, at any given time, will be more or less in or out of focus and all of which will be organized, integrated, and apprehended as a specific "set" of events only in and through the very act by which we narrate them as such. [P. 225]

Finally, Smith offers a new way to evaluate and perhaps ultimately distinguish different types of narrative, a way which for the time being rejoins discourse of the real and discourse of the imaginary: "what must be described and explained is not how . . . a narrator can *re*arrange the chronology of a given set of events but rather how, on what bases, and, sometimes, whether his audience will infer from his narrative and chronology of some set of events that is *not given*" (p. 226).

The key to my response to White and my commentary on Smith has by now, I hope, become clear. Prior distinctions, drawn from essentially Europocentric research, between historical and fictional narrative and among various types of historical texts and "narratives" must be abandoned until the Europocentrism of narratology and its focus on fiction begin to give way. We need to overarch prior distinctions with a minimalist definition of narrative that will allow us to look at new and broader data with an open mind, a definition that does not rigidly separate narrative from other discourse—a definition akin to Smith's: "we might conceive of narrative discourse most minimally and most generally as verbal acts consisting of *someone telling someone else that something happened*" (p. 228).[14] Smith herself does finally say that on the basis of this definition history should be included as part of all narrative; furthermore she attempts to make some meaningful distinctions, as when she observes that:

> . . . *the extent to which* a narrator takes or claims responsibility for the veridicality of his tale [the traditional mark of historiography] will serve different interests and, accordingly, have a different sort of value for himself and his audience depending on the nature and constraints of the transaction between them and, conversely, that different situations and structures of motivation will elicit and reward different *kinds and degrees* of truth claims. . . . What these observations suggest is that a number of key problems of narrative theory that are commonly posed and analyzed in philosophic terms—for example, as questions of the "truth value" or fictional "propositions"—could be profitably reformulated in terms of the variable constraints, conventions, and dynamics of verbal transactions and explored accordingly. [P. 231]

As I have argued elsewhere, issues such as these should determine the future direction of the study of historical narrative in particular and of all narrative in general.[15]

14. See also Pratt, *Toward a Speech Act Theory,* and my *Toward a Theory of Historical Narrative,* chaps. 1 and 7.
15. See my *Toward a Theory of Historical Narrative,* chap. 7.

Critical Response

III

The Narrativization of Real Events

Hayden White

In their commentaries on my "Value of Narrativity in the Representation of Reality," Marilyn Waldman and Louis Mink raise issues having to do with the scope of my examples, on the one side, and what might be called my categorical confusion, on the other. Waldman suggests that if I had not depended so heavily on European materials but had examined other traditions of historical writing, I would have been better able to make the case for the annals form as a kind of narrative and would not have slipped into the error of regarding the kind of narrative favored by modern Western historians as the model against which all other kinds of historical representation are to be measured. I must, in my ignorance of matters Arabic, accept what she has to say about the cultivation of the annals genre in Islamic centers which boast of both a high degree of literacy and a manifest consolidation of political and social authority. She is certainly right in suggesting that the decision to use the annals or list form of historical representation should not be taken as evidence either of ignorance or stupidity in all cases but may well be, in those cases in which prospective audiences possess the appropriate level of reading competence, a sign of the establishment of conventions for conveying meanings that are every bit as full and sophisticated as anything produced by modern Western historians.

I am less sanguine about the prospects of resolving the problems raised by narrative theory by collapsing the distinction between discourse and narrative on the basis of their shared status as acts or transactions between authors and their readers governed by different kinds of contractual obligations. While this kind of "speech-act" approach to the problem of narration, narrativization, and narrative may no doubt lead to greater understanding of the social conventions that render different kinds of discourse appropriate or inappropriate ("felicitous" is the term favored by speech-act theorists), it will not, I surmise, give us much insight into the psychological, aesthetic, or moral appeal of different *forms* of discourse. Above all, this contextual, conventionalist, or situational approach to the problem of discourse offers no prospect at all of accounting for the appeal of those forms of discourse that are manifestly infelicitous vis-à-vis the normal expectations of audiences but are nonetheless effective for *changing the rules* under which different kinds of discourse are construed to be felicitous or infelicitous. Speech-act theory, like the theory of evolution before the advent of modern genetics, can tell us a great deal about why genres persist but virtually nothing about variations or changes in generic formations.

I believe, conversely, that the study of narrative as a form of discourse preeminently suited to mediate between alternative notions of what the moral order should consist of offers the prospect of accounting, at least in part, for changes in what audiences regard as the appropriate modes of discourse as well as the appropriate contents or referents of different modes of representation. One can find any number of possible meanings in a given genre by imputing to real or imagined audiences a competence to do with a text whatever it takes to make that text meaningful. Thus when considering what can or should count as a narrative per se, the use of a contextual, historical, or empirical approach can only result in the conclusion that anything can so count as long as the social context in question decides that it is a narrative and not something else. One can confidently predict, I think, that the prosecution of the speech-act or reader-competent approach to the problem of genre will only result in a list of examples as long and as lacking in order as the list of different contexts identified. As Roland Barthes points out in his "Introduction to the Structural Analysis of Narratives," the path of empiricism can lead only to confusion. Why not, as Barthes suggests, follow the lead of linguists (who, in their study of languages, have taken a resolutely deductive approach) by first postulating hypotheses and then seeing what insights and understanding result from their application to specific cases.[1]

Since I have taken this deductive path in my own consideration of the value of narrativity in the representation of (historical) reality, I am

1. Roland Barthes, "Introduction to the Structural Analysis of Narratives," *Image, Music, Text*, trans. Stephen Heath (New York, 1977), pp. 80–82.

Hayden White, professor in the program in the history of consciousness at the University of California, Santa Cruz, is the author of *The Tropics of Discourse: Essays in Cultural Criticism* and *Metahistory: The Historical Imagination in Nineteenth Century Europe*.

perfectly willing to entertain the notion that my suggested model may contribute nothing to the understanding of any specific kind of narrative practice. The question is, Does ascribing to narrative a moralistic or moralizing function, rather than a primarily cognitive or aesthetic function, yield any insight into *some* narrative practices and specifically into the narrative practices of historians in the West? And because I have taken the deductive rather than the empirical path (the examples I gave of annals, chronicles, and histories being *illustrative* of the principles informing my hypotheses, not universal paradigms), I am especially vulnerable to the criticism Mink has made of my essay. For the thrust of Mink's criticism, as I understand it, has to do with a confusion of categories, on the one hand, and a failure to demonstrate the "necessity" or "universality" of the linkage between "narrativization" and "moralization," on the other.

I assume we agree that narrativization is what Fredric Jameson calls "the central function or *instance* of the human mind"[2] or what Mink himself calls, in an essay on "Narrative Form as a Cognitive Instrument," "a form of human comprehension" that is productive of meaning by its imposition of a certain formal coherence on a virtual chaos of "events," which in themselves (or as given to perception) cannot be said to possess any particular form at all, much less the kind that we associate with "stories."[3] The question is, With what *kind of meaning* does storying endow those events which are products of human agency in the past and which we call "historical events"?

Mink believes that the transformation of events into stories endows them with cognitive meaning. In fact, as he has argued, the very notion of event is so ambiguous that it makes no sense at all to speak of an *event per se* but only of *events under description.*[4] In other words, the kind of descriptive protocol used to constitute events as facts of a particular sort determines the kind of fact they are considered to be. For Mink, narrativity is a mode of description which transforms events into historical facts by demonstrating their ability to function as elements of completed stories. Thus the question he must address in this context is why this demonstration of an event's capacity to function as an element in a completed story should constitute grounds for claiming its cognitive authority rather than its moral suasion or aesthetic satisfaction.

This question has more significance for modern philosophy of history than for modern historiography since modern historiography (unlike its classical prototypes) unfolds under the imperative to provide

2. Fredric Jameson, *The Political Unconscious: Narrative as a Socially Symbolic Act* (Ithaca, N.Y., 1981), p. 13.

3. Louis O. Mink, "Narrative Form as a Cognitive Instrument," in *The Writing of History: Literary Form and Historical Understanding,* ed. Robert H. Canary and Henry Kozicki (Madison, Wis., 1978), p. 132.

4. See ibid., pp. 145–47; all further references to this essay will be included in the text.

more than the aesthetic satisfaction of its rhetorical clothing. In its aspiration to the status of a kind of science, again unlike its medieval prototypes, it specifically eschews the impulse to be morally edifying, except of course to the extent that truth is conceived to be morally edifying in itself—the "the truth shall make you free" syndrome. At the same time, however, those who defend historiography as an instrument of cognition (rather than a product of cognition) have had to admit that if history is a science, it is a damned strange science and possibly not even a science at all in any modern, and theoretically established, sense of the term. This is why modern philosophers of history generally insist that historical knowledge is the province of the understanding rather than of reason, where true science takes its rise. In their view, understanding is a kind of knowledge which, while not having the rigor, testability, and precision of scientific knowledge, nonetheless yields insight into the way things—and especially things human—*really* are. And if we are to give a name to the ground in consciousness of this kind of knowledge which, while not exactly rational and not exactly scientific, is nonetheless *real* knowledge, we may call it "common sense."

It is not surprising, then, that Mink argues for common sense as the kind of cognition the narrative form serves. Thus he writes:

> Both historians and writers of imaginative fiction know well the problems of constructing a coherent narrative account, with or without the constraint of arguing from evidence, but even so they may not recognize the extent to which narrative as such is not just a technical problem for writers and critics but a primary and irreducible form of human comprehension, an article in the constitution of common sense. ["Narrative Form," p. 128]

And on the question of the kind of truth to which historical narratives lay claim, he writes:

> Inseparable from the question of how narratives aggregate is a second problem about the sense in which a narrative may be true or false. This question arises only if a narrative as such does have holistic properties, that is, if the *form* of the narrative, as well as its individual statements of fact, is taken as representing something that may be true or false. . . . It is an unsolved task of literary theory to classify the ordering relations of narrative form; but whatever the classification, it should be clear that a historical narrative claims truth not merely for each of its individual statements taken distributively, but for the complex form of the narrative itself. ["Narrative Form," p. 140]

I find nothing in these quotations with which to disagree; in fact, I could have cited them as buttresses to my own argument on the moralizing function of historical narrativity. For it seems illuminating to me to construe narrative as a form which, as used in historical representations, "represent[s] something that may be true or false"; and this "something," I would agree, is nothing other than that set of commonplaces comprised of beliefs about the meaning or ultimate nature of reality, shared by the average members of any given culture—what we call common sense. But I would also contend that what we must mean by common sense (if the term is not to be construed so generally as to include science, art, philosophy, religion, and everything else that we normally contrast with it) is more particularly that sense which we have in our function as members of particular cultures; that is, I would contend that the world has a specifically moral, as well as a determinative physical, meaning. Story forms, or what Northrop Frye calls plot structures, represent an armory of relational models by which what would otherwise be nothing but chains of mechanical causes and effects can be translated into moral terms. They are not, as Mink suggests in his response to my essay, merely devices allowing us to accommodate the notion of human intentions, aims, and purposes in our representations of human affairs. Story forms not only permit us to judge the moral significance of human projects, they also provide the means by which to judge them, even while we pretend to be merely describing them. And Mink suggests as much when he remarks:

> Only by virtue of such [narrative] form can there be a story of failure or of success, of plans miscarried or policies overtaken by events, of survivals and transformations which interweave with each other in the circumstances of individual lives and the development of institutions. ["Narrative Form," p. 140]

If this were only a technical matter (this business of "failure or of success, of plans miscarried or policies overtaken by events," etc.), if only a contribution to our understanding of the instrumental and operational difficulties involved in realizing plans, executing projects, and the like, narrativization could not claim a cognitive authority different in kind from, although every bit as important as, the sort of authority claimed by disciplines that do not utilize its techniques. It is only by virtue of what it teaches about moral wisdom, or rather about the irreducible moralism of a life lived under the conditions of culture rather than nature, that narrative can claim cognitive authority at all. As Mink points out, precisely because the same set of events can be plausibly narrativized as either tragedy or comedy, either romance or farce, narrative has the power to teach what it means to be *moral* beings (rather than machines endowed with consciousness) more or less capable and shrewd enough to carry out our intentions as we conceive them. Nobody ever learned to be more *efficient* in carrying out intentions or realizing goals by reading historical narratives. What can be learned from them is what it means to have intentions, to intend to carry them out, and to attempt to do so; and this meaning, or our sense of it, may well find a place in our commonsensical notions of the way things really are. However, that place is not presided over by the cognitive but by the moral faculty; that is what makes it common.

Of course all I have said, I have said on the authority of common sense; accordingly, rather than offer arguments in defense of it, I should rest content with the conviction that since "everybody knows this," only those with uncommon sense will disagree with me. One of the consolations of common sense is that it signals its validity by the anticipated agreement accorded by "persons of goodwill." Indeed, one of its virtues is the conviction that informs it: agreement with its dicta is the very mark of goodwill. And so it is with the narrativization of real events: this conviction, like all convictions, can only be a moral one.

Space prohibits here a lengthy comment on Mink's discussion of annals as "unsolicited memory." I agree that the list of events he has summoned up from his own memory can tell us much about his personal interests, values, and beliefs but very little about his conception of historical reality. But this is not due to the list *form* but to the fact that the list is comprised of items drawn from personal rather than public memory. The fallacy in considering a historical account as a kind of collective autobiography derives from a confusion of personal with public memory. So, too, the moral sense that is conveyed by the representation of past public events differs from that conveyed by the representation of personal memories. The reason why a narrativization of personal memories tells us little about one's conception of history is that it is too full of one's *personal* moral beliefs. An annalistic account of public memories, by contrast, tells us a great deal both about the annalist's conception of history and about his or her conception of public morality. It is the "publicity" that makes the difference.

Critical Response

IV

The Telling and the Told

Nelson Goodman

Some passages in Barbara Herrnstein Smith's "Narrative Versions, Narrative Theories" intimate that my paper "Twisted Tales; or, Story, Study, and Symphony" is incompatible with what I have urged in *Ways of Worldmaking* and other writings. To clear away any misunderstanding, let me show that nothing in my paper makes any concession to absolutism, "dualism", or "deep structure".

In distinguishing between order of telling and order of occurrence, I am not supposing that order of occurrence is an absolute order of events independent of all versions but am rather drawing the distinction between order of the telling and order of the told. Consider some brief tales:

1. Lincoln's assassination preceded Kennedy's.
2. Kennedy's assassination followed Lincoln's.

In (1) the orders of the telling and the told agree: On the other hand, in (2) the order of telling reverses the order of the told, and we have a twisted tale. But the twisting is with respect not to an absolute order of events independent of all versions but to what this version *says* is the order of events.

This essay and the following essay by Seymour Chatman are responses to Barbara Herrnstein Smith's "Narrative Versions, Narrative Theories."

1. See my "Twisted Tales; or, Story, Study, and Symphony."

The distinction between order of the telling and order of the told holds equally for false as for true tales. For instance:

3. Kennedy's assassination preceded Lincoln's.
4. Lincoln's assassination followed Kennedy's.

In (3) the orders of the telling and the told agree, while in (4) the order of telling reverses the order of the told. Although both (3) and (4) are false, (4) is twisted while (3) is not.

The tales may even be entirely fictional:

5. Washington's assassination preceded Truman's.
6. Washington's assassination followed Truman's.

In this case, orders of the telling and the told agree in (5) but differ in (6).

Thus the distinction between order of the telling and order of the told does not imply truth, or that events told of occurred in a given order, or even that there are any such events. This holds equally well where the order of the told is implicit or inferential rather than explicit. Consider the following:

7. Don Quixote attacked the windmill. He was defeated.

In this tale, the two orders agree; but interchanging the sentences gives a twisted tale. In other cases, such as (3) and (6), what might otherwise be the implicitly told order is overruled by an explicitly told order.

All this would have been clearer had I written "*told* order of occurrence" rather than simply "order of occurrence" in my paper. Still, fictional examples like the Jacopo del Sellaio and the Piero di Cosimo paintings are plain evidence of what I meant.

One further point: if I say that the geocentric and the heliocentric systems describe the same motion, I do not imply that there is some absolute motion that both systems describe but only that the two systems are related in a certain way. If I say that two terms have the same or

---

Nelson Goodman, emeritus professor of philosophy at Harvard University, is the author of, among other works, *The Structure of Appearance* and *Ways of Worldmaking.* His previous contributions to *Critical Inquiry* are "The Status of Style" (Summer 1975), "Metaphor as Moonlighting" (Autumn 1979), and "Twisted Tales; or, Story, Study, and Symphony" (Autumn 1980).

virtually the same meaning, I am not saying that there is any such entity as a meaning that they have but am only speaking of a relation between the terms. And when I speak of several versions of the same or virtually the same story, I am by no means conceding that there is some underlying story, some deep structure, that is not itself a version.

Critical Response

V

Reply to Barbara Herrnstein Smith

Seymour Chatman

When it comes to narrative, God knows there's enough to keep the most diversified interests busy, as the Chicago narrative symposium demonstrated. My own interest—which fate has decided to call "narratological"—focuses on the question, What is narrative per se? What properties must a text have to be called a narrative, and what properties disqualify it? Realizing the difficulty of the question and the importance of bringing a broad range of experience to bear on it, I invited readers of my *Story and Discourse* to cross-examine a theory based on an amalgam of Anglo-American narrative study (James, Lubbock, and Booth) and Russian and French literary semiotics. A number of scholars have accepted the invitation. Barbara Herrnstein Smith's spirited "Narrative Versions, Narrative Theories" is the latest examination and the one most in need of reply, since it strikes at the heart of the theory and beyond at basic tenets of linguistics and semiotics as we know them.

Smith argues that structuralist narrative theory is "afflicted . . . with a number of dualistic concepts and models, the continuous generation of which betrays a lingering strain of naive Platonism and the continued appeal to which is both logically dubious and methodologically distracting" (p. 209). Let me begin with the "naive Platonism." I am no classical philosopher, but I always understood Platonism to be rather monist in its dualism, to reject phenomena in favor of noumena. According to Runes' *Dictionary of Philosophy,* "Platonism is characterized by partial contempt for sense knowledge and empirical studies, . . . by a longing for another and better world, by a frankly spiritualist view of life, by . . . a method of ever more profound insights rather than the formal logic of

258

Aristotle, and . . . by an unswerving faith in the capacity of the human mind to attain absolute truth." Now I admit to days when I long for another and better world. But I must ask, in all reasonableness, whether my book or books like Gérard Gennett's *Narrative Discourse: An Essay in Method,* Tzvetan Todorov's *The Poetics of Prose,* and Roland Barthes' *S/Z* could possibly be described as "spiritualist," contemptuous of "sense knowledge and empirical studies," or unduly marked by a belief in the possibility of "absolute truth." Books not merely peppered with examples but literally chained to texts: to the texts of Joyce, Balzac, and Proust, to the *Thousand and One Nights.* Structuralists, surely, are pragmatists to a fault. Aristotle, not Plato, is our mentor (he is the star of *Story and Discourse*). Dualists we are, but dualists who burrow for the structures precisely for the sake of the precious surfaces, the better to understand and appreciate them. Our intention, then, whatever Smith thinks of our performance, is not Platonic but anti-Platonic.

On the substantive charges of logical dubiety and methodological distraction: Smith objects particularly to two postulations made by structural narratologists (there are actually important differences between us, but since she does not distinguish, I shall presume—with due temerity— to speak for the field as a whole). The first objection is to narratology's view that a given narrative, both story and discourse, can be actualized in different media (*Cinderella* as verbal tale, as ballet, as comic strip, etc.). This, she claims, is wrong on two counts. For one thing, it begs the question of what constitutes a given "story." She reminds us of the estimable research of the British Folklore Society which collected 345 versions of the tale, from the familiar Grimm Brothers' version to those of Africa and the Middle East. The large number and considerable variation among these versions, she implies, undercuts any narratologist's Ur-Cinderella—which she describes, with evident distaste, as "a version-less version . . . unembodied and unexpressed, unpictured, unwritten and untold . . . occup[ying] a highly privileged ontological realm of pure Being within which it unfolds immutably and eternally" (p. 212). Narratologists, being mere human beings, cannot of course find the "real" *Cinderella* among all those texts. But I don't recall any of us wanting or needing to. Narratology is not interested in the question, which belongs rather to comparative folkloristics. It does seem unfair to accuse a theory of not doing what it never purported to do. (I am excepting Vladimir Propp and followers like Alan Dundes here, for they are concerned not only with the definition of a specific genre of narrative, the fairy tale, but also with what comparative techniques can tell them about it.) All

Seymour Chatman is a professor in the department of rhetoric at the University of California, Berkeley.

that narratology argues is that any given text, say, the Grimm Brothers' version or the Syrian version or version 129 in the British Folklore volume, could occur indifferently, with minimal variation in discourse and story properties, as a ballet or puppet show or comic strip or in some other shape. There is in every story, regardless of its medium of representation, a portion which is *purely* narrative in structure, independent of that medium, that portion having its own structure—in natural language, in the language of dance, in the language of comic-strip drawing, or whatever. Narrative structure is a *construct* (which is *not* a Platonic idea), a construct of features drawn by narratologists from texts generally agreed to be narratives. The proposal seems so modest, so little more demanding than the constructs that pass effortlessly through pages of literary history and criticism (the Romantic movement, the baroque, the metaphysical lyric), that it is hard to believe it is being challenged.

Smith's second objection to the separation of story and discourse is that the fact of variety among plot summaries cannot thereby be accounted for. Here it is necessary to demur at her representation of our position. In arguing the possibility of distinguishing story from discourse in any given version of *Cinderella* (or any other narrative text), the narratologist says nothing about plot summaries. Smith is incorrect in inferring that the narratologist claims "it is the fact that each of us would construct the *same* plot summary of *Cinderella* that demonstrates our intuitive apprehension of its basic story" (p. 212). Nowhere in *Story and Discourse* or in any other narratological account that I know is such a claim made, for the simple reason that the theory does not presume to account for the actual performance of plot summarizers (just as transformational-generative grammar does not presume to account for the actual performance of speakers of the language). There is no more reason for a theory of the nature of narrative (concerned with the question, What is narrative as opposed to other kinds of texts?) to account for individual tellings of a story than for a phonological theory to account for individual variations in the pronunciation of the vowel diphthong of the word "house." The pronunciation of that diphthong differs across the population of English speakers for precisely the kinds of reasons that Smith cites for variations among versions of a story: speakers' prior experiences of hearing "house," ways in which they've learned to talk about those pronunciations, general constraints on the act of describing phones and phonemes in general, and so on. Of course the differing ways we each pronounce a phoneme is a function of our differing life histories; but what has that to do with phonemic theory? The phonemes are as real as their actualizations on people's lips; they are not some fuzzy Platonic idea but a reality, a construct derived by linguists from actual utterances and attributable to the configuration of articulational and semantic features. Just as linguistics argues for a logical model, not a behavioral account of actual speech performance, narratology offers a theory which assumes the task of defining its subject (all and only narratives in the universe of texts) on a logical model, with no reference to the contingent life histories of those who make or partake of stories. (That is why the real author and the real reader are not included as components of the narrative transmission—only the implied author and the implied reader, the narrator and the narratee.) So story, the content element, and discourse, the form element, are posited as constructs separable by easy mental operations from stories actualized in concrete representations. Story is not plot summary: a plot summary is itself a version, a concrete representation (the medium is words) of the whole narrative—story and discourse. Barthes, Genette, and the rest of us no more deal in the realms of pure being than did Ferdinand de Saussure, Leonard Bloomfield, or Roman Jakobson.

Smith's second objection is an objection to the dualistic explanation of what Genette calls anachrony—the assumption that discourse-time can be at odds with story-time with respect to order, duration, and frequency: longer than, shorter than, reversed (as in flashback), and so on. Her argument needs to be quoted at length:

> One would not deny, of course, that the time it takes someone to read *War and Peace* may differ from the time it took the Russians to defeat Napoleon. . . . It is certainly also the case that a narrator may relate events in a non-chronological order, telling us, for example, about someone's funeral before telling us about his childhood, as Tolstoy does in "The Death of Ivan Ilych." The question at issue, however, is neither the existence of these possibilities nor their interest and significance in the experience of narrative. Rather, it is whether either of these temporal disparities—or both of them taken together—requires us to posit the existence of two distinct, independent time orders for every narrative. . . .
>
> With respect to the . . . difference between the *durations* of discourse-time and story-time . . . it is not clear what makes this disparity especially remarkable, or especially relevant to narrative, or especially relevant to narrative time. After all, there is also a difference between the length of time occupied by the siege of Moscow and the length of time it takes to *say* "the siege of Moscow." [P. 220]

Durational discrepancy, however, is a general narrative-structural question and not simply a matter of verbal expression. It is precisely because language *can* independently represent the lengthy event in a split-second word or phrase, without any reference to a narrative text at all, that it is necessary to see the discrepancy as a narrative and not merely linguistic event, at the risk of confusing structure with articulating medium. Again: narratives are not simply sets of words. A narrative can be expressed without using a single word, as in a mime show, or a comic strip without bubbles or captions, or a silent movie without titles, like F. W. Murnau's *Der Letzte Mann.* Smith's narrative theory is totally language oriented, privileging verbal narrative at the expense of all the other ways of communicating stories: "we might conceive," she writes, "of narrative discourse most minimally and most generally as verbal acts consisting of *someone telling someone else that something happened*" (p. 228). Even if it were possible to prove that the first narrative was verbal, historical precedence would still not be an adequate reason for making words the central or even a necessary component of a narrative theory. Words, I argue, are not the ultimate components of narratives; those ultimate elements are, rather, events and existents in a chain of temporal causality or at least contingency. Words are no more privileged than any other second-order signs for conveying the first-order narrative elements—events, characters, props, and setting. Since the visual media do not possess neat and "natural" ways for summarizing events over a long duration, since they have no progressive tense or battery of expressions like "for a long time," they must resort to special devices to communicate such meanings. One camera shot would not suffice to show the burning of Atlanta, but the simple sentence "Atlanta burnt for days" would suffice for the verbal version. A filmmaker would have to use some special device to show the passage of time—a peeling calendar, perhaps, or a "transition-montage" of shots accompanied by dolorous music, or the like. Clearly, then, the summary of the duration of a story event is a function of the narrative structure per se, quite independently of the problem of its representation in any specific medium.

To deny the need for different temporal orders of story and discourse is, further, to leave us with a complex list of all the possibilities; whereas, as Genette has shown, these can be explained in terms of a minimal number of relations and functions (duration, order, frequency; "equals," "is greater than"; etc.). The capacity to explain the maximum number of phenomena in the simplest way is, I take it, a sign of the power of a theory.

Smith's alternative to the structuralist model is a speech-act model. I am sure all students of narrative welcome another approach to this intricate subject; nothing but good can come from a plurality of approaches, providing they respect each other's limits. Clearly, every aproach will privilege some matters over others. Smith's interest in the "circumstantial and psychological variables" under which stories come to be recounted will certainly be better satisfied by a narrative theory based on ideas like those advanced by the ordinary-language philosophy of J. L. Austin, John Searle, H. P. Grice, and others. To the extent that such a theory is less concerned with the definition of narrative text as such and more with the conditions for the production of narratives, perhaps it should be called "narrative pragmatics" rather than "narratology" (but what's in a name?). Smith outlines her alternative project as follows:

> For any narrative, these conditions would consist of (1) such circumstantial variables as the particular context and material setting (cultural and social, as well as strictly "physical") in which the tale is told, the particular listeners or readers addressed, and the nature of the narrator's relationship to them, and (2) such psychological variables as the narrator's motives for telling the tale and all the particular interests, desires, expectations, memories, knowledge, and prior experiences (including his knowledge of various events, of course, but also of other narratives and of various conventions and traditions of storytelling) that elicited his telling it on that occasion, to that audience, and that shaped the particular way he told it. [P. 222]

I can see the value of an elaborate inquiry into the narrator's background and motivations for work in socio- and psycholinguistics, like that of William Labov's, and, to a lesser extent, for folkloristics. But I'm not sure I see its relevance for literary narrative, say, for the modern novel. Of course, if the narrator is a character in the novel, then a study of the context and motives of his/her narration is obviously relevant to the interpretation of his/her character, as it is to the larger structure of the text. (Structural narratology is not mute on these questions, as Smith seems to suggest. There is the excellent work of Gerald Prince on the narratee, and in my own book I argue the need to analyze character traits, including, of course, those of character-narrators since their personalities so influence our decisions about the reliability of their accounts.) But if the narrator is anonymous (as in classical eighteenth-century omniscient-narrator novels) or self-evidently minimized (as in some of Hemingway's stories), how much can we really expect (or want) to learn about him/her and the material conditions of the narration? (If Smith means by "narrator" the author, real or implied, the inquiry seems even more irrelevant and also subject to the biographical and affective fallacies.)

What I see least in Smith's own theory is any concern for that stubborn but essential question, What is narrative per se, and how does it differ from other kinds of discourse—description, exposition, argument, and so forth? In fact, she seems convinced that distinctions are not possible:

> It is also important to recognize that narrative discourse is not necessarily—or even usually—marked off or segregated from other discourse. Almost any verbal utterance will be laced with more or less minimal narratives, ranging from fragmentary reports and abortive anecdotes to those more distinctly framed and conven-

tionally marked tellings that we are inclined to call "tales" or "stories." Indeed, narrative discourse is, at one extreme, hardly distinguishable from description or simply assertion. That is, "telling someone that something happened" can, under certain circumstances, be so close to "saying that something is (or was) the case" that it is questionable if we can draw any logically rigorous distinction between them or, more generally, if any absolute distinction can be drawn between narrative discourse and any other form of verbal behavior. [P. 228]

Again, Smith confuses the surface medium, language, with the deep structure of the text, which is a logical structure. Narrative subsists in an event chain, operating through time. Its logic is *xRy,* where *R* is temporal succession. In film this succession is usually actualized in the mere sequence of two shots, the splice between which represents translocation and, temporally, anything from simultaneity to gross ellipsis, unless, of course, the context communicates the flashback effect. In a verbal narrative, there is not only the sequence of sentences but also verb tense and a wide variety of other grammatical and lexical clues to mark the event or situation depicted by the sentence as occurring somewhere along the event chain of the narrative as a whole. To illustrate from *Pride and Prejudice* (my italics):

> The whist party *soon afterwards breaking up,* the players gathered around the other table.

> Elizabeth *was sitting* with her mother and sisters . . . when Sir William Lucas himself *appeared.*

> Miss Bingley's letter *arrived, and put an end to* doubt.

But of course verbal narrative, established in its broad lines by such normative sentences, can accommodate sentences which taken alone would suggest another kind of discourse, for example, description: "Mr. Collins was not a sensible man"; or philosophical generalizations: "It is a truth universally acknowledged that a single man in possession of a good fortune must be in want of a wife"; and so on. In such cases, we say that the descriptive or generalizing sentence operates *at the service of* the deep narrative structure.

Chapter 14 of Coleridge's *Biographia Literaria* is, in its main lines, its deep structure, an exposition. Its characteristic mode is found in sentences like:

> A poem *contains* the same elements as a prose composition.

> The poet, described in ideal perfection, *brings* the whole soul of man into activity.

> Good Sense *is* the Body of poetic genius, Fancy its Drapery, Motion its Life, and Imagination the Soul that is everywhere.

The expository text establishes in broad lines a logic of $x = y$, most simply phrased in language by the copula and the simple present tense: "Good Sense *is* the Body of poetic genius." But once established, the expository text can accommodate sentences which occurring alone would suggest a narrative:

> *During* the first year that Mr. Wordsworth and I were neighbours, our conversations *turned* frequently on the two cardinal points of poetry.

> The thought *suggested* itself—(to which of us I do not recollect)— that a series of poems might be composed.

> In *this* idea *originated* the plan of the *Lyrical Ballads*.

Narrative at the service of exposition, a familiar enough pattern. But what I am urging is that the text mode inheres not in the language, the surface manifestation, but in the logical tie of assertion, $x = y$, which could equally be conveyed nonverbally (as in a filmic metaphor: Kerenski = a peacock, Charlie Chaplin's spoons = the legs of a dancer).

It is not that the sentence characteristic of the narrative mode, with its "then" or "next" or "afterward," *becomes* an assertion or a description or whatever when it occurs in an expository or descriptive text, or vice versa; it is rather that any sentence, suggestive of any mode, can operate *at the service* of the underlying deep structure of a text. The notion of the surface manifestation being at the service of the deep structure is crucial to textual analysis and permits a degree of logical rigor that Smith is too ready to give up.

Index